RE-ORGANISING SERVICE WORK

Re-Organising Service Work
Call centres in Germany and Britain

Edited by
URSULA HOLTGREWE
Chemnitz University of Technology

CHRISTIAN KERST
Gerhard-Mercator-University Duisburg

KAREN SHIRE
Gerhard-Mercator-University Duisberg

LONDON AND NEW YORK

First published 2002 by Ashgate Publishing

Reissued 2018 by Routledge
2 Park Square, Milton Park, Abingdon, Oxon, OX14 4RN
711 Third Avenue, New York, NY 10017, USA

Routledge is an imprint of the Taylor & Francis Group, an informa business

Copyright © Ursula Holtgrewe, Christian Kerst and Karen Shire 2002

The editors have asserted their moral right to be identified as the authors of this work in accordance with the Copyright, Designs and Patents Act, 1988.

All rights reserved. No part of this book may be reprinted or reproduced or utilised in any form or by any electronic, mechanical, or other means, now known or hereafter invented, including photocopying and recording, or in any information storage or retrieval system, without permission in writing from the publishers.

Notice:
Product or corporate names may be trademarks or registered trademarks, and are used only for identification and explanation without intent to infringe.

Publisher's Note
The publisher has gone to great lengths to ensure the quality of this reprint but points out that some imperfections in the original copies may be apparent.

Disclaimer
The publisher has made every effort to trace copyright holders and welcomes correspondence from those they have been unable to contact.

A Library of Congress record exists under LC control number: 2002071160

ISBN 13: 978-1-138-71843-2 (hbk)
ISBN 13: 978-1-138-71841-8 (pbk)
ISBN 13: 978-1-315-19581-0 (ebk)

Contents

List of Figures and Tables		vii
List of Contributors		viii
List of Abbreviations		xii

1	Re-Organising Customer Service Work: An Introduction *Karen Shire, Ursula Holtgrewe and Christian Kerst*	1

PART I
INSTITUTIONS AND CONTEXTS:
THE MAKING OF AN INDUSTRY?

2	Call Centres: Constructing Flexibility *Sandra Arzbächer, Ursula Holtgrewe and Christian Kerst*	19
3	Consolidation, 'Cowboys' and the Developing Employment Relationship in British, Dutch and US Call Centres *Peter Bain and Phil Taylor*	42
4	Call Centres in Germany: Employment, Training and Job Design *Susanne Bittner, Marc Schietinger, Jochen Schroth and Claudia Weinkopf*	63
5	Call Centres as Organisational Crystallisation of New Labour Relations, Working Conditions and a New Service Culture? *Nestor D'Alessio and Herbert Oberbeck*	86

PART II
RATIONALISATION, SKILLS AND CONTROL

6 Skill Formation in Call Centres 105
  Paul Thompson and George Callaghan

7 Capitalising on Femininity: Gender and the Utilisation
  of Social Skills in Telephone Call Centres 123
  Vicki Belt

8 Call Centres and the Contradictions of the
  Flexible Bureaucracy 146
  Carsten Dose

PART III
CUSTOMER SERVICE WORK AND INTERACTION

9 Call Centre Consumption and the Enchanting Myth of
  Customer Sovereignty 163
  Marek Korczynski

10 Quality Time and the 'Beautiful Call' 183
   Catrina Alferoff and David Knights

11 Co-Production in Call Centres:
   The Workers' and Customers' Contribution 204
   Kerstin Rieder, Ingo Matuschek and Philip Anderson

Index 228

List of Figures and Tables

4.1	Number of Jobs and Employees in Call Centres	65
4.2	Sectoral Distribution of Call Centres According to Results of Various Studies	67
4.3	Shares of Women by Hierarchical Level and Function	69
4.4	Examples of the Training Received by Call Centre Agents in a German Bank	75
4.5	Share of Part-time Employment in the FREQUENZ Call Centres	77
4.6	Approaches to Work Enrichment in Call Centres	80
6.1	Previous Jobs of 17 Employees	112
7.1	Employee Profiles in the Case Study Call Centres	131
8.1	Organizational Structure of the Newly Established Back-office Units	151
11.1	Four-Cell Scheme to Depict Potential Constellations of Service Interactions in Call Centre Work	220

List of Contributors

CATRINA ALFEROFF is a Research Assistant in the Department of Management at Keele University on an ESRC-funded project investigating work in call centres. Areas in which she has researched and published include discrimination in employment and training for older workers, employment and training for people with disabilities, direct mail and the problem of privacy, and out-of-hours health service provision. She has lectured in Sociology and HRM at Staffordshire University.

PHILIP ANDERSON is Research Assistant on the project 'Service Work as Interaction' at the Chemnitz University of Technology. His research interests include intercultural communication and associated stress factors in service work as well as various themes in the field of migration studies.

SANDRA ARZBÄCHER was a Researcher in the project 'Call Centres: Organisational Boundary Units between Neo-Taylorism and Customer Orientation' at the University of Duisburg. She is now working as a Human Resource Manager with the IT subsidiary of a financial services company.

PETER BAIN lectures in the Department of Human Resource Management at the University of Strathclyde, and worked in the engineering and car industries before entering the groves of academe. Areas in which he has researched and published include occupational health and safety, technological change in the workplace, and contemporary developments in trade unionism. He is a lead member in a joint Scottish universities' project researching work in call centres and software development, funded under the Economic and Social Research Council's 'Future of Work' programme.

VICKI BELT is a Research Associate at the Centre for Urban and Regional Development Studies (CURDS), a multi-disciplinary research centre at the University of Newcastle, UK. Her research and publications cover the changing nature and experience of work and employment in the service economy and the nature of women's employment with a specific focus on call centres, and the implications of the growth of call centres for regional economic development.

SUSANNE BITTNER is Researcher in the research group 'Flexibility and Social Security' at the German Institute for Work and Technology (IAT). Her main topics of research are services, labour market and employment.

GEORGE CALLAGHAN is a Staff Tutor working with the Open University in the United Kingdom. His PhD is in the labour process field through a study of flexibility, mobility and skills in the labour market. More recent research has included a project, funded by the UK's Economic and Social Research Council, into the work organisation of call centres.

NESTOR D'ALESSIO is Staff Tutor at the Sociological-Research-Insitute at the University of Göttingen. His main areas of research are: structural changes of the service sector, ecology, the finance sector, sociology of labour and organisation.

CARSTEN DOSE is a Policy Administrator at the Wissenschaftsrat (German Science Council), Cologne. He studied sociology at the University of Frankfurt/Main and was a member of the graduate school 'Technology and Society' at Darmstadt University of Technology from 1998-2000 with a scholarship from the DFG. His research interests lie in the fields of sociology of work and technology.

URSULA HOLTGREWE is Principal Investigator (with Hanns-Georg Brose) in the project 'Call Centres: Organisational Boundary Units between Neo-Taylorism and Customer Orientation' at the University of Duisburg. Until the end of 2001 she was a fellow in the Lise-Meitner post-doctoral program. She is now working at Chemnitz University of Technology in the Faculty of Economics and Business Administration, Department of Innovation Research and Sustainable Resources. Her recent research and publications include organisational fields, boundaries, subjectivity in organisational change, and experiences and value commitments between the spheres of work and other activities.

CHRISTIAN KERST was a Researcher in the project 'Call Centres: Organisational Boundary Units between Neo-Taylorism and Customer Orientation' at the Gerhard-Mercator-University Duisburg, Institute of Sociology. His research is in the field of the sociology of work and organisations, industrial relations, and the sociology of technology and innovation. He is now working at "Hochschul-Informations-System" (HIS), Hannover.

DAVID KNIGHTS is Professor of Organisational Analysis and Head of the School of Management at Keele University. He is the editor of the journal Gender, Work and Organisation and his recent research and numerous publications range from post-humanist feminism, resistence, control, trust, power and identity in organisations, ICT and virtuality, call centres, financial services, education and social exclusion. He is the co-author (with H. Willmott) of *Management Lives: Power and Identity in Work Organisations* (Sage Publications) and co-editor (with H. Willmott) of *The Reengineering Revolution: Critical Studies of Corporate Change* (Sage).

MAREK KORCZYNSKI teaches employment relations and the sociology of work at Loughborough University Business School. He is author of *Human Resource Management in Service Work* (Palgrave and MacMillan), and co-author of *On the Front Line: Organization of Work in the Information Economy* (Cornell University Press). He continues to write and research in the sociology of production and consumption in services.

INGO MATUSCHEK is Researcher in the DFG research group 'New Media in Everyday Life: From Individual Use to Socio-Cultural Change' at the Chemnitz University of Technology. He coordinates the research project 'Autonomy and Standardization in Media-Related Boundary Unit Work-Informatised Conversation Work in Communication Centres'. Together with two colleagues he edited *Neue Medien im Arbeitsalltag. Empirische Befunde – Gestaltungskonzepte – theoretische Perspektiven* (Westdeutscher Verlag). He is interested in conversation analysis, the sociology of time, new forms of service and media-related work and subjectivity of workers.

HERBERT OBERBECK is Professor of Sociology at the Technical University of Braunschweig. His main areas of research are: structural changes in industry, structural changes of the service sector, changes of social structure and social conflicts about ecology.

KERSTIN RIEDER is a Researcher at the Leopold-Franzens University of Innsbruck, Psychological Institute. Her PhD is a study of work conditions, the guiding principles of society and work identity in nursing. She is an associated partner of the research project 'Service Work as Interaction' at the Chemnitz University of Technology. Her research interests include the customer's role in service interaction as well as stress factors for service workers.

MARC SCHIETINGER is Researcher in the research group 'Flexibility and Social Security' at the German Institute for Work and Technology (IAT). His main topics of research are services and working time.

List of Contributors

JOCHEN SCHROTH was Researcher in the research group 'Flexibility and Social Security' at the German Institute for Work and Technology (IAT) until October 2001. He is now working for a trade-union.

KAREN A. SHIRE is a Professor of Sociology and Japanese Studies, and managing director of the Institute of East Asian Studies at the Gerhard-Mercator-Universität Duisburg. Her research and publications cover work and organisation in knowledge and information-intensive services, in comparative perspective. She is the principle investigator of two projects for the German Ministry of Education and Research program on the Future of Work – one on the organisation of knowledge and information-intensive services and an second on virtual organisations. She is also the principle investigator of a DFG project on Employment Diversification in Japan. She is co-author of *On the Front-Line:Organization of Work in the Information Economy* (Cornell University Press).

PHIL TAYLOR is a Senior Lecturer in Industrial Relations/HRM in the Department of Management and Organization at the University of Stirling. Areas of recent research and publications include call centres, employment relations in microelectronics, occupational health, student part-time employment, trade unions and HRM and the white-collar labour process. Current call centre research includes projects on health and safety, international employment relations and trade union organising. He is a lead member of an Economic and Social Research Council 'Future of Work' project based across three Scottish Universities investigating the meaning of work in two emerging sectors, call centres and software development.

PAUL THOMPSON is Professor of Organisational Analysis in the Department of Human Resource Management at the University of Strathclyde. His research and publishing interests focus on organisational analysis, the labour process and workplace innovation. Recent published work includes *Workplaces of the Future* (edited with Chris Warhurst, Macmillan, 1998) and *Organisational Misbehaviour* (Sage, 1999, with Stephen Ackroyd). He is a co-organiser of the International Labour Process Conference and Editor for the Palgrave Series, *Management, Work and Organisations* and *Critical Perspectives on Work and Organisations*.

CLAUDIA WEINKOPF is Senior Researcher and coordinator of the research group 'Flexibility and Social Security' at the German Institute for Work and Technology (IAT). Her main topics of research are services, labour market and employment.

List of Abbreviations

ABN-AMRO	Dutch Bank
ACD	Automatic call distribution
BT	British Telecom
CCA	Call Centre Association (UK cross-sectoral employers' organisation)
CCA	Call Centre Academy (North Rhine-Westphalia)
CCO	Call Centre Offensive (governmental programme in the German federal state of North Rhine-Westphalia)
CSA	Customer Service Advisor
CSC	Customer Service Centre
CSR	Customer service representative
CTI	Computer-telephone-integration
CWA	Communication Workers of America
CWU	Communication Workers Union (UK)
DAG	German white collar union, (*Deutsche Angestelltengewerkschaft*)
DFG	Deutsche Forschungsgemeinschaft (the German National Research Council)
DIHT	National Chamber of Commerce in Germany (*Deutscher Industrie- und Handelstag*)
DTI	Department of Trade and Industry (UK)
ecmc	European Centre for Media Competence, located in Marl, Germany
FNV	*Federatie Nederlandse Vakbeweging* (the largest trade union confederation in the Netherlands)
GDR	German Democratic Republic
HBV	Union of service, banking and insurance workers, Germany (*Gewerkschaft Handel, Banken, Versicherungen*)
IAM	International Association of Machinists and Aerospace Workers (USA)
IDS	Incomes Data Services (London-based research organisation)
IHK	Chamber of Commerce (Germany, *Industrie- und Handelskammer*)
KLM	Dutch Airline
NRW	North Rhine-Westphalia
NVQ	National Vocational Qualification (Britain)
SNT	Dutch call centre outsourcing company

STEC	Nijmegen-based industrial research organisation
UNIFI	Union for Finance and Insurance (UK)
ver.di	United Services Union (Germany) (*Vereinigte Dienstleistungsgewerkschaft*)
WERS	Workplace Employment Relations Survey (1998) (fourth in a series of UK surveys)

Chapter 1

Re-Organising Customer Service Work: An Introduction

Karen Shire, Ursula Holtgrewe and Christian Kerst

Call centres are the area of front-line information work, which most closely approximates the model of regimented or Taylorised service work organisation (Frenkel, Korczynski, Shire and Tam, 1999; Taylor and Bain 1999). Research about call centres is relatively recent and the sociological findings to date tend toward the negative imagery of call centres as the digital communications factories of the post-industrial service economy. Yet call centres embody two logics – rationalisation and customer orientation – whereby the concern for service quality poses a limit on the extent of service standardisation (Korczynski 2000a, 2000b, in this volume). The introduction of highly integrated information and communications systems in call centres for managing customer relations opens the way for more pervasive forms of labour process control, such as real-time performance measurement and monitoring. Interactive and informed work in call centres creates a demand for new mixes of worker skills and competencies, not easily integrated into the traditional occupational classifications and training schemes, which have been the basis for recognition and reward. The highly measured and very flexible forms of work in call centres and the presence of large numbers of part-time and temporary workers pose issues for improving and regulating work and employment conditions, which go beyond the usual range of labour and industrial relations issues. While rationalisation, technology, skills, control, segmentation and industrial relations are the traditional ingredients of sociological studies of work and organisations, the study of interactive service work in call centres poses new dimensions for understanding work and employment in the service economy.

Call centres are specialised organizations. The act of establishing a call centre typically involves either a re-organisation of customer contact into a separate organizational unit or outsourcing call services to an external provider. This volume aims to explore the sectoral and cross-national diversity of the call centre organizational form and its impact on the nature of service work employment. While the task of taking and making calls is nothing new, in the past 15 years, telephone-mediated services have evolved from mail-order and directory information services into highly informated and specialised interactive customer relations centres engaged in a range of advising, transaction, sales and marketing activities. From the point of view of managers, call centres are a strategy for standardising service encounters while making service provision more flexible. From a work and employment perspective however, call centres are sites of strongly regimented, stressful jobs, primarily taken up by young, female, low-skilled workers or by those with atypical work biographies, who eschew traditional forms of interest representation.

While the contributions in this book cover a number of national contexts, the focus is explicitly on Germany and Britain. At the extremes of the range of regulated and deregulated economies in the European Union, the contrastive study of the German and British cases offers important lessons for the rest of Europe as well. With an earlier establishment of call centres, Britain is frequently seen as an example for the successful expansion of service employment. In Germany, white-collar work has traditionally been embedded in the specific traditions of occupational training and co-operative industrial relations which define the German Model. Call centres present a strategic challenge to this model. Their expansion has been at the forefront of changes aimed at making employment more flexible in Germany. The focus on Britain and Germany permits a more conceptual comparison of service employment within a liberal-capitalist and a non-liberal, socially embedded economy, while posing the question of continued national diversity or more uniform liberalisation.

The contributions in this book originated in a workshop entitled *'Are Regimented* Forms *of Work Inevitable? Call Centres and the Chances for an Innovative Organisation of Service Work in Europe'* funded by the Anglo-German Foundation for the Study of Industrial Society and held at the Gerhard-Mercator University Duisburg, Germany in December 2000.[1] At the time of the workshop, German research on call centres was underdeveloped in comparison to British research and an explicit aim was to learn from the more advanced state of British call centre research. This volume is the first presentation of German research on call centres in English and presents an opportunity to consider the cross-national differences in the development of call centres, but also the differences in research issues, concepts and findings among German and British sociologists of work and organisations.

---

[1] The workshop was organised by the editors, together with Carsten Dose and Sandra Arzbächer. With the exception of the chapter by Bittner, Schietinger, Schroth and Weinkopf, all the chapters in this book were originally contributions to this workshop.

The findings presented in this volume advance research on call centres and service work in several respects. In Part I, the focus on call centres and the re-institutionalisation of employment relations points to the importance of trade-union renewal and the necessity for going beyond the traditional bargaining issues in re-regulating service work. This is no simple matter, since call centres, as organisational rationalisation strategies, are often keen to evade traditional regulations and enact a more flexible employment environment. The focus on recruitment, skill formation and gender relations in Part II uncovers a gap in perceptions of call centre agents' skills as perceived by managers and experienced by workers. While managers focus on recruiting workers with 'social skills' and a customer orientation, workers report the overwhelming importance of emotional management in customer and co-worker relations and the lack of recognition of the complexity of their competencies. In Part III, the role of customers in the 'production process' of call centres and the tensions arising from competing standardisation and customer orientation strategies are treated as central issues for understanding the experience of service work.

In this introductory chapter, we outline the development of call centres, conceptualise the German–British comparisons and review previous sociological research on call centre work and employment.

The Heterogeneous Development of Call Centres

The first *call centre* was established in the United States in the 1960s, ironically in the manufacturing sector, when a federal court advised the Ford Motor Company to set up a toll-free telephone line in order to facilitate information exchange about the re-call of defective automobiles (Bagnara, 2001). From the beginning the rise and expansion of call centres was linked to technical developments in communications and later integrative information technologies. The availability of toll-free numbers was utilized by mail-order and information services to expand customer contacts over telephones. However, call centres are a rationalisation strategy for customer service work associated with the development of personal computers, networking capabilities and software innovations linking communications and information technologies. Aside from technological factors, privatisation of public service utilities and strategies for increasing service flexibility and access stand out as important influences on the establishment of call centres.

Up until the mid-1990s, call centre work tended to be dedicated to standardized services, with agents engaged primarily in order-taking and simple transactions. Organisational changes, especially the recognition of the rationalising potential of new technology for more complex service tasks, led to an organizational upgrading of call centres within those sectors, such as finance, where they had already been established, as well as the expansion into other sectors of both more qualified and standardized customer relations work. The privatisation of telecommunications and the deregulation of energy markets created an enormous and sudden need for customer sales units, in response to which, call centres provided an efficient organisational solution, avoiding investments in a new and costly branch structure. Software developments allowed for extremely complex routing of calls, as well as the integration of customer data, products and process information across the entire range of organizational activities and services. Call centres were used by banks, for example, to cut back on the more expensive operation of local branches and to rationalise back-office work (see Dose, in this volume); developments which were at least in part supported by the centralisation and dispersed access to customer, product and process information.

The elevation of call centres to centres of customer communications with strategic importance for organisations was typically associated with their (re-) establishment as market-oriented profit centres. The development of management information systems generated real-time statistics on a range of activities, such as number of calls, transactions and sales, as well as work process related measures, such as average length of calls. The organisational up-grading of call centres is also associated with greater managerial concern for the quality of call centre services, expressed in greater investments in recruitment, personnel assessments and evaluations.

Comprehensive and reliable statistics on the number and breakdown of call centres are difficult to come by in Germany or Britain. Bittner, Schietinger, Schroth and Weinkopf (in this volume) gather together a number of industry studies to present an overview of call centres in Germany, while British scholars often rely on an expensive industry source, the Datamonitor, for an overview of call centres in Britain. Most of the contributions in this volume are based on empirical case studies; to date, the most reliable, albeit less than comprehensive source of information about work organisation and employment relations in call centres.

The evidence available in Germany, Britain and other national contexts points to the importance of the finance industry, especially banks, for the early development, expansion and further re-organisation of call centres. Estimates place roughly 30 per cent or more of all call centre employment in Germany and Britain in this sector, with evidence of future growth in jobs. Here, both the rationalisation and flexibility impulses behind this re-organisation of service work are most clear. The establishment of call centres are associated with the closing of bank branches, the shifting of white-collar and back office jobs to call centres, the pioneering of 24-hour direct banking services, the breaking of restrictions on Sunday and holiday work and the evasion of collective bargaining agreements (Arzbächer, Holtgrewe and Kerst, in this volume; Bain and Taylor, in this volume; D'Alessio and Oberbeck, in this volume; Dose, in this volume). Other sectors of importance are telecommunications, where unionisation is more likely, and more recently, outsourcing companies, which have come to represent the least qualified and lowest cost sector of call centre employment.

A number of the contributions in this volume point to the heterogeneity of call centres. Aside from the usual variables which differentiate organisations and the labour process from a sociological perspective – size of establishment, industrial sector, product market conditions and work complexity/skill level – call centres are further differentiated by the focus on inbound or outbound services, and more importantly, by whether they are company-internal or external outsourced call service providers. The latter point seems most tied to the overall nature of call centre employment. Arzbächer, Holtgrewe and Kerst (in this volume) argue that internal providers, which engage in services considered part of the core competency of their parent organisations are most likely to take a high quality path of call centre development, based on improved working conditions and employee development. At the other end of the spectrum are the external (outsourcing) call centres, which compete on the basis of price and are more likely to populate the low-cost, low-skilled end of the call centre spectrum. These are the *cowboys* at the 'frontiers of control' with roughshod employment conditions, according to Bain and Taylor (in this volume).

Union representation and collective bargaining coverage are factors which influence employment relations in call centres and may further differentiate call centres. The likelihood of unionisation tends to depend on the levels of unionisation common to the particular industry prior to the establishment of call centres. Here, telecommunications plays a leading role in the unionised sector of call centre employment. In Germany, because the postal and telecommunications union represented a single employer before privatisation, the union was not able to ignore the representation of early call centre workers, as was the case in banking (Arzbächer, Holtgrewe and Kerst, in this volume). Even in the USA, where national unionisation rates are nearing 10 per cent, the sectoral strength of the communication workers' union has led to some spectacular victories in the representation of qualitative issues in the regulation of call centre work (Bain and Taylor, in this volume).

Nonetheless, evading unionisation is often at the core of management strategy in the establishment of call centres. In the German finance industry, where unionisation rates are high, call centres are typically established as subsidiaries, which then do not join the employers' association, in order to evade collective bargaining coverage. The five largest banks in the Netherlands quit the employers' association in order to place themselves outside the sectoral agreements, while call centre hubs in the US tend to be in 'right-to-work' states where closed shop unions are prohibited (Bain and Taylor, in this volume).

Complexity of work and unionisation are characteristics closely associated with the nature of work in call centres. Many of the authors in this volume refer to a quality versus quantity spectrum, where either service quality is maximised through job enrichment, skill development and worker participation or quantity is foregrounded through high volume, standardised and low-cost service provision. While we are able to discern several dimensions of national diversity (see below), call centre work and employment seems quite similar by sector across national contexts (Bain and Taylor, in this volume; see also Frenkel, Korczynski, Shire and Tam, 1999). Yet common to all but the most high-skill call centres is the reliance on management information systems for the generation of performance measures, typically the numbers and duration of calls.

Call Centres between De-regulation and Re-regulation

In the 1980s, comparative research on work organisation in Germany and Britain found systematic differences in the levels of Taylorisation and social division of labour, with the contrast between the social embeddedness of firms in Germany versus the deregulated and liberal employment relations in Britain (Maurice, Sellier and Silvestre, 1986; Lane, 1989). Even with the introduction of new micro-electronic technologies and the adoption of lean management, German work organisation continued to pose an alternative to Taylorisation (and Toyotism) through the emphasis on high quality production and skilled workers (Streeck, 1992; Jürgens, Malsch and Dohse, 1988; Sorge and Warner, 1986). In the 1990s however, internationalisation and competitive pressures have turned attention to the liberalisation of industrial relations in Germany (Streeck, 1997; Hassel, 1999).

The emerging patterns of work and employment in call centres deviate in important ways from those of the standard German model of the skilled industrial worker with strong employment protections. Despite the comparatively low employment rate of women in Germany, the proportion of female workers in call centres is estimated between 50 and 73 per cent (Bittner, Schietinger, Schroth and Weinkopf, in this volume), similar to Britain and other countries. Students are another available and low-cost supply in Germany of call centre labour (Arzbächer, Holtgrewe and Kerst, in this volume).

Call centre workers are often skilled and highly educated workers, but unlike their counterparts in traditional and professional occupations, are recruited for their personality traits and social skills rather than for their formal or technical qualifications. Skill levels are, on average, higher in Germany, where frequently call centre agents have formal vocational training in clerical or service occupations. In both Germany and Britain, however, call centres recruit on the basis of other criteria, and use these formal qualifications without having to pay for them (Arzbächer, Holtgrewe and Kerst, in this volume; Bittner, Schietinger, Schroth and Weinkopf, in this volume; Thompson and Callaghan, in this volume; see also Kerst and Holtgrewe, 2001). Though part-time and temporary employment have been historically more regulated in Germany, and have not expanded at the same pace as in more liberal employment systems, such new employment forms are common in German call centres. Bittner, Schietinger, Schroth and Weinkopf (in this volume) report that between 40 and 50 per cent of call centre employees are part-timers, most of them women. Despite a higher proportion of part-time work in the British economy (23 per cent compared to 17.6 per cent in Germany (OECD, 2001, p. 38), the proportion of British part-time call centre agents is lower than in Germany (27 per cent, according to Belt, Richardson and Webster, 2000).

German call centres are often quite explicit in avoiding union coverage. Regional efforts to attract call centres exclude union representatives and involve the loosening of local restrictions on working times (Arzbächer, Holtgrewe and Kerst, in this volume). While call centres in Germany, like in Britain, tend to locate in the old bastions of industrial strength, now in industrial decline, it seems that very few of the traditional institutions or corporatist practices are carried over into the regulation of service work. Instead, we observe that call centres prove to be able social actors, who shape their own flexible labour sources through recruitment practices and place themselves in less regulated employment environments. Much of the evidence in this volume suggests that employment relations in German call centres are disembedding from the traditional regulatory constraints, thus moving in the direction of the more liberal employment model of the British economy (see also Lane, 2001).

Important institutional differences continue to exist however. These are also reflected in differences in the research focus of the German and British contributions to this volume. Most importantly, the German Works Constitution Act guarantees workers the right to establish works councils and co-determinate a range of workplace issues, including the use of new technology for performance measures. Additionally protections are provided in privacy of information regulations in Germany. Thus, the use of new technology for pervasive performance monitoring of workers seems less of a workplace issue in German compared to British call centres. Nearly all of the British contributions cite statistical benchmarking of individual performance and monitoring as a major source of work intensification and stress (see also Taylor, Mulvey, Hyman and Bain, 2002). German scholars agree that the repetitive nature of call centre work is a problem, but focus more on work design reforms (e.g. job enlargement) for improving the quality of working life and issues of training and employee development, in order to move organisations toward a 'high-road' service quality emphasis (Arzbächer, Holtgrewe and Kerst, in this volume; Bittner, Schietinger, Schroth and Weinkopf, in this volume).

While call centre workers are not recruited on the basis of their formal qualifications, as noted above, most German workers have some prior training or occupational certification. We are not able to observe a specialisation of German call centres in higher end services, but the German market seems more restricted than the British at the 'quantity' end of the call centre spectrum where competition is based on high volume at low cost (Bain and Taylor, in this volume). There is however, one relevant exception. A number of outsourcing call centres have been established in the 'new federal states' of the former GDR, where different employment conditions and a looser institutional framework represent deviations from the tighter regulation in the 'old federal states'. Thus, there is little evidence of a German boom in outsourced call centres, as is happening now in Britain. In the terminology of Bain and Taylor (in this volume), the German call centre sector seems to be weak on *cowboys*.

In both countries, the development of call centre employees' skills tend to be company-based and on-the-job. We suspect however, that the range of external training centres in Germany, though well short of being integrated into the dual-system of vocational education, diverge from the much weaker forms of certification of British call centre agents (Thompson and Callaghan, in this volume). In general, the British experience seems to confirm the traditional contrasts with Germany – the lack of skilled labour, price-based competition, short-term orientation in technological investments for quick returns in productivity and more adversarial labour relations.

None of the contributions in this volume is based on a direct German-British matched study of call centre work and employment – an obvious weakness for conceptualising the contours of national diversity. The evidence from the German cases however, points to both a logic of de-regulation and a trend toward re-regulation on the basis of continuing institutional resources. Nonetheless, re-regulation seems to result in a 'status quo minus' (Bode, Brose and Voswinkel, 1991), whereby the old mechanisms of social integration are not as yet, clearly being replaced in new regulatory patterns while new forms of social inequality are becoming apparent. Institutional resources are not completely absent in Britain. While criticised by trade-unions, the new Employment Relations Act, for example, has proven to give call centre agents a resource in their right to be accompanied by a union representative when disciplined, as often happens when performance and measurement determines that workers fall short of unilaterally determined targets (Bain and Taylor, in this volume). We conclude however, that both participation rights and an infrastructure for employee skill development are much less developed in British call centres, compared to German ones. Further, the limited use of performance targets and monitoring in Germany clearly indicates that social institutions have effects on work organisation and practices of labour process control.

Nonetheless, the impact of de-regulation on institutional complementarities, organisational practices and social outcomes is a complex and open-ended process, which should remain a central concern of comparative service work research in the future. The globalisation of call centres, which has become more evident very recently, could further impact on service working conditions in comparative contexts. Bain and Taylor (in this volume) find evidence of the export of US 'cowboy' call centres to the Netherlands, for example. Recent media reports of US call centre services locating in low-wage India, where local workers are schooled in speaking and acting like US-Americans is further evidence of pressures for de-regulation (Steinberger, 2001). The limited market for German-language call centre services may mean that such global location strategies only prove relevant for English-language call centre services.

Work, Control and Customer Relations in Call Centres

Towards the second half of the 1990s call centres came to interest researchers across Europe from diverse streams of industrial and organisational sociology and labour process theory. This new form of work and organisation appeared to epitomise a range of both 'old' and 'new' issues in the context of shifts to a service and knowledge-based economy. Early research both in Britain and Germany pointed out a return of Taylorist organisation and control in call centres under headings such as 'the new sweatshops' or the standardisation of white-collar work (Fernie and Metcalf, 1998; D'Alessio and Oberbeck 1999). The linking of computer and telecommunications technology appeared to enhance the possibilities of technological/informative monitoring and control to panoptic proportions (Fernie and Metcalf 1998). In Germany, where white-collar work has also followed the German Model of skilled and secure employment, call centres were seen as dividing previously integrated work organisations (Baethge 1999; D'Alessio and Oberbeck, in this volume). The early focus on call centres was in line with Ritzer's (1993) emphasis on rationalisation as standardisation, the expansion of self-service and the deskilling of service work.

More recent research however, has shown that call centre work is more complex. At the centre of this complexity lies the fact that call centre work is interactive customer service work. As organisational strategies, call centres are surely attempts to rationalise service work, but at the same time compete on the basis of improved service quality. Subject to the dual logics of rationalisation and customer orientation, the development of call centres and the experience of call centre work are subject to a range of tensions, contradictions and dilemmas (Korczynski, 2000a, 2000b, in this volume; Holtgrewe and Gundtoft, 2000; Kerst and Holtgrewe, 2001; Alferoff and Knights, in this volume).

Recent research on call centres makes clear that both *customers*, as participants in the co-production of all types of interactive service work (Leidner, 1993; Rieder, Matuschek and Anderson, in this volume) and *workers*, in the skills and subjective dispositions they bring to interactive service work, play a central role in balancing the contradictions of the 'customer-oriented bureaucracy', (Korczynski, 2000a, 2000b; Holtgrewe, 2001a). Nonetheless, as a number of the authors in this volume note, research on the skills and tensions of interactive service work and on the role of the customer in 'co-production' remains underdeveloped. The concept of 'emotional labour' (Hochschild, 1983) is often used to analyse the nature of call centre work, but as Thompson and Callaghan (in this volume) argue, workers are in fact engaged in 'emotional management' rather than the performance of emotional states.

As anyone who is a regular call centre user knows, call centre service is not necessarily satisfying for customers, though organisations go to great lengths to present their call centres as responses to customers' needs and demands. Thus, call centre workers and their customers must engage in what Korczynski (in this volume) calls the 'management of disillusionment' which arises from the 'myth of customer sovereignty'. Workers may indeed turn the managerial rhetoric of customer-orientation around in order to resist standardisation and control, focussing instead on truly giving good service (Alferoff and Knights, in this volume). In fact, call centre workers mainly derive satisfaction from customer relations (Korczynski, Shire, Frenkel and Tam, 2000; Rieder, Matuschek and Anderson, in this volume).

The issue of service quality has been discovered as a crucial 'contested terrain' between management and workers in call centres. On the one hand, management discourses about quality, emphasized in training and evaluation measures (McCabe et al, 1998; Sturdy, 2000) tie agents' subjectivity into the production of service work (Macdonald and Sirianni, 1996). On the other hand, workers' subjectivities are not as responsive as managers would perhaps prefer. Workers, being addressed as subjects and providers of service quality, make their own sense of these demands. In nearly every case study of call centre work, agents are found defending spaces of discretion, insisting on personal authenticity in their interactions with customers and guarding the social and temporal requirements of satisfactory interactions (Tyler and Taylor 2001; Korczynski, Shire, Frenkel and Tam, 2000; Knights and Odih 2000, Alferoff and Knights, in this volume). Once again, researchers have learned not to overrate the success of managerial discourses.

These claims to service quality and its recognition are central to collective struggles as well (Taylor and Bain 2001; Holtgrewe 2001b; Alferoff and Knights, in this volume). Here, the 'new' issues of service quality, discretion to deviate from standards and targets and recognition of social skills are added to the more traditional bargaining issues of pay, working hours, holidays etc. which, as Bain and Taylor (Taylor and Bain 1999; Taylor and Bain 2001 and in this volume) have frequently pointed out, are as equally relevant for call centres as for other more traditional sectors of trade union organising.

Organisation of this Volume

The three parts of this volume follow the logic of a movement from the macro-institutional (Part I), to the workplace organisational (Part II), and micro-interactive (Part III) levels of analysing work in call centres.

The four chapters appearing in Part I – Institutions and Contexts: The Making of an Industry? – focus on the impact of call centres on institutional frameworks in Germany and Britain. Arzbächer, Holtgrewe and Kerst, in Chapter 2, analyse the re-institutionalisation process unfolding with the development of call centres in Germany. Using the concept of organisational fields and taking an action perspective they follow institutional change and argue that re-regulation is evident in call centre industrial relations, regional efforts to attract call centres and employee recruitment and development practices. Bain and Taylor, in Chapter 3, compare call centre industrial relations in the US, Britain and the Netherlands, in three industries where call centre workplaces are common – telecommunications, finances and outsourcing services. While unionisation is central to democratising employment relations in call centres, unions have been slow to take up a range of new issues, central to the regulation of work in this service context. Chapter 4 by Bittner, Schietinger, Schroth and Weinkopf presents an overview of call centre development and employment relations in Germany. In this national context, work re-design and employee training and development are seen as key issues for the qualitative development of services and the improvement of working life. D'Alessio and Oberbeck, Chapter 5, is one of the earliest studies of call centre work in Germany. In their view, call centres represent the rationalisation of white-collar work, more or less consistent with a Taylorisation thesis.

Part II – Rationalisation, Skills and Control – turns the focus to the work organisational level, in analysing the impact of rationalisation on the nature of skills and the means of labour process control in call centres. All three of the chapters in this section challenge the view of call centre work as de-skilled and focus on the contradictions of rationalised service work. In an in-depth empirical study of a banking call centre, Thompson and Callaghan (Chapter 6) focus on skill development and emotional labour in interactive service work. They argue that a considerable gap exists between the behavioural characteristics recruited by managers, who believe that social skills are what the work demands, and call centre workers, who understand their main competence as the management of emotions and stress. Their contribution makes clear that interactive service work is not a simple case of de-skilled white-collar work, and that the emphasis on social skills as well as the concept of emotional labour do not go far enough in understanding the nature of call centre workers' competencies. In Chapter 7, Belt focuses specifically on female labour in call centres and explores the extent to which employers draw on 'female assets' in the construction of call centre work relations and skills. In case studies of eleven call centres, located in four different industries, Belt finds that while employers do recruit women for their 'people skills', female call centre agents complained that the repetitive nature of their work prevented them from actually making use of their social and communicative competencies. Echoing the emphasis on 'emotional management' stressed by Thompson and Callaghan, Belt finds that resilience, self-control, coping and providing emotional support for others were the skills perceived by call centre agents to be central to effective working. These skills were not however, recognised or rewarded by management. In Chapter 8, Dose challenges the view put forth in Chapter 5, that call centres are a simple Taylorisation of white-collar work. He argues that call centres take the form of a 'flexible bureaucracy', more responsive than traditional service organisation to customer demands, though not necessarily leading to improvements in service quality or working conditions of service workers.

All of the chapters in Part III focus on the role of the customer in call centre work. Chapter 9 by Korczynski deconstructs the 'enchanting myth of customer sovereignty', which motivates the service orientation of call centre workers. Drawing on his concept of the 'customer-oriented bureaucracy', which has come to characterise the nature of the dual-logic of call centre organisation, he argues that workers are put in a tense situation, where they must be both deferential and authoritative, propagate the myth of customer sovereignty, as well as manage customers' disillusionment with the myth. The study of a telecommunications call centre by Alferoff and Knights in Chapter 10 focuses on how call centre workers attempt to foreground service quality over quantitative performance measures, by reappropriating managers' rhetoric of the 'beautiful call'. In so doing, workers effectively resist management surveillance of their work and engage in creative strategies to reconstruct call centre work as truly customer-oriented. The final Chapter 11 by Rieder, Matuschek and Anderson focuses on the role of the customer in the co-production of interactive service work. Breakdowns in service quality occur not only as a consequence of the competencies and goals of call centre workers, but also when customers prove incompetent or pursue different goals from those of the service organisation and its workers. Especially Chapters 9 (by Korczynski) and 11 (by Rieder, Matuschek and Anderson) point to the importance in the future of studying service work from the perspective of customers – as co-producers, subjects and social actors in their own right – in the context of service interactions.

Acknowledgements

The editors would like to thank two reviewers – Heidi Gottfried and Arndt Sorge – for comments, which contributed a great deal to improving the introduction and presentation of this book. We relied completely on Maiko Kuchiba for numerous edits and the formatting of the camera-ready text for publication. Finally, we would like to thank the contributing authors, for both participating in the original workshop and for their patience in the longer-than-expected process of editing and collating texts between two countries. The British contributors, immediately after their arrival in Duisburg, Germany for the workshop in December 2000, were put through a harrowing schedule, which included a visit to a German call centre, a tour of a shutdown steel mill, led by a former employee who insisted we all climb to the top of the 60 meter high oven in the rainy darkness, and dinner in a restaurant, which only serves potatoes. At the end of the workshop, it was the British authors who encouraged us to undertake the co-publication of German and British call centre research. We hope our readers will find the effort warranted.

References

Baethge, M. (1999), 'Subjektivität als Ideologie. Von der Entfremdung in der Arbeit zur Entfremdung auf dem (Arbeits-)Markt?', in Schmidt, G. (ed.), *Kein Ende der Arbeitsgesellschaft. Arbeit, Gesellschaft und Subjekt im Globalisierungsprozeß*, Berlin, Edition Sigma, pp. 29-44.

Bagnara, S. (2001), *Entwicklungstrends von Call Centern in Europa*, report to the project EURO-TELEWORK, Dortmund, IuK-Institut.

Belt, V., Richardson, R. and Webster, J. (2000), 'Women's Work in the Information Economy: The Case of Telephone Call Centres', *Information, Communication and Society*, Vol. 3(3), pp. 366-385.

Bode, I., Brose, H.G. and Voswinkel, S. (1991), 'Arrangement im Status quo minus', *Soziale Welt*, Vol. 42, pp. 20-45.

D'Alessio, N. and Oberbeck, H. (1999), '"Call-Center" als organisatorischer Kristallisationspunkt von neuen Arbeitsbeziehungen, Beschäftigungsverhältnissen und einer neuen Dienstleistungskultur', in *Jahrbuch sozialwissenschaftliche Technikberichterstattung 1998/99. Schwerpunkt: Arbeitsmarkt*, Berlin, Sigma, pp. 13-61.

Fernie, S. and Metcalf, D. (1998), *(Not) Hanging on the Telephone. Payment Systems in the New Sweatshops?*, Centre for Economic Performance, CEP-discussion paper 390, London, (http://cep.lse.ac.uk/pubs/download/dp0390.pdf, downloaded 22.7.01).

Frenkel, J., Korcyznski, M., Shire, K.A., Tam, May. (1999), *On the Front Line: Organization of Work in the Information Economy*, Ithaca, N.Y., Cornell University Press.

Hassel, A. (1999) 'The Erosion of the German System of Industrial Relations', *British Journal of Industrial Relations*, Vol. 37(3), pp. 483-505.

Hochschild, A. R. (1983), *The Managed Heart. Commercialization of Human Feeling*, London, University of California Press.

Holtgrewe, U. (2001a), 'Organisationsdilemmata und Kommunikationsarbeit. Callcenter als informatisierte Grenzstellen', in Matuschek, I., Henninger, A. and Kleemann, F. (eds.), *Neue Medien im Arbeitsalltag. Empirische Befunde, Gestaltungskonzepte, Theoretische Perspektiven*. Wiesbaden, Westdeutscher Verlag, pp. 55-70.

Holtgrewe, U. (2001b), 'Recognition, Intersubjectivity and Service Work: Labour Conflicts in Call Centres', *Industrielle Beziehungen. The German Journal of Industrial Relations*, Vol. 8(1), pp. 37-54.

Holtgrewe, U. and Gundtoft, L. (2000), 'Call Center – Rationalisierung im Dilemma', in Brose, H.-G. (ed.), *Die Reorganisation der Arbeitsgesellschaft*, Frankfurt, Campus, pp.173-203

Jürgens, U., Malsch, T. and Dohse, K. (1988) *Moderne Zeiten in der Automobilfabrik: Strategien der Produktionsmodernisierung im Länder- und Konzernvergleich*, Berlin, Springer Verlag.

Kerst, C. and Holtgrewe, U. (2001), Flexibility and Customer Orientation: Where Does the Slack Come From?, paper presented at the Work, Employment and Society Conference, Nottingham University, 11-13 September 2001.

Knights, D. and Odih, P. (2000), ' "Big Brother is Watching You!: Call centre surveillance and the time disciplined subject', presented at the Annual British Sociological Association Conference, Making Time, Marking Time, York University, 17 – 19 April, to be published in Crow, G. and Heath, S. (eds.), *Times in the Making: The Political Economy of Time Change*, Palgrave, forthcoming.

Korczynski, M., Shire, K., Frenkel, S. and Tam, M. (2000), 'Service Work in Consumer Capitalism: Customers, Control and Contradictions', Work, Employment and Society, Vol 14(4), pp. 669-687.

Korczynski, M. (2001a), 'The Contradictions of Service Work: Call Centre as Customer-Oriented Bureaucracy', in Sturdy, A., Grugulis, I. and Willmott, H. (eds.), *Customer Service, Empowerment and Entrapment*, Basingstoke and New York, Palgrave, pp 79-101.

Korczynski, M. (2001b), *Communities of Coping: Collective Emotional Labour in Service Work*, paper presented at the Work, Employment and Society Conference, University of Nottingham, 11 -13. September 2001.

Lane, C. (1989), *Management and Labour in Europe: The Industrial Enterprise in Germany, Britain and France*, Hants, England, Edward Elgar.

Lane, C. (2001), 'Understanding the globalization strategies of German and British multinational companies: is a "societal effects" approach still useful?', in Maurice, M. and Sorge, A. (eds.), *Embedding Organizations: Societal Analysis of Actors, Organizations and Socio-Economic Context*, Amsterdam, John Benjamins Publishing Company, pp. 189-208.

Leidner, R. (1993), *Fast Food, Fast Talk: Service Work and the Routinisation of Everyday Life*, Berkeley, UCP.

Macdonald, C.L. and Sirianni, C. (eds.) (1996), *Working in the service society*, Philadelphia, Temple University Press.

Maurice, M., Sellier, F. and Silvestre, J.-J. (1986), *The Social Foundations of Industrial Power*, London, MIT Press.

McCabe, D., Knights, D, Kerfoot, D., Morgan, G. and Willmott, H. (1998), 'Making sense of "quality"? Toward a review and critique of quality initiatives in financial services', *Human Relations*, Vol. 51. pp. 389-411.

Ritzer, G. (1993), *The McDonaldization of Society*, London and Thousand Oaks, California, Sage.

Sorge, A. and Warner, M. (1986), *Comparative Factory Organization. An Anglo-German Comparison of Management and Manpower in Manufacturing*, Gower, WZB Publications.

Steinberger, K. (2001), 'Bei Anruf Schock', *Süddeutsche Zeitung*, 31 December 2001, p. 3.

Streeck, W. (1992), *Social Institutions and Economic Performance*, Newbury Park, Cal., Sage.

Streeck, W. (1997), 'German Capitalism: Does It Exist? Can it Survive?', in Crouch, C. and Streeck, W. (eds.), *Political Economy of Modern Capitalism*, London, Sage, pp. 33-54.

Sturdy, A. (2001), 'Servicing Societies? - Colonisation, Control, Contradiction and Contestation', in Sturdy, A., Grugulis, I. and Willmott, H. (eds.), *Customer Service. Empowerment and Entrapment*, Basingstoke and New York, Palgrave, pp. 1-17.

Taylor, P. and Bain, P. (1999), '"An assembly line in the head": Work and employee relations in the call centre', *Industrial Relations Journal*, Vol. 30, pp. 101-117.

Taylor, P. and Bain, P. (2001), 'Trade unions, workers rights, and the frontier of control in UK call centres', *Economic and Industrial Democracy*, Vol. 22, pp. 39-66.

Taylor, P., Mulvay, G., Hyman, J., Bain, P. (2002), 'Work Organisation, Control and the Experience of Work in Call Centres', forthcoming in *Work, Employment and Society*, (http://www.strath.ac.uk/Other/futureofwork/publications.html).

Tyler, M. and Taylor, S. (2001), 'Juggling Justice and Care: Gendered Customer Service in the Contemporary Airline Industry', in Sturdy, A., Grugulis, I. and Willmott, H. (eds.), *Customer Service. Empowerment and Entrapment*, Basingstoke and New York, Palgrave, pp. 60-78.

PART I
INSTITUTIONS AND CONTEXTS:
THE MAKING OF AN INDUSTRY?

Chapter 2

Call Centres: Constructing Flexibility

Sandra Arzbächer, Ursula Holtgrewe and Christian Kerst

Introduction

The development of call centres as a flexible interface between firms and their environments has been seen as exemplary or even symptomatic of flexible capitalism. This paper explores the interrelations of organisational and institutional changes towards deregulation which are both prerequisites and consequences of the development of call centres. Yet we contend that de-institutionalisation is only part of the story. With the emergence of call centres as an organisational field initial moves of de-institutionalisation are followed and complemented by tendencies of re-institutionalisation. The paper presents results from the project 'Call Centres: Organisational Boundary Units between Neo-Taylorism and Customer Orientation'[1] which explores the establishment and development of call centres on the levels of institutions, organisations and work. The research is based on interviews with institutional and management experts and with call centre agents, six case studies of call centres in contrasting industries, and a survey of call centre workers' demographic characteristics, careers and work experience. In this paper we present an institutional analysis and draw on case studies of two banking call centres, both of which belong to large banks in Germany. They handle telephone requests for their banks' branches, operate a support hotline for online banking, and offer direct brokerage services by phone. Bank 2 offers telephone banking as well. Both employ between 300 and 600 call centre agents.

At first, it is important to stress the strong dynamics of this field of economic activity. The dimension of time and timing is decisive for researching of call centres. In Germany the expansion of the call centre sector beyond operator services, mail-ordering and direct marketing has taken place

---

[1] The project is funded by the Deutsche Forschungsgemeinschaft (DFG) as part of the SPP197 '*Regulierung und Restrukturierung der Arbeit in den Spannungsfeldern von Globalisierung und Regionalisierung*'. It started at the University of Duisburg in April 2000 and ran until March 2002.

since the mid-1990s. The first direct bank (the former Bank 24) started operations in autumn 1995. The development was triggered by interrelated technological and institutional factors coming together in the mid-1990s: The liberalisation of the telecommunication and energy markets, the strong growth of mobile telecommunication and the diffusion of internet access into private households led to the emergence of new markets, new packages of goods and services, new types of customers (e.g. the customer for electricity) and new information needs.

Data on the number of call centres in Germany or employment are difficult to obtain (cf. Bittner et al., in this volume). There are between 100,000 and 225,000 jobs in German call centres employing 200,000 – 400,000 people. Because of the rapid growth of call centre businesses and employment, the lower figures may indeed be underestimated.

Internationalisation of call centre operation in Germany is limited because communication services are language based and customers appear to require native speakers on the phone.[2] Therefore, competition for call centre investments takes place within the national boundaries between German federal states (*Länder*). Nearly every region facing structural change and losses in industrial employment sees a chance to gain employment opportunities in the call centre boom.

Looking at the regional distribution, about 25 per cent of the call centres in Germany are located in North Rhine-Westphalia (which indicates a slight overrepresentation in relation to the total population). Other strong locations are around Bremen (Baumeister, 2001) and in the northern part of the former GDR.[3] The main reason for this regionalised pattern of locations is that call centres seek locations with two major properties: a large labour market with low labour costs, and vicinity to universities. Bremen as well as the Ruhr area seem to meet both conditions excellently. Indeed, in these regions both students' participation in the labour force and unemployment rates are well above the West German average (Schnitzer et al., 2001, p. 288). Especially the very dense university landscape in the Ruhr area provides call centres with a large number of student part-time workers. In these cities, call centres are also seen as an important element of (and indicator for) structural change from an industrial towards an innovative service economy. Duisburg, Essen, Bochum and Dortmund as major cities in

---

[2] Exceptions can be found in Ireland where some German-speaking agents live (also in some hispanic tourist areas), and in the Netherlands close to the German border. In the latter case, German employees commute to Dutch locations.

[3] Two main development paths can be distinguished: In the eastern regions (*neue Bundesländer*, former GDR) call centres include the more simple services (retail, simple information desk and marketing services). More complex and qualified services are located in the western part of Germany.

the Ruhr area all have many call centres. In Duisburg alone, 3,600 employees work in about 30 call centres. Comparably high numbers of employees can be found in Dortmund and Essen. Among these neighbouring cities, some specialisation has developed. Duisburg has a main focus on call centres in the financial industry, while Dortmund's focus lies on technical support services.

This paper investigates the processes of de- and re-institutionalisation under the perspective of flexibility. The following chapter outlines theoretical framework for understanding the dynamics of institutional flexibility of organisations. Then we explore the double flexibility of call centres: Both the organisations' flexibility related to market environments and their internal flexibilisation correspond with institutional flexibility. In the remaining parts we demonstrate the shaping of institutional flexibility empirically through three exemplary subjects: industrial relations in and around call centres, the management of internal flexibility through personnel policies, and call centres in their regional context.

Theoretical Framework: Organisational Fields and Strategies Under Construction

The theoretical perspective on call centres in this paper uses concepts of neo-institutional organisation theory (cf. Meyer and Rowan, 1977; Powell and DiMaggio, 1991; Scott, 1995) and of strategic action (Crozier and Friedberg, 1979; Oliver, 1991) to explore the integration and (re)constitutive role of call centres in the larger context of an organisational field under construction.[4]

From an organisational perspective, the establishment of call centres or use of call centre services responds to organisations' need to balance flexibility and stability in relation to their environment. This is inherently dilemmatic for any organisation. Call centres promise both increased openness to customers' needs and protection of the organisations' core practices and routines. While they thus produce flexibility for their internal or external customers, they are faced with their expectations and embedded within

---

[4] 'By organizational field we mean those organizations that, in the aggregate, constitute a recognized area of institutional life: key suppliers, resource and product consumers, regulatory agencies, and other organizations that produce similar products or services' (DiMaggio and Powell, 1991, pp. 64). The structuring and empirical existence of a field is plausible, if there are intensive interactions between the field organisations, 'interorganizational structures of domination and patterns of coalition' emerge, organisations face a field-specific information density, and a mutual recognition exists of being involved in a common doing (DiMaggio and Powell, 1991, p. 65).

institutional arrangements and contexts which they in turn seek to change. As new, recently established organisations they present themselves as innovative and are perceived in this way. Norms and expectations of innovation legitimise change and enable such organisations to position themselves in and act strategically upon their newly emerging institutional environments.

Neo-institutionalism argues that new organisational forms are established not only due to their superior rationality or technologically excellent efficiency. Without positioning themselves in an institutionalised organisational field and answering to its perceptions and expectations, new organisational forms are not viable. The attribution of an organisation to a specific field by the organisation itself and by relevant other organisations and actors provides the organisation not only with the necessary legitimacy, but also gives certainty in mutual expectations and works as a source of meaning. Such institutionalised expectations are grounded on cognitive, normative and regulative pillars (Scott, 1995). Of course, this model should not be misunderstood as a model of pure adaptation to existing institutions. Organisations enact their environment and strategically act upon it, try to shape the expectations of others contributing to the creation and change of institutional environments. Organisational change and institutional change are thus interdependent. Also one organisation's change is another's change in their environment to which e.g. unions, politics or education organisations must react. Hence, institutional flexibilisation is a double-sided construct, in which organisational and institutional enactment of relevant environments, attempts at strategic action and negotiation of expectations interrelate.[5]

Oliver (1991) especially draws attention to the point that organisations are not pure victims of institutional pressure. Instead, she suggests a continuum of organisations' strategic responses to institutional pressure which ranges from passive acquiescence over compromise, strategies of avoidance, escape, and defiance to very active strategies of manipulation, influence or control of institutions.[6] Young organisations in an emerging

---

[5] In so far, it would be misleading to refer only to the tendencies of organisational fields towards isomorphy. If we acknowledge that organisational decisions and institutional constraints are loosely coupled and organisations have some space to enact such constraints and act upon them, institutional theory offers far more than a simple theory of diffusion and adaptation. It has its strength in covering the whole range of evolutionary processes which may lead to innovative social practices as well as the reproduction of well established routines and institutional structures.

[6] For her argument she draws on both resource dependency and neoinstitutional theory. Therefore, she avoids underestimating power in interorganisational relations while clearly seeing that the exercise of power is contingent on the institutionalised

organisational field have chances to gain access to a broader range of these strategic options. During the constitution of a new organisational field then processes of (re)institutionalisation occur and narrow the available range of strategic options.

Flexible Positioning in Institutionalised Organisational Fields

In many cases, call centres have been founded as new firms or as the result of an outsourcing decision. These decisions over a redrawing of organisational boundaries are traditionally explained by transaction cost theory. Transaction cost theory suggests that call centres working with sensitive data and strategically important knowledge will tend to remain part of the firm or the business group (Nippa, 1999). External call centre service providers will be used for overflowing calls and for information gathering operations which are more removed from an organisation's core competencies and knowledge bases. Also, moving call centres outside the scope of collective agreements (as a consequence of an outsourcing decision) may be considered to reduce transaction costs. However, both in new and changing organisational fields and in services transaction cost arguments give only a limited orientation.[7] For example, the trade-off between lowering costs by getting rid of collective agreements and the loss of trust and legitimacy is difficult to evaluate.

In the early developmental stage of a new service more options for institutional choice between market, hierarchy and network appear to be realistic since obviously superior solutions have not yet been identified. Consequently, initial choices are frequently modified or even reversed contributing to the turbulence of the field. For example, some companies have already begun to re-integrate formerly outsourced call centre services. Thus, there is no unilinear tendency from hierarchy to market. This supports the institutionalist view that institutional choices as well as institutional and organisational change are not determined by transaction cost economics, but the logic of appropriateness (March and Olsen, 1989) and the maintenance of social legitimacy in turn influences the perception of cost.

Referring to the concept of organisational fields raises the question, whether call centres as a new type of service organisation are located in

---

acknowledgement of an actor's position within an organisational field. Institutions thus are both resources and restrictions.

[7] For an overview of criticism of transaction cost economics see Ortmann, Sydow and Türk (1997, pp. 25). Especially, in front line service work it may be very difficult to distinguish between production (service) cost and transaction (information) cost.

existing organisational fields or establishing a new one. This is mirrored by the debate, whether call centres constitute an new industrial branch. Parts of the call centre population perceive themselves as a branch, namely the call centre service companies. Other call centres count themselves as parts of existing branches (e.g. retail, financial service, telecommunication, tourism). However, outside observers have tended to view call centres as a more or less undifferentiated type of organisation. Because of this divergence of internal and external observation, the semantic of an industry branch or an industrial sector has become dominant. Consequently, if call centres are addressed as a whole, a new type of service organisation, they become compatible (*anschlussfähig*) with the routines of training institutions, agencies for business promotion, employment agencies or governmental policies. This institutional perspective on call centres opens up new options for them. As a collective unit they are able to successfully claim public and political support. And this again puts the question of the newly constructed industry's image and reputation on the agenda. Therefore, it is plausible to talk about the organisational field of call centres, even if they do not constitute a classical industrial branch.[8] An open question then is whether this field is stabilising in the long term or will be disappearing again.

Flexibility and flexibilisation in and of the organisational field thus works in distinct arenas.

(1) Flexibility against market environments means increased permeability of organisational boundaries. Viewed from the point of view of the customer, call centres multiply the possibilities to contact the firm. In the temporal dimension, service time is extended and reaction to communicative demands speed up. Materially services are becoming more differentiated, socially more communication channels and media are accepted and communication is informalised. The organisation presents its flexible side to the environment. From the perspective of the organisation, new marketing strategies and possibilities emerge (value-added services, direct marketing, cross-selling, data mining, telephone-internet-combinations), that are to allow even more flexible reactions on perceived customer demands.

(2) Internally, organisations need to manage that flexibility. Information and communication technology, routines of recruitment, training and coaching must be balanced with the demands for flexible work and control.

---

[8] This does not mean that organisational field and industry branch are the same concept. The field approach is broader because it encompasses numerous organisations that are not covered by the branch concept. But in many cases a classical branch (that may be found in statistical classification systems) is a kind of field core. In the case of call centres this core is less stable and institutionalised and it has weaker boundaries.

In the process, a call centre-specific labour market emerges, and is enacted by organisations which, in turn, adapt to that market. High employee turnover rates ('churn rates') for example, can in the long run turn out to be a major organisational problem or a major mechanism for maintaining flexibility.

(3) Call centres both promote and exploit flexibility with respect to institutions (e.g. industrial relations and system of collective agreements, specific labour markets, education and vocational training). They are less exposed to strong, formalised expectations than organisations in old and well established fields. This is why they can develop alternative behavioural strategies against institutional pressure and indeed, they have been established to widen the range of strategic options (cf. Oliver, 1991). The positioning of call centres in the industrial relations system can be described as escape and defiance. Here, outsourcing has widely been used to escape from existing collective agreements and challenge them. With respect to the institutions of vocational training and occupations the early strategic response has been based on avoidance. Call centres are widely indifferent to their employees' formal qualifications.

Nevertheless, processes of re-institutionalisation occur. Call centre fairs and journals structure and organise communication within the organisational field. Managers, unions and researchers discover and promote examples of good practice, but also agents circulate information about good jobs. Both call centre associations and 'markets' for reputation emerge. Recruitment shows clear isomorphic tendencies towards a mix of university students and working mothers. Also, recruitment instruments such as assessment centres are spread via journal articles and the evolving consulting scene.

These examples show that institutional flexibility is not unbounded and the levels of flexibility are interdependent. While organisations and institutions move through stages of de- and re-institutionalisation, windows of opportunity open up which enable processes of both social opening and social closure. Our argument is that the call centre sector in Germany after a period of social opening is gradually shifting to social closure and institutional consolidation. We will illustrate this point in more detail for different areas of institutional life: industrial relations, managing internal flexibility and call centres in regional contexts

Regulating Flexibility: Industrial Relations

Industrial relations in Germany are similar to other Northern European countries, characterised by the vertical system of trade/industrial unions with counterparts in corresponding industrial employers' associations (cf. Weiss, 1992).

The system of industrial relations works on two levels, the industry level and the plant level. The legal base of the industry level are different laws within labour legislation. Most relevant is the 'Collective Agreement Law' (*Tarifvertragsgesetz*) which defines industrial unions and employers' associations as social partners and commits them to collective bargaining. Collective agreements are usually negotiated for industries and regions. They may regulate wages, working time and some aspects of working conditions. Collective agreements formally apply only to association members. By not joining or leaving employers' associations, companies may avoid the industry-wide agreements.

The legal base of industrial relations on the plant level is the 'Works Constitution Act' (*Betriebsverfassungsgesetz*) which regulates co-determination. In companies with five or more employees, both unionised and non-unionised workers are represented by an elected works council with information, consultation and co-determination rights.[9] Works councils co-determine payment systems (but not wage rates, which are negotiated on the collective level), work-schedules, qualification and – important in the case of call centres – new technology that could be used to control workers performance and behaviour. Works councils must be informed and/or consulted over issues of work organisation, job content and personnel policy and -planning. Management must negotiate with the works council over all issues considering co-determination; arrangements are fixed in 'plant-specific agreements' (*Betriebsvereinbarungen*) and apply to all employees.

The two levels of industrial relations complement one another. Workers' interest in general is represented by the union and plant-specific affairs are the domain of works councils that are legally bound to exercise their rights in the interest of social peace. Both types of collective actors depend on one another: Works councils need the structure and knowledge of unions to be successful, and they are the first step for unions to organise employees and establish a bargaining position for collective agreements.

When call centres were beginning to be established, unions were fairly slow to identify new demands and respond to them. Suffering from a decrease of membership at the time, they retained their focus on their traditional clientele of (male) full-time workers in large companies. They failed

---

[9] Such councils are not mandatory, but elections must be called when demanded by either three employees or by a union with at least one member in the company. For plants with more than 200 employees, a certain proportion of works council members are exempted from their regular jobs, and work full-time for the works council. In smaller plants, works councils serve voluntarily, but conduct necessary duties on company time.

to perceive the development of this new organisational field. Emerging new markets demanded considerable changes from unions, which were at the time struggling with their own internal structure and competing with one another over the organisation of new industries.

For instance, the union of service, banking and insurance workers (HBV) was in charge of companies offering mail-ordering. When companies in the 1980s extended the times for mail-ordering in order to improve customer service they started to route certain calls to small, external service companies. Works councils and the union kept silent to avoid the politically delicate issues of work at night and on Sundays in those companies they represented.

> 'It started when they routed overflows to external services. We didn't talk about it. We were glad that it wasn't necessary to work in company XY on Saturdays and Sundays. Looking back from today, you can say we externalised problems.' (Union rep. HBV)

Such a policy of preserving privileges (not-in-my-backyard policy) can be described as the avoidance of environmental pressure by the unions. They ignored the multitude of small service companies that were hard to unionise anyway. In a certain way, private sector unions underestimated the potential of the service sector and the repercussions of these changes on their traditional strongholds. Thus they missed opportunities to influence and shape these developments at an early stage.

In contrast, the post and telecommunications union (*Deutsche Postgewerkschaft*) which traditionally had been a public sector enterprise union (*Betriebsgewerkschaft*) could not afford such an avoidance strategy. The union had to change considerably in the 1990s when the telecommunication sector was deregulated and transformed; from the public to the private sector, from a single company to an industry and from very co-operative industrial relations to a more flexible approach. Their tradition, however, was both a constraint and a resource. The post and telecommunications union played a crucial role in call centre organising since they traditionally had to regulate round-the-clock shift work and had experience in co-determining shift patterns, staffing levels etc. which were new to other industries. On the other hand, the union found itself confronted with very different types of employees in the new companies.

With the opening of the telecommunication market and the establishment of the first direct banks, reorganisation and new forms of labour were obviously no longer limited to small plants in a basically rather obscure sector of 'new services', but they invaded into a traditional union field. Here, unions became active trying to have works councils elected in the call centres of these sectors, but were hampered by the competition of different industrial unions and the German white collar union (DAG) over domination in each new company. Which union succeeded in which company depended either on traditional co-operative relations or on the union's willingness to compromise in order to dominate the company. This competition was partly replaced by co-operation at least among white-collar unions who in the spring 2001 amalgamated to form the world's largest service union *ver.di (= Vereinte Dienstleistungsgewerkschaft/United Services Union)*. In the preliminary stages of the merger unions established a flexible and co-operative project framework to address particular issues such as representing call centres. Call centre specialists in the unions have co-operated to develop new instruments of regulation such as 'framework collective agreements' leaving space for company specific arrangements.

All of this has indeed led to an improvement of unions' position in the organisational field. Call centres are increasingly seen as both a challenge and an opportunity to gain inroads in new and traditionally weakly unionised industries:

> 'Where else do you have 300 and more people with similarly problematic work situations?' (Union rep. DPG)

At present, works councils are fairly normal in call centres close to established industries and no longer a rarity in new ones. The most problematic areas in the view of unions are 'new' call centres in marketing and services but also in telecommunications. In telebanking and telecommunications the respective unions made co-ordinated efforts. This was easier since such companies were established fairly simultaneously: in response to competitors' actions in the case of telebanking and in response to deregulation in the telecommunication sector. These efforts have been fairly successful and in these industries a considerable share of call centres have elected works councils with at least some union influence.

In banking, this has frequently been a struggle and it seems that the unions' success frequently was based on failed management schemes to prevent it. In Bank 1 in our sample, a works council was established by a small active group 'just like that, without a need or particular incident' (Works Council Chair, Bank 1) a few month after the project of a telebank had started. In Bank 2, which also started as a new telebank enterprise, a chaotic start gave rise to disappointment with working conditions. 'On the night shifts, the idea was born to make an appointment with the union' to get advice on the establishment of a works council (Works Council Chair, Bank 2). Here, management tried first to delay talks with the union. Then they announced a plant assembly for the organisation of works council elections themselves in order to beat the unionised employees to it. In the election, both union and non-union representatives were elected, but later on, the management-oriented faction resigned under the mistaken assumption that that would dissolve the works council. In fact, Bank 2 ended up with a complete union works council, which now is fairly well established and successful but in quite a conflictual relationship with management.

In marketing, unions first targeted the market leader with branches all over Germany, a company which used to be fairly notorious in the industry for wage dumping and using self-employed workers. This had the double advantage of setting a warning example and gaining more or less silent support from the company's competitors.[10]

> 'We said at the start let's take on the bad guy. And were sort of supported by the other call centres, they smiled and said, go ahead and good luck to you.' (Union rep. DPG)

The provisions of the Works Constitution Act in Germany give works councils considerable power. These powers are rooted in the tradition of German industrialism and the question is how useful and appropriate they are to new(ish) fields of employment. The specific conditions of call centre work and the workforce limit the use of these powers. The high share of part-timers obviously means that interest and involvement in workplace participation are often low. Even where works councils are established, their members are not necessarily unionised and most of their constituency is not either. But also where the prerequisites for interest representation are in place, competent negotiation and bargaining requires a certain expertise and experience with the rules of the game. Unions currently are faced with inexperienced actors on both sides, and representatives suggest that part of management's frequent anti-union stance results from that as well:

> 'Both sides ... don't know how to handle co-determination. Both sides are young. Often students doing business courses and thinking they have to show the boss what's what, or law students practising learning through examples.' (Union rep. DPG)

---

[10] In 2001 a major competitor of the market leader started bargaining with *ver.di* over a collective agreement on plant level in order to set up standards for the competition and restrict price competition. In November 2001, in Hamburg the union *ver.di* and the retail employers' association concluded a wage agreement that put all employees in retail call centres under the umbrella agreement of Hamburg's retail industry.
(cf. http://www.labourcom.uni-bremen.de/callcenternetz/download/TarifvertragCall-CenterHH.pdf).

Also, for established works councils dealing with newly established call centres with their working times, specific skill demands and workforces are a new matter. In both cases, the need for union support and consultation is high.

The most successful issues for the works councils in our experience have been wage-negotiations and prohibiting individual performance monitoring. Here, the right of works councils to co-determine new technology and work organisation comes in useful both in its own right and as a bargaining chip for other points. Works councils often have succeeded in increasing wages by a few Marks per hour, establishing premiums for night and weekend work in between 20 – 40 per cent and they are influencing the modes of control and quality management as well. In the call centres we studied, individual measurement of performance in terms of call times, sales figures etc. is limited with the exception of call centres in direct sales. Works councils are also working on online rights and trying to bargain agreements which limit the monitoring of e-mail and internet use.

There is some insecurity among different works councils over the regulation of working times. This is where the very experience and tradition of the telecommunications union may turn into a liability. Telekom works councils tend to approach working time in the traditional Fordist way, limiting anti-social working hours and distributing loads and compensation evenly. With workforces with diverse working time needs and preferences, the question arises anew of what to regulate and where to establish corridors of self-determination by teams and workers themselves while still avoiding self-exploitation in the process.

Quality management and coaching however is generally accepted both by employees and works councils. Works councils and unions are aiming for appropriate recognition of qualitative dimensions of work. For instance, performance-related pay systems in their view should mirror demonstrated competencies rather than measured performance.

In sum, there is no denying that employers have moved ahead when it comes to flexibilising labour conditions by escaping established systems of industrial relations. Still de-institutionalisation was also favoured by the condition and non-strategy of the unions at the time. Since trade unions have reorganised and flexibilised themselves, their influence has improved and co-determination has increased again. The flexibilisation of industrial relations has turned out to be a process of trial and error with actors negotiating flexibilisation and its limits and changing themselves in the process rather than pursuing a unilateral strategy.

Managing Flexibility: Recruitment and Coaching

On the organisational level, flexibility may be seen as a key product of call centres. In order to deliver that product, a considerable part of the flexibility/stability dilemma is transferred to the actual work situation of call centre agents. Even if their work is highly regimented and strictly controlled, they have to articulate both sides of bureaucracy and customer-orientation (Korczynski, 2001): standardisation and empathy, swift task completion and competent problem-solving. Organisational control thus can and does not dissolve the flexibility/stability dilemma. While 'doing flexibility' is left to agents' agency, organisational control works on it, frames and shapes it. Recruitment and on-the-job training in Bank 1 and Bank 2 show how organisations are modifying the initial logic of de-skilling in the light of labour market pressures. Recruitment addresses the prerequisites and quality management the outcomes of agents' work performance in multiple and subtle ways.

This, in our view, explains why control in call centres has so aptly been described as 'info-normative' (Frenkel et al., 1999), performed both through 'hard' measurements and 'soft' cultural and normative controls, a careful cultivation of informal work cultures. However, this distinction is fluid in itself. The figures of capacity, performance etc. often are a matter of interpretation and management is about contextualising them and assessing their relevance. On the other hand, communicative quality is translated into sophisticated evaluation systems. Managing flexibility thus means to combine performance data, quality evaluation, training and control and to continuously modify this combination according to (perceived) need and demand.

Recruitment

Firstly, a considerable part of the workforce consists of the typical part-time workers, i. e. mothers returning to work and/or students. Both these groups have particular temporal needs and their skills and demands do not need to be fitted smoothly into the traditional German model based on formal training and recognised occupations.[11] The escape from traditional industries thus gave companies an opportunity to tap a different type of labour market.

---

[11] This model does not just apply to industrial labour but to clerical and service work as well. However, the recruitment of skilled women for routinised jobs is a fairly traditional means of flexibilisation, both downgrading work and keeping skills in reserve (Gottschall et al., 1985).

From an institutional perspective it is worth noting that in Germany, university students are an attractive workforce for call centres. This is a result of de-institutionalisation and deregulation in the organisational field of higher education from which call centres (and possibly other new service industries) profit. Traditionally, working students are exempted from social security payments and provisions and thus present cheap labour. In the 1990s, cuts in student grants have increased the need to earn a living. Currently in Germany 65 per cent of students work an average of 13.9 hours during term time (Schnitzer et al., 2001, p. 277). With low skilled and temporary jobs they earn a median of 7.66 € which is slightly below the low end of call centre wages in West Germany. The length of university courses in Germany and their often fairly un-regulated character especially in the humanities give students the time and motivation to work during their studies. On the subjective side, a university education is frequently less a distinct phase in the lifecourse but an extended lifestyle in which studies, work and other commitments are pursued simultaneously, eventually leading to degrees and/or a regular career or not. This is especially true in the Ruhr area, where the opening of new universities in the 1970s was part of a government policy towards structural change. Working-class students cannot afford not to work and mature students frequently hold down jobs. Indeed, Ruhr area students have the highest rates of participation in the the labour market, above 70 per cent.

Call centres have come to find out through labour turnover and training costs that call centre work requires particular skills and competencies for which the socio-demographic characteristics of their prospective workforce are not sufficiently predictive.[12] Thus, sophisticated recruitment procedures have been established (cf. Thompson and Callaghan in this volume). Phone interviews are an obvious means of screening applicants, but often they are followed by one-day recruitment events involving group presentations, phone simulations and other assessment centre exercises. The evaluation criteria are continuously evaluated and modified in the light of anticipated changes in work roles and demands. Such changes are seen in the inclusion of e-mail, multimedia communication and in an increasing orientation towards sales (cf. Knights and McCabe, 1999).

> 'Eventually we are required to reconsider employees' profiles. This is not a problem as all our instruments are designed to allow for short-term success evaluation. ... If we find that through recruiting we do not get the right kind of people we adapt the instrument immediately. The questionnaire for the phone

---

[12] It is worth noting that the traditional ascription of social skills and graces to women, while still existent (cf. Belt in this volume), does not appear natural any longer.

interview is refined continuously. We used to strongly distinguish between inbound as less sales-oriented and outbound. Now we set great store by customer-orientation in inbound as well, the readiness to actively approach customers.' (Bank 2, Personnel)

Recruitment for the right skills and personality traits is thus geared towards the selection of an employee *habitus* (Bourdieu, 1982) which enables agents to move between tight regimentation and flexibility, matter-of-factness and friendliness, subordination and responsibility (cf. Holtgrewe, 2001a). The exact emphasis on these respective elements is left open to continuous modification which mirrors the call centre's perceived position in both the market and the strategic outlook of the organisation.

Coaching

The shaping of the day-to-day performance of these balancing acts is the domain of quality management. Firstly, training and coaching sessions are scheduled to fit in with the immediate demands of incoming calls. Orientation towards quality is thus pursued in the slack periods and 'pores of the working day'.

Bank 1 is currently implementing a coaching system which simultaneously evaluates and trains workers according to detailed quality criteria which have been laid down for each service specifically. Each agent is to be coached ten times per year with each session lasting 50 minutes and feedback given immediately. The results form part of the pay-relevant performance appraisal as well.

Here, agents are expected to see evaluation under the perspective of self-improvement (cf. Grey, 1994; Newton, 1996) and as a chance for organisational recognition of their competence (cf. Holtgrewe, 2001b). This view is supported by agents' statements. Accordingly, they take over parts of training and quality management as well. Agents are put in charge of certain subjects for which they offer their colleagues training and 'fresh-up' sessions. Trainers are also recruited from the ranks of agents with psychology or education courses or degrees. Beyond coaching and training, the density of communication and reflection of quality in this bank is quite impressive. There are quality circles, round tables with management and workers etc.

This kind of job enrichment ties up with students' extrafunctional skills or skills which they are currently learning. It also ties up with a willingness to consider exams and evaluations as an integral part of skill formation and personal development, which is shaped in university socialisation. The recruitment of students enables the organisation to mobilise the norms and dispositions of (future) highly-skilled and professional workers in a less than professional field.

Managing flexibility in terms of personnel selection and quality management thus positions employees in such a way that they are able to move competently between regimented work, customer empathy and an 'entrepreneurial' perspective on the demands of the organisation. The way they do this is in turn closely observed and evaluated by the organisation, and control and technologies of the self are interlaced.

Locating Flexibility: The Case of North Rhine-Westphalia

We argued above that call centres have been able to exploit institutional expectations to gain public support and resources. Here, regional and political sources of support were most important.

Today, nearly all German federal states (*Bundesländer*) have their own regional policies to support the development of a vital call centre scene. Among the first to set up such a programme was North Rhine-Westphalia.[13] In 1997, a governmental programme called '*Call Center Offensive*' was started here. It offers communication, qualification and training, and locational promotion services to call centres. Each has different implications for institutionalisation.

The establishment of communication structures among persons and organisations interested in call centres presents a rather weak form of institutionalisation. Nevertheless, in the early stages of the development of the organisational field it has been important in order to lay seeds for a professional community.[14] At the same time workshops and round tables at the local level quite successfully advertised the new public policies. An official of the governmental program comments:

> 'The call centre practitioners were happy that someone looked after them and offered them a communication platform.' (CCO-Official 2, p. 2)

---

[13] For Bremen cf. Baumeister 2001.
[14] The integration of the '*Call Center Offensive*' into the much broader programme of '*media nrw*' was another important element of the communication strategy. This programme presents government efforts to initiate innovation and give support in new media and information technology applications. Here, call centres are (at least) symbolically connected to other parts of the so-called high-tech industries with their connotations of modernity, innovation, and long-term prospective investments. Yet call centres retain the additional charm of offering larger amounts of medium-skilled jobs.

Also, the publication of brochures, a website, and visits of government representatives in newly established call centres intensified the public awareness of the booming sector. On the other hand, skepticism about the quality of the new jobs soon came up. Consequently, politicians and managers soon identified the relatively bad image of call centre work as a major obstacle for the growth of call centres. Therefore, the interests of call centre companies and politicians are meeting in the improvement of the image. Nevertheless, the case of Citibank's closure of the Bochum call centre caused considerable loss of trust among employees and the public (cf. Holtgrewe, 2001b).

The certification of training institutions was a second important element of the *Call Center Offensive*. The training centre of the Chamber of Commerce in Düsseldorf in co-operation with local call centre representatives developed a first curriculum for a six-week-training for call centre agents in 1997. On the basis of this curriculum the Call Centre Academy North Rhine-Westphalia (CCA) was founded to disseminate the curriculum to training institutions all over North Rhine-Westphalia. So far, local training centres in 21 North Rhine-Westphalian cities offer these courses, especially to the unemployed. Local Chambers of Commerce hold the examination and gives out a certificate. By the end of 2000 approximately 3000 people had successfully attended them. The rate of successful entry into call centre jobs is estimated at up to 70 per cent.

The concept of the CCA was to achieve comparable training standards across the country.[15] In some cases the network between employment agency, local training centres and companies establishing call centres worked very quickly and successfully. In Dortmund and Siegen for example, large call centres had some hundred employees trained and recruited through CCA courses within a few months.

While some call centre managers criticise the curriculum for not providing skills up to their company's standard, the CCA-courses appear to fulfill important functions for call centres as well as for political actors. They take over part of the personnel selection especially for those call centres with relatively low skill requirements. In co-operation with local employment agencies, the training centres scan the local labour market, especially the unemployed for those who could be interested and suited for call centre jobs. Political actors, on the other side, are interested in such

---

[15] The approach of standardisation is not restricted to the *Bundesland*. The national Chamber of Commerce (*Deutscher Industrie- und Handelstag, DIHT*) also adopted the curriculum and offers it to the training centres of its member chambers. A distinct feature of the North Rhine-Westphalian CCA is the attempt to control and evaluate the correct transformation of the curriculum into course schemes. Yet there is some controversy over the success of this evaluation.

creation of employment. And for the employment agency call centre training opens up another option to offer their clients and to demonstrate activity.

Starting with the certification of call centre agent training by the chambers of commerce call centre training is on its way into the formal German system of vocational training and advanced training. This certificate is formally comparable to those in other occupations. A second step is now the institutionalisation of training for supervisors and middle managers and – more importantly – the accessibility of vocational and advanced training in clerical occupations for experienced call centre agents. There is some controversy over a third step, namely the call centre agent as an occupation or a training module within the German dual system of a three-year vocational training. Pilot projects have been started.

The third element of the North Rhine-Westphalian *Call Center Offensive* (in co-operation with local agencies for business promotion) is the concrete support of call centres that are willing to locate in the *Bundesland*. It offers an initial business consulting for potential start-ups. More than 600 companies and entrepreneurs have had contact with the programme.

Here, the usual means of local business promotion (especially the procurement of buildings and connection to public transport) are used. Additionally, in some parts of the Ruhr area investment aids from EU funds are available.[16] In this respect, call centres were treated like companies from other branches willing to base themselves in North Rhine-Westphalia. Interviewed call centre managers and relevant representatives from the institutional context agree that these financial subsidies play only a minor role for locational decisions. In their view, the location service itself is more important with respect to labour market, transport infrastructure and the quick availability of suitable office buildings.

There is one remarkable example of direct pressure from call centres in North Rhine-Westphalia for 'hard' institutional change. This concerns the deregulation of legislation on work on Sundays and holidays which is relatively strictly regimented by law. Exceptions have to be confirmed individually, under participation of union representatives. In May 1998 the Government of North Rhine-Westphalia granted call centres a general exemption from this rule and allowed them to work on Sundays and public holidays. This gave the government a welcome opportunity to demonstrate the seriousness of their commitment to call centre development. Other federal states showed isomorphic tendencies and followed suit, but for a

---

[16] A special situation in Eastern Germany sharpens regional competition. In the Eastern *Länder* not only EU investment aids are available but additionally wages may be subsidised.

while this was a significant advantage in the regional competition for call centre employment. However, work on these days still comes under co-determination by works councils.

Not accidentally, the unions were kept out of the 'Call Center Offensive', at least in the beginning. This is surprising in a region were unions are traditionally strong and under a social-democratic-lead government. A reason may be that the structural change of the North Rhine-Westphalian economy generally lowered unions' influence. The promotion of young, technology- and media-based entrepreneurship, of media industries, advanced technological application in microelectronics, software and e-commerce is hardly compatible with traditional union structures and attitudes. On the other hand, it is not unlikely that government has strategically excluded unions in order to demonstrably initiate a development path outside the traditional locked-in clusters of heavy industries. As we pointed out above, in the early stages of the call centre boom the unions themselves underestimated this development.

In terms of regional economic change the growth of call centres is clearly related to institutional change and the building of new institutions. Probably the most important institutional effect is the emergence of call centre specific regional labour markets (Scott and Storper, 1992, p. 18). For a regional labour market it is particularly important to develop a common 'fund of knowledge that help participants screen and evaluate the information they receive' (ibid.). Interviewed experts confirmed this argument. They consider the local labour market to be the main reason for locational decisions of call centres. This labour market works in the interest of workers as well. They tend to change jobs according to pay and conditions and to establish networks of information on employers. Especially universities are a place of vivid exchange of information on the quality of call centre jobs.

Other institutional effects of call centre growth in the Ruhr area remain somewhat speculative. For a traditionally very strong agglomeration of the old economies (steel, coal mining, construction) the change from industrial production clusters to service clusters is perceptible and may have extensive consequences in the future. The fact that thousands of university students in the Ruhr area are gaining direct experiences in service work may contribute to changed cultural attitudes towards service work. The rapid growth of call centres so far has given student workers the chance to move into middle management positions for which staff used to be recruited internally. For the first generation of call centre agents their jobs may turn out to offer a long-term perspective. Whether this leads to a career path remains open at the moment.

The outlined shaping of a call centre specific landscape in the Ruhr area and the considerable investments in personnel may in turn contribute to a stronger territorial integration (Asheim, 1992, p.59) of a supposedly very mobile industry. Another incentive for this not only functional but also territorial integration of call centres is the discovery of potential 'forward linkages' of call centres to existing important clusters (Coffey, 1992, p. 142). In Duisburg, linkages between logistics (another important sector of the economy because the city is also the location of Europe's largest inland port) and call centres are discussed; Essen is traditionally strong in retail and wholesale; and Dortmund has discovered connections between its university, its considerable software sector and some call centres specialising in technology-oriented services. Hence, institutional interdependencies may emerge and tighten the territorial integration of call centres and their embeddedness in local economies.

Conclusion

The construction of flexibility both in call centres and in and through the emerging organisational field thus does not constitute a linear move towards deregulation. Rather, we find interlaced loops of de- and re-institutionalisation, of discontinuity and continuity through which standards, actors, employment and work relations are structuring one another. The examples we sketched show that the departing point has frequently been a breach with traditional arrangements under the heading of flexibilisation. Organisations and their subsidiaries escaped from collective agreements and occupational structures, the NRW government yielded to the pressure to exempt call centres summarily from the regulation of Sunday work. Unions found themselves in the unattractive role of defending previous arrangements while constrained by their focus on traditional full-time skilled work.

So the establishment and diffusion of call centres indeed shook up the foundations of work and employment relations which were perceived as too inflexible. It effectively challenged traditional status rights and limitations to flexibility and forced workers both in call centres and in companies employing call centres to make concessions both through actual outsourcing and the threat of outsourcing. It was firmly brought home that any rearrangements would amount to a *status quo minus* (cf. Bode, Brose and Voswinkel, 1991). Improvements from there have been mostly relative but should not be underestimated.

After initial steps of deregulation, re-institutionalisations on more flexible terms set in. Companies are learning, often by default, that call centre work cannot summarily be deskilled without incurring costs at other points. Thus skill and its development and certification are becoming focal points for the organisational field to negotiate. The same is the case for the image of call centre work.[17] In turn, a not-unskilled workforce enables call centres to add value to their services and extend their fields of operations in order to utilise a larger share of agents' skills.

Call centre *managers* have accumulated an amount of experience with call centre operations – including the high reflexivity of reorganisation – which may empower them to claim strategic expertise in customer relations management in relation to both internal and external customers. The orientation of a part of call centre management towards service quality and innovation thus has strategic reasons. They are coming to control a 'relevant zone of uncertainty' (Crozier and Friedberg, 1979) for their organisation or customers.

Assumedly contingent *workers*, confronted with dire working conditions and tightened control are frequently coming to see the uses of interest representation. *Unions* are getting the point that boundaries between core employees as their clientele and contingent labour are eroding and their traditional focus on the full-time/skilled/breadwinner groups is becoming outright dangerous. *Politicians* attributing job gains to their successful attraction of call centres find themselves questioned as to the quality and sustainability of these new jobs.

These instances contain the makings of a 'modernisation alliance' of unions, progressive management and consultants and politicians, of which academic research is likely to become a part. The actual implementation of a high-quality path of call centre development along the lines of skilled work, sophisticated interest representation, worker participation and state-of-the-art workplace design is, however, contingent upon specific conditions and organisations' enactment of these conditions. This includes a closeness of call centre operations to organisations' core competencies and thus a strategic relevance, a critical mass of call centres in a region which leads to a functioning labour market offering job alternatives and career prospects, opportunities for circulation of knowledge and communication of experiences among both management and workers, political, public and academic attention to the field, an encompassing system of company-internal and external training including options for further training, the exploration of networking with customer branches and attention to service innovation.

---

[17] This is quite usual for a-typical industries and occupations cf. Voswinkel and Lücking (1996) for the building and restaurant trades.

This is by no means a naturally emerging process of organisations isomorphically drifting towards the high-quality path of service innovation. The development of identifiably good practices, of standards and guidelines has been the result of conflictual and political struggles (at least) as well as of state-moderated discourses and enlightening research. Bad examples (e. g. Citibank cf. Holtgrewe, 2001b) and public outrage over closures and escape from collective agreements ('*Tarifflucht*') have played their part in these processes as well.

Thus this sketch should not be taken to suggest that all is well in the German call centre scenery. The outlined modernisation alliance represents the possibilities of the bright side of the picture. Embracing it too euphorically as researchers has its own dangers. We need to be especially attentive to processes of segmentation in the field (along gender, ethnicity and class lines and industry lines as well) which may come to exclude bad jobs and their holders further from the high-quality road. The enlightened management and interest representation discourse is not purely ideological, though. We are arguing that it is becoming institutionally and organisationally effective through *Leitbilder* of quality and competence, through the struggles around them, and through actors' reflexive self-positioning in the field.

References

Asheim, B.T. (1992), 'Flexible specialisation, industrial districts and small firms: A critical appraisal', in Ernste, H. and Meier, V. (eds.), *Regional Development and Contemporary Industrial Response*, London and New York, Belhaven, pp. 45-63.

Baumeister, H., (2001), *Call Center in Bremen. Strukturen, Qualifikationsanforderungen und Entwicklungstendenzen*, Bremen, Arbeitnehmerkammer.

Bode, I., Brose, H.G. and Voswinkel, S. (1991), 'Arrangement im Status quo minus', *Soziale Welt*, Vol. 42, pp. 20-45.

Bourdieu, P. (1982), *Die feinen Unterschiede*, Frankfurt, Suhrkamp.

Coffey, W. (1992), 'The role of producer services in systems of flexible production', in Ernste, H. and Meier, V. (eds.), *Regional Development and Contemporary Industrial Response*, London and New York, Belhaven, pp. 133-146.

Crozier, M. and Friedberg, E. (1979), *Macht und Organisation*, Königstein/Ts., Athenäum.

DiMaggio, P.J. and Powell, W.W. (1991), 'The Iron Cage Revisited: Institutional Isomorphism and Collective Rationality', in Dimaggio, P.J. and Powell, W.W. (eds.), *The New Institutionalism in Organizational Analysis*, Chicago, University of Chicago Press, pp. 63-82.

DiMaggio, P.J. and Powell, W.W. (eds.) (1991), *The New Institutionalism in Organizational Analysis*, Chicago, University of Chicago Press.

Frenkel, S.J., Korczynski, M., Shire, K.A. and Tam, M. (1999), *On the Front Line. Organization of Work in the Information Economy*, Ithaka, New York and London, Cornell University Press.

Gottschall, K., Mickler, O. and Neubert, J. (1985), *Computerunterstützte Verwaltung*, Frankfurt/Main and New York, Campus.

Grey, C. (1994), 'Career as a Project of the Self and Labour Process Discipline', *Sociology*, Vol. 28, pp. 479-497.
Holtgrewe, U. (2001a), 'Organisationsdilemmata und Kommunikationsarbeit. Callcenter als informatisierte Grenzstellen', in Matuschek, I., Henninger, A. and Kleemann, F. (eds.), *Neue Medien im Arbeitsalltag. Empirische Befunde, Gestaltungskonzepte, Theoretische Perspektiven*, Wiesbaden, Westdeutscher Verlag, pp. 55-70.
Holtgrewe, U. (2001b), 'Recognition, Intersubjectivity and Service Work: Labour Conflicts in Call Centres', *Industrielle Beziehungen, The German Journal of Industrial Relations*, Vol. 8(1), pp. 37-54.
Knights, D.; McCabe, D. (1999), 'Are There No Limits to Authority?' TQM and Organisational Power, *Organizations Studies*, Vol. 20, pp. 197-224.
Korczynski, M. (2001), 'The Contradictions of Service Work: Call Centres as Customer-Oriented Bureaucracy', in Sturdy, A., Grugulis, I. and Willmott, H. (eds.), *Customer Service. Empowerment and Entrapment*, Basingstoke, Macmillan, pp. 79-101.
March, J.G. and Olsen, J.P. (1989), *Rediscovering Institutions. The Organizational Basis of Politics*, New York, Free Press.
Meyer, J.W.; Rowan, B. (1977), Institutionalized Organizations: Formal Structure as Myths and Ceremony, *American Journal of Sociology*, Vol. 83, pp. 340-363.
Müller, H.P. (2001), 'Über die Mühen der Profilfindung einer Dienstleistungsgewerkschaft. Entstehungsgeschichte der Multibranchengewerkschaft "Ver.di" im Spannungsfeld von Organisationskonflikten und Programmsuche', *Industrielle Beziehungen, The German Journal of Industrial Relations*, Vol. 8(1), pp. 108-137.
Newton, T.J. (1996), 'Resocialising the Subject? A Re-reading of Grey's "Career as a Project of the Self"', *Sociology*, Vol. 30, pp. 137-144.
Nippa, M. (1999), 'Call Center strategiegerecht organisieren', *Harvard Business Manager*, Vol. 6, pp. 86-93.
Oliver, C. (1991), 'Strategic Responses to Institutional Processes', *Academy of Management Review*, Vol. 16, pp. 145-179.
Ortmann, G., Sydow, J. and Türk, K. (eds.) (1997), *Theorien der Organisation. Die Rückkehr der Gesellschaft*, Opladen, Westdeutscher Verlag.
Scott, A.J. and Storper, M. (1992), 'Regional development reconsidered', in Ernste, H. and Meier, V. (eds.), *Regional Development and Contemporary Industrial Response*, London and New York, Belhaven, pp. 3-24.
Scott, W.R. (1995), *Institutions and Organizations*, Thousand Oaks, London and New Delhi, Sage.
Schnitzer, K., Isserstedt, W. and Middendorff, E. (2001), *Die wirtschaftliche und soziale Lage der Studierenden in der Bundesrepublik Deutschland 2000*, Bonn: BMBF.
Voswinkel, S. and Lücking, S. (1996), 'Normalitätsmanagement', *Soziale Welt*, Vol. 47, pp. 450-479.
Weiss, M. (1992), 'Structural Change and Industrial Relations: The Federal Republic of Germany', in Gladstone, A., Wheeler, H., Rojot, J., Eyraud, F. and Ben-Israel, R. (eds.), *Labour Relations in a Changing Environment*, Berlin and New York, De Gruyter, pp. 243-250.

Chapter 3

Consolidation, 'Cowboys' and the Developing Employment Relationship in British, Dutch and US Call Centres

Peter Bain and Phil Taylor

Introduction

The massive and sustained growth in both the number of call centre operations and in the size of the workforce has been one of the most significant developments in the changing structure of employment in north America and western Europe over the last decade. In the three countries which form the focus of this paper, recent research puts the number of call centre employees at between four and almost nine million in the USA (three to six per cent of the total workforce), 600,000 in the UK (2.3 per cent), and 200,000 in the Netherlands (almost three per cent) (Roncoroni, 2000; Datamonitor, 1998, 1999). Although most current indicators suggest that call centre employment will continue to expand, at least in the medium-term (the next five years), the impact of a serious, world-wide economic recession in halting growth or producing contraction, cannot be discounted.

Obviously, the emergence of the internet is an important factor in influencing the future development of the call centre, and it is clear that there has been an increase in the number of customers conducting on-line transactions. However, all available evidence shows that these trends have led, not to the inevitable demise of the call centre as some journalists under the sway of technological determinism would have it (Financial Times, 10 August 2000), but to the emergence of integrated, 'one stop' contact centres in which telephone-based customer facilities are provided alongside internet, email and fax services (Parle, 1999; Neff, 2000). Even before the 'crash' of the dot.com companies in 2000, to the extent that e-commerce and internet services had increased, it was apparent that they were accompanied by the growth of telephone based customer operations.

Throughout this period of expansion, the employment relationship in call centres has been characterised by the adoption of a diverse range of policies and practices. At one extreme, some organisations have chosen, or accepted union demands, to incorporate their call centre workforce into existing representational and bargaining arrangements. At the opposite extreme, rejecting the path of negotiation or participation, some companies have endeavoured to impose a relationship upon their employees firmly rooted in the conviction that management should enjoy an unfettered right to manage. Between these two polarities, lie gradations in managerial approach, style and strategy.

These differences are a reflection of two sets of factors. Firstly, as we have emphasised elsewhere (Bain and Taylor, 2000; Taylor and Bain, 2001a), despite common defining characteristics, call centres are not homogeneous. Differences exist in relation to a number of important variables; size of the operation, the industrial sector involved, product or service market conditions, complexity of service and call cycle time, nature of operations (inbound, outbound or combined), inherited patterns of industrial relations – all of which might influence management's approach to the employment relationship. Secondly, and more directly, there persists amongst many employers a genuine uncertainty as to the preferred method of dealing with a host of general and workplace-specific employment relations' issues which have emerged in the relatively new and often volatile environment of the call centre.

This paper will first set out the overall patterns of call centre development in the UK, Netherlands and the USA. In the process, particular sectoral and locational characteristics will be identified (Bain and Taylor, 1999a; Datamonitor, 1998, 1999; STEC, 2000). However, drawing upon recent research carried out by the authors in these three countries, the paper will then focus mainly on management's efforts to deal with both the routine and problematic issues arising from the specific conditions, content and organisation of call centre work. These range from the ways in which 'bread and butter' aspects of the employment contract, such as pay, hours and holidays are processed and resolved, to attempts by organisations to address enduring and endemic problems such as employee 'burnout' and high labour turnover.

In terms of managerial practice and subsequent outcomes, it will be argued that a key influence is whether or not trade unions are recognised by employers for bargaining purposes and, consequently, whether or not companies are able to unilaterally impose and change working practices and conditions. Inevitably, in this respect, the wider industrial relations context is of great significance and here union density serves as one useful, *albeit* imperfect, indicator of the way the employment relationship is perceived and conducted. US aggregate union density is considerably lower than in both the Netherlands and Britain, whilst differing cross-sectoral constraints also influence and shape the strength and efficacy of union organisation. An important related factor in those organisations where unions are present is the scope of the bargaining agenda (Taylor and Bain, 2000).

We will conclude our analysis by assessing the prospects for industrial relations in call centres in the light of some recent and significant trends and developments. These include the activities of some particularly determined anti-union employers and the huge growth in outsourcing in Europe and in the USA, the withdrawal by certain employers from longstanding sectoral bargaining agreements in the Netherlands, and the potential impact of the Employment Relations Act in Britain.

Sectoral and Locational Developments

Sectoral Developments

Common historical roots can be identified in the sectoral development of call centres in the three countries. The re-configuration of work that became the embryo of the call centre originated in large, often public sector, corporations, and was established to provide customer inquiry and/or servicing facilities by means of the telephone. Typical early operations were located in the travel industry (airlines, rail and bus), in utilities such as electricity, gas and water, and in the telephone companies. However, these early examples of servicing a mass customer base through the medium of the telephone would not satisfy current commonly-accepted definitions of a call centre (Taylor and Bain, 1999, p. 102), pre-dating as they do, the utilisation of 'real time', inter-active, personal computers in the workplace whose widespread diffusion only commenced in the early 1980s.

One important aspect of call centre development, common to the Netherlands, USA and Britain, is the pivotal role played by the banking industry in its expansion (Bain and Taylor, 2002). For example, the phenomenal growth of call centres in Britain in the mid-1990s can be attributed, in large part, to the earlier adoption by the finance sector of this highly profitable innovation in the conduct of customer transactions, which took place alongside an extensive programme of closing local branches. Financial institutions came to utilise information and communication technologies in their day-to-day, centralised, customer servicing operations, long before the widespread investment in call centres which took place in virtually every industry during the mid-1990s. Particularly significant in focusing interest in the potential of call centres were the commercial successes of the innovative, round-the-clock First Direct (banking) and Direct Line (insurance) operations, established in 1989 and 1988 respectively (BIFU, 1996, pp. 5, 12). Although early call centre initiatives were not confined to financial services, there is no question that these celebrated examples from banking and insurance made the greatest impact, leading to emulation throughout almost every sector of industry.

It remains the case that, in the USA, UK and Netherlands, more call centre jobs are located in finance than in any other economic sector. Datamonitor (1998) estimated there were 44,400 agent positions in financial services in 1997, constituting 27 per cent of the total UK call centre workforce, projected to rise to 66,000 positions by 2000.[1] Since, due to shifts and part-time work, Datamonitor assumes there are two workers for every agent position, this implied a total of approximately 132,000 jobs by the year 2000. Mitial's (1999) estimate of the number of agents in finance sector call centres was 53,060 (35 per cent of UK call centre employment) in 1995, increasing to 86,400 (32 per cent) by 1998 – not far from Datamonitor's estimate in a sector whose parameters are difficult to define. In 1997, Datamonitor (1998) reported that financial services (27 per cent) was the most important locus of call centre employment in the Netherlands while, in the USA, the 366,000 employed in the sector in 1999 was predicted to increase to 430,000 by 2003.

Another characteristic of call centre development which transcended national boundaries was the introduction of 'toll-free' telephone numbers. The largest Dutch outsourcing company, SNT, has attributed the significant growth of call centres in the early period as being in no small measure due to the introduction of 0800/0900 numbers in the Netherlands in 1986 (SNT, 2000). Similar free-phone measures, encouraged by the giant telecommunications companies, were likewise influential in stimulating call centre development and expansion in the USA and UK.

A more recent common trend internationally has been the spectacular growth of outsourcing operations (Datamonitor, 1998, 1999; STEC Groep, 2000). Companies providing such a facility seek to persuade potential clients that their customer servicing functions would be more effectively conducted by contracting out, on either a permanent or short-term campaign basis, to an experienced, specialist call centre. Clearly, in such situa-

---

[1] It should be noted that Datamonitor's research routinely refers to 'agent positions' or 'seats', and not to the number of agents employed. As we point out, they then assume – based upon the proliferation of '24/7' and other extended hours operations, and on the incidence of part-time working - that two call centre workers are employed for every agent position.

tions, cost is a key consideration, and clients seek reassurance that there will be savings for them if they proceed along this path. However, cost may not be the only criteria, as firms also need to be convinced that the outsourcing call centre will deliver levels of customer satisfaction which protect the reputation of the client company. In addition, outsourcing may be advantageous to any company seeking to circumvent union presence and existing collective bargaining arrangements.

Many outsourcing organisations place particular emphasis on holding labour costs as low as possible, since these account for more than half of total call centre costs (CCA, 1999). Further incentives to reduce labour costs come, firstly, from competitive pressures emanating from potential client companies and from fellow outsourcers, and, secondly, from the frequently ruthless and aggressive pursuit of profits symptomatic of the outsourced sub-sector. For similar reasons, there are good grounds for believing that increasing numbers of companies who currently run in-house call centre operations are either considering, or have already turned to, dedicated outsourcing organisations. While fuller evidence in support of this statement will be presented below, two examples of the trend will suffice at this stage. According to SNT (2000), the number of outsourced agent positions in the Netherlands has been growing at 30 per cent per annum. In Scotland, the number of outsourced call centres more than doubled (from 18 to 42), and the workforce increased from 2,905 to 9,010, between 1997 and 2000 (Taylor and Bain, 2001b).

However, as might be expected in such a diffuse and rapidly growing area of employment, there are also some nationally deviant sectoral developments. For example, a distinctive feature of the more recent phase of expansion in the Netherlands has been the strong presence of trans-national companies, particularly, but not exclusively, US-based, who established many multi-lingual call centres in the 1990s to handle their pan-European operations. Datamonitor (1999) ascribed the significance of the Manufacturing, Distribution and Consumer Products [MD&CP] sector, which accounts for 21 per cent of all call centre jobs, to the Netherlands' role as a distribution hub for Europe. While the trans-nationals were undoubtedly motivated by the need to gain entry to the massive new markets within the boundaries of the European Union, it is clear that the multi-lingual capabilities of the Dutch population have continued to be a significant factor in choosing the country of location. The sophistication of these language skills is reflected also in the size of the Dutch travel and tourism sector which accounts for 14 per cent of all call centre jobs (Datamonitor 1998).

Locational Developments

Successive studies have shown that the most important factors which organisations identify when considering the location of a new call centre are those related to the availability and perceived competence of the local labour force, and to the provision of technologically suitable office accommodation (Taylor and Bain, 1997; Mitial, 1999). Bristow *et al.* (2000, p. 19), in explaining patterns of development, conclude that there has been a 'propensity to site call centres close to existing concentrations of allied activity, with preferences for densely populated areas mediated by needs to maintain employee access and avoid staff turnover problems'. For these reasons, large conurbations were initially the main loci for call centres, typically either in city centres or in peripheral business parks. Despite some geographical dispersal to rural hinterlands, the pattern of urban concentration remains, often in areas which have experienced industrial decline and relatively high levels of unemployment. In addition, the spatial distribution of call centres has been shaped, in all three countries, by the support and subsidies of economic development agencies. While competition undoubtedly occurs between the centralised agencies of nation-states, it is often fiercest within an individual country's borders as regional and local agencies seek to attract new call centre investment to their area.

In the Netherlands, the importance of these factors was reflected in rapid initial growth being strongly based in the 'randstad', the 'rim' formed by the western cities of Amsterdam, The Hague and Rotterdam. However, by the late 1990s, as labour market conditions tightened, expansion was taking place at a slower rate in the 'randstad' than in adjacent areas and in the more far-flung border regions of the country (STEC Groep, 2000). It has been argued that the outsourcing companies, in particular, are attracted by the level of public funding for new developments in the peripheral, older industrial areas, where unemployment also tends to be higher. In 2000, the entire eastern border, from Maastricht in the south to Groningen in the north, was described as a 'hot spot' for call centre development (Nijenhuis, 2000).

In the UK, the economically over-heated London area has generally fared less well than other big regional conurbations in attracting call centre investment, although multi-lingual operations have proved an important exception to this rule (Mitial, 1999). However, while some recent research has suggested that the significance of the south-east has been under-estimated (IDS, 2000), for most of the 1990s, a number of other big UK cities vied for the accolade of the most highly rated location by investing companies. Amongst the most enduring candidates for the title of call centre capital have been Leeds, Glasgow and Belfast, but considerable and growing clusters have also developed in South Wales, Liverpool, and in North-East England around Newcastle and Sunderland.

Compared to Europe generally, call centre development in the USA is more likely to be located in a context of regional, rather than national markets. Examples include the many banking, telecommunications, airline and utility companies whose business has a regional orientation, and who tend therefore to site their operations in the bigger cities of the state or region. However, to the extent that call centres do operate nationally across the USA, the heavy concentrations in the west, around Omaha and Phoenix for example, can be explained, in part, by their location in non-union, 'right to work' states.[2] It is also argued that, in national telesales operations, the western accent is regarded as neutral and acceptable (Folts, 2000). As in other parts of the world, a combination of the massive expansion of call centre operations alongside ever-tighter labour market conditions, has resulted in the establishment of many new facilities in hitherto relatively under-developed areas, such as in Southern cities like Birmingham, Mobile, Nashville and Tampa.

Employment Relations Issues

Whilst call centres are defined, in essence, by the integration of computer and telephone technologies, it is necessary to emphasise the many differences that exist in work organisation and call complexity (Kinnie *et al.*, 2000; Batt, 2000). Particularly crucial distinctions arise from the degree to which management prioritises the quantity or quality of their employees' calls, and operations range from the simple, volume-driven and routinised, to the complex and customised (Taylor and Bain, 2001a). Notwithstanding these organisational and functional differences, management has sought to establish 'frontiers of control' which, in the majority of call centres, means repetitive, routinised work, embodying new Taylorist developments.

As competitive pressures have grown, an earlier ethos of customer service has been increasingly subordinated to the imperatives of sales figures and statistical benchmarking, for example, in the finance sector. As a consequence, many call centre workers have come to experience work as intensive, target-driven and generally stressful, and attribute the compulsion

---

[2] About half of all individual states have introduced 'right to work' legislation which undermines union organization by allowing employees not to join a union even where it has won a workplace ballot. At the same time, the union must represent any non-members employed in the bargaining unit.

to meet targets as the principal source of pressure in the performance of daily tasks (Taylor and Bain, 2000). Other aspects of the labour process are also widely regarded as contributing to the pressures of the job – the lack of time between calls, the repetition and monotony of tasks, the infrequency and brevity of breaks, the strict interpretation of performance measurements, and the stress arising from the requirement to continuously perform emotional labour (S. Taylor, 1998).

Many of these production-related issues are, of course, acknowledged by call centre employers. However, when these matters are considered in conjunction with the need for management to provide acceptable rates of pay, hours of work, holidays, and the many other items integral to the employment contract, it becomes clear that the creation and maintenance of a stable industrial relations climate can be a formidable task. The questions, therefore, of management philosophy and style, and the nature of the prevailing employment relations system, are of particular importance in the frequently volatile environment of the call centre.

As call centre employers have become increasingly conscious that these matters have to be addressed, there have been growing signs that they are doing so on a collective basis. Although these tendencies are generally at a formative stage, historically, employers' associations have been depicted as

> '…reactive institutions which have come into being to protect members from the activities of unions or the state or both…(and) have sought to regulate trade and competition, to provide a united front in negotiations, and to provide a range of services.' (Plowman, 1991)

In the Netherlands, the five largest outsourcing organisations formed a national association in 1999, primarily to represent their interests in matters such as employment legislation and access to training funds (Sprenger, 2000). In the UK, the national Call Centre Association (CCA) boasts 420 corporate members, including many large trans-nationals from a variety of sectors, as well as many organisations from the fast-expanding outsourcing and public sectors (CCA, 2000a). Partly in response to some hostile media coverage, but also because of concerns over employment relations issues such as the new legislation and the BT call centre strike, the CCA (2000b) produced a 'Standard for Best Practice' which its members agreed to adopt. This sets out processes which have the declared aim of ensuring that the treatment of both customers and employees is of the highest standard, and the standard has been endorsed by the Department of Trade and Industry (DTI).

Another significant and related trend has been the formation of local employers' groups in areas of high call centre concentration, such as

Glasgow and Leeds. These groups meet regularly to discuss issues and developments in their areas, and there is no doubt that pay and conditions of employment are high on the agenda (Parle, 1999). 6,000 miles away, in the booming, 'sun belt' city of Phoenix, Arizona, where no fewer than 90,000 people were employed in 160 call centres in the year 2000, similar meetings take place (Flynn, 2000). In the older, industrial city of Birmingham, Alabama, while there was no evidence of collaboration between the longer-established call centre operators (Bell South, the banks, Social Security Administration, etc.) and recent inward investors (who include outsourcing companies, Sitel and Teletech), the Metropolitan Development Board produced regular updates on local wage rates and labour availability (MDB, 2000).

A key question in all of these developments is, of course, the extent to which the workforce have the opportunity to actively engage in the process of influencing the terms and conditions under which they are required to work and, in particular, whether or not there is an effective trade union presence. The role of trade unions in call centres has been largely neglected yet, as we have argued elsewhere, their presence in the UK is far more widespread than popularly imagined, with evidence of recent and significant recruitment activity (Bain and Taylor, 1999b). Members see the union as important in negotiating what might be described as the conventional bargaining agenda of pay, hours, holidays, health and safety, etc. However, as indicated above, workers' experience of the call centre labour process suggests that an effective bargaining agenda needs to incorporate a range of issues which have remained largely outside the domain of union action.

We shall now assess the arrangements for dealing with, firstly, the 'traditional' conditions of work and, secondly, the specific issues generated by the particular form of labour process and experience of work in the call centre.

Employment Relations: The 'Traditional' Bargaining Agenda

In aggregate terms, union membership covers 14 per cent of the workforce in the USA, 28 per cent in the Netherlands, and around 30 per cent in the UK. Collective bargaining coverage is much higher than union density in the Netherlands and UK, and slightly higher in the USA (IDS, 2000; FNV, 2000; Certification Officer, 2000; WERS, 1998). Whilst the tripartite, 'polder' model of government, employer and union collaboration still holds in the Netherlands, both the UK and US industrial relations systems have undergone considerable change under the impact of neo-liberal, de-regulating and anti-trade union governments. However, as will be discussed, there are significant inter-sectoral differences, with union recognition and collective bargaining far more likely to exist in call centres where these practices have been widely established throughout the company prior to the start-up of their call centre facilities.

Conversely, companies and sectors, where there is no or limited union recognition and collective bargaining, are likely to have these policies extended to their call centres. In the latter category, we can identify two types of company. Firstly, those, including a number of trans-nationals, which have displayed a longstanding aversion to unions and collective bargaining and have adopted an exclusionist version of human resource management. Secondly, there exists a layer of recently established companies which hold an extreme unitarist concept of the employment relationship, in which the employee's role is perceived to be confined to unquestioning obedience of managerial decisions. Amongst these can be found a number of organisations which genuinely deserve the appellation of 'cowboy' because of the roughshod manner in which they treat their workforce.

Telecommunications

In sectors such as utilities and telecommunications, which were characterised until the 1980s or 1990s by the existence of mainly public monopolies, there exist significant clusters of unionised call centres. In the USA, for example, AT&T and the 'baby Bell' companies not only continue to negotiate pay and conditions with the Communication Workers of America (CWA), but also incorporate their call centre employees into company-wide grading structures and comprehensive collective agreements. As a consequence, agreements can be both detailed and lengthy, with that between Bell South and the CWA extending to 313 pages. Such agreements set out in detail how every imaginable substantive element (pay, hours, shifts, holidays, seniority benefits etc.) in the employment contract will be applied, as well as establishing procedures for resolving disputed matters. Similar arrangements apply in British Telecom in the UK, and in KPN, the Dutch telecommunications giant.

However, the deregulation of telecommunications has presented the unionised call centres with threats to their conditions from two sources. First, there are challenges from new entrants to the industry. For example, with the ending of the Bell monopoly there are now 250 companies in the state of Alabama registered to provide telecommunication services (Camp, 2000). Second, from outsourcing organisations keen to secure contracts for customer handling functions from the existing companies. This sense of external competition is conveyed to employees by management, and is experienced in the form of work intensification, threats to outsource contracts and/or to automate certain functions, and in the perennial efforts to hold down pay and conditions. However, one difficulty for some of the more militant employers is the fact that the unions tend to retain considerable strength in the most profitable business segment of company operations, where the most senior and skilled operators are concentrated. As a result, while employers have sought to dictate the terms of what is still regarded by call centre staff as a 'bargaining' agenda, the combination of strong collective bargaining traditions in sectors such as telecommunications, the potential industrial muscle of strategic groups of union members, and tight labour market conditions generally, has made it more difficult for management to achieve many of their strategic objectives.

Finance

A much more divergent picture is evident in the finance sector. Firstly, unionisation in the sector in the USA is estimated to stand at around 2 per cent and is concentrated in a few of the more highly unionised states. Accordingly, there appear to be few formal mechanisms in place for call centre staff in the US finance sector to influence decisions on pay and working conditions, with opportunities perhaps restricted to periodic employee attitudinal surveys or one-to-one interviews during the annual, or often less frequent, reviews. In the UK, union recognition and presence varies hugely from company to company, with very strong organisation in some firms and little, or nothing, in others. In contrast, until the year 2000, the terms and conditions of employment for all Dutch finance sector workers were covered by a single sectoral agreement.

Having unilaterally jettisoned national negotiations in the sector in the 1980s, UK banks now deal with their employees on a company by company basis, either through a union, by management *diktat,* or through consultative machinery. During Barclay Bank's annual pay and conditions negotiations with the unions in 1997, when the company tried to impose new conditions which would have adversely affected employees' pensions, Barclaycard call centre workers in Liverpool were amongst those who took strike action. In 1999, Barclay's became one of many British companies to sign a 'partnership' agreement with a union (UNIFI). Under this kind of agreement, management and union commit themselves to a collaborative, problem-solving, approach to the employment relationship. However, despite the agreement, the company continued to deny UNIFI recognition and bargaining rights in three of its call centres. After threats of industrial action by the union, the company finally agreed to ballot employees on the issue, on the same basis as that proposed under the new Employment Relations Act[3] on its implementation. On a 76 per cent staff turnout, 89 per cent voted in favour of union recognition. While management has accepted this decision, it remains to be seen whether the outcome will result in improvements to the work regime in what has been a very troubled environment.

In the Netherlands, attempts were made by both ABN-AMRO, one of the 'big five' banks, and by KLM, the national airline, to set up new call centres in 1996, with terms and conditions inferior to those determined by the existing sectoral agreements. Although the industrial court ruled against ABN-AMRO, and in favour of KLM, the latter did not proceed with their plans. However, in January 2000, the 'big five' banks announced their withdrawal from the sectoral agreement, and the unions were compelled to accept this decision (EIRR, March 2000). There is no doubt that the sectoral agreement was seen by the big banks as inhibiting the introduction of significant innovations which they desired, including the abandonment of joint regulation and the introduction of more flexible working arrangements in their call centres. For example, one clause identified for removal by ABN-AMRO concerned the agreed practice by which the company pays 11.80 € (£7.40) towards the cost of all meals for employees working at the weekend (de Rooy, 2000). As is the case throughout Dutch industry, employees are entitled to consultation on company plans through the works council structure. However, ABN-AMRO has tried to distance the call centre workforce from the rest of their operations by establishing a separate works council in one of their call centres, with the clear objective of encouraging a generally more flexible approach from employees.

Outsourcing

Two distinct approaches to the employment relationship reflect important trends occurring in the context of the growth of outsourcing. On the one hand, as some organisations found themselves able to expand in conditions of tightening labour markets over prolonged periods of time, they decided it was necessary to introduce improvements in the contractual relationship with their employees, partly in response to their own recruitment and re-

---

[3] The Blair government's Employment Relations Act was generally disappointing to the British trade union movement, but nevertheless contained clauses, enacted in 2000, which were perceived by the unions to offer some possibilities of improving their chances of recruitment and organization. These were, first, an encouragement to employers and unions to voluntarily reach agreement concerning collective bargaining rights but, failing such agreement, the establishment of balloting mechanisms leading to automatic recognition if the union gained the support of '50 per cent plus one' in the bargaining unit. Second, a right for individual workers to have outside representation, if they so desired, in grievance or disciplinary cases.

tention problems. In the year 2000, for example, SNT, the biggest Dutch outsourcing company, initiated a policy of offering longer-term (three-year) contracts and company shares to their staff, while the call centre employment agency, Randstad Callflex, negotiated its first collective agreement with the unions.

On the other hand, the approach to employment relations adopted by the Arizona-based outsourcing company, Excell Multimedia, attracted widespread media publicity and hostility from trade unions and public bodies in the UK. This company, formed in 1994, expanded rapidly in the USA, Canada and Mexico, before securing their first UK contract in 1996. A rising tide of complaints from their UK employees concerning pay, conditions and the quality of customer service was ignored, and leading union activists were dismissed, in a repeat of events in Arizona and Canada. In March 2000, the main client, Cable and Wireless, terminated their contract with Excell and replaced them with Vertex, another outsourcer. Vertex quickly established contact with the Communication Workers Union (CWU), a decision influenced by their earlier experiences in another call centre they operate in the utilities sector. In this case, following Vertex's unilateral removal of collective bargaining rights from call centre staff in 1996, the workforce voted overwhelmingly to return to this method of pay determination four years later (IDS, 1999).

Some of the most extreme examples of dictatorial management styles have emanated from outsourcing companies in the USA, especially those operating in the short-term, telesales business. These are widely regarded as unstable, temporary operations, offering low wages, long hours, Dickensian working conditions and little job security (Folts, 2000). While such call centres may be perceived to be typical 'cowboy' outfits, they are growing both numerically and proportionally. Workers find themselves at the mercy of managers unconstrained by union presence, and any signs of organised employee discontent are dealt with ruthlessly (McGrath, 2000). Employees who have experience of working for this type of company contrast the lack of equity in their treatment, with the clear ground-rules and representational rights laid down in unionised establishments.

Employment Relations: The 'Production Issues' Bargaining Agenda

There is widespread acknowledgement throughout the sector internationally that a major problem exists in relation to employee 'burnout'. This is particularly the case at the high-volume, low-value, quantitative end of the call centre spectrum, where the causal relationship with the nature of work organisation is most obvious. A combination of the need to achieve both quantitative and qualitative targets, the requirement to constantly expend emotional labour, the impact of extensive monitoring and the experience of long periods of often repetitive, routine work can generate intolerable pressures. These stressful aspects of work organisation may well be compounded by poor environmental and ergonomic conditions. Furthermore, where no collective mechanisms exist for the pursuit of remedial measures, the severity of the problems facing employees becomes ever more acute.

In the industry's jargon, 'burnout' is widely perceived to be related to high levels of employee turnover, or 'churn'. Our own research suggests that attaining accurate turnover information from call centre employers is extremely difficult and that the most reliable figures are often to be found at the extremes. Call centres with low turnover rates are often keen to publicise them, while those with very high rates acquire notoriety within the industry (Bain and Taylor, 1999a). Although these related problems of burnout and churn are widely acknowledged by employers and managers and can lead to the adoption of participatory and 'softer' management styles, the effectiveness of these measures remains highly circumscribed. In all three countries, the weight of evidence is compelling that management, from senior levels to supervisory and team leader grades, ascribe overwhelming significance to statistical benchmarking as key performance indicators. The transmission belt downwards of target imposition - from corporate level to the individual call centre, to the team and, finally, to the individual operator - results, in the final analysis, in an intensification of work.

This observation, of the central role and importance of target-setting, is a recurring theme of our research and informs our critique of Frenkel *et al.* (1999) who emphasise the 'facilitative' nature of supervisory activity. In many call centres, non-fulfilment of individual targets by employees leads to disciplinary action. For example, commenting on the punitive regime in the lower-end, routinised operations in Bell South where she had been employed, the president of CWA Local 3902 commented 'I would rather flip hamburgers than work under these new harsher conditions' (Abbott, 2000). Widespread and systematic monitoring provides the statistical evidence for the exercise of these disciplinary measures. The competitive imperatives which drive this top-down imposition of targets are found not merely at the highly quantitative end of the spectrum in outsourced organisations, where they might be expected, but also in some operations that might be regarded as tending towards the quality end. For example, in early 1999, 75 per cent of the staff at a Prudential Assurance greenfield site call centre in the UK were on disciplinary charges for non-fulfilment of targets (Finance Sector Unions, 1999).

Even where they have a significant presence and full collective bargaining rights, unions, for the most part, have neglected to negotiate proactively over questions relating to the organisation and content of work, and have tended to concentrate exclusively on a pay and conditions agenda. However, the concerns which call centre operators express, arising from their daily experience of an intensive and pressurised labour process, are increasingly those which they want their unions to raise in addition to the items covered by the 'traditional' agenda. Reduced targets, more and longer breaks, relaxed call handling times, a negotiated use of statistics, and higher staffing levels are demands which relate directly to the pace and intensity of work and which, to date, have largely remained outside the scope of bargaining.

By way of contrast, there are a number of examples which demonstrate an alternative approach by unions, and which show how they can intervene in order to ameliorate imposed target-setting and unacceptable monitoring practices. The one-day strike by 4,000 British Telecom call centre employees, in November 1999, was specifically directed at the company's insistence on strict employee adherence to tight targets of 285 seconds per call and, more generally, against a harsh management style perceived to be reflected in their ready use of disciplinary measures. During negotiations, the CWU succeeded in convincing BT to remove individual targets for employees, and gained a commitment that managers would adopt a more consultative and sympathetic approach to production-related problems. It was also agreed to establish a pilot scheme in which employees would be allowed to resolve customer problems without being subject to time targets. (CWU, 2000)

Monitoring of employee performance is tightly defined and severely restricted under the CWA-Bell South agreement signed in August 1998. If an individual's calls are to be sampled by management, then s/he must be informed and given the choice of remote or 'side-by-side' monitoring. On the other hand, if the company wishes to randomly sample performance of the work process by remotely logging on to an employee's computer, then, only in the event of having committed a very limited range of offences of a serious nature can the employee be subjected to disciplinary action. Further, no action can be taken over a first offence. The company has indicated that it wishes to re-visit this agreement in the next round of negotiations. (Camp, 2000)

Compared to any previous arrangement, the IAM-Southwest Airlines agreement of November 1997 enables workers to exercise a greater degree of control over the shifts they choose to work. This is an issue of considerable importance to (particularly) women workers, as they seek to juggle the competing demands of work and childcare. As call centre managers respond to variable peaks in customer demand, it is a common complaint that shift changes at short notice throw precariously constructed childcare arrangements into chaos, as these are often dependent on the availability of family members. While companies typically claim, with varying degrees of commitment and justification, to try to accommodate employees' domestic and social needs, the IAM-Southwest agreement provides a method and structure which allows call centre staff considerable flexibility in choosing when to work. Based upon seniority and length of service, a worker can select the shifts she wants to work and arrange an exchange with another worker of the same grade. They then inform the performance desk of this change, with no intervention by any supervisory or managerial grade. In the Phoenix call centre, which employs 1,100 people, a huge board, covered with exchange proposals for weeks ahead, is testament to the success of union intervention and the popularity of this measure.

Finally, the willingness of trade unions to defend individual call centre employees facing disciplinary cases has been a notable development, perceived by the unions as a basic and key means of building membership. In all six case studies involved in our study of UK finance sector call centres, the unions and staff associations described instances where non-members, previously indifferent or antipathetic to collective organisation, were convinced of the need to join when represented at disciplinary hearings by workplace activists (Taylor and Bain, 2000). In the case of Excell Multimedia's Glasgow call centre, it was the company's harsh and widespread use of disciplinary procedures that enabled the union activists to begin to act as effective representatives. The measure contained in the Employment Relations Act, enacted in September 2000, which allows workers on disciplinary charges or pursuing a grievance to be accompanied by a representative, is consciously being utilised by unions keen to raise their profile in a number of unorganised call centres.

Conclusions

Notwithstanding national peculiarities, and acknowledging that call centres originated in the USA, their development and sectoral profile display remarkable similarities in the three countries in our study. Firstly, significant growth occurred in both the finance and telecommunications industries, followed by the diffusion of operations throughout virtually all branches of the economy as companies sought to emulate the cost-efficient re-organisation of service delivery, whilst expanding the range of services provided. Secondly, there is the comparable, recent and extremely rapid growth of outsourced call centres providing services on behalf of client companies, with competitive pricing a key strategic consideration. Thirdly, whilst making allowances for differences in the size of national markets and geography, similar locational patterns have emerged, with concentrations in the large conurbations modified, to an extent, by the role of investment agencies as they have sought to attract capital to their particular favoured loci.

What is also particularly striking is the similarities in the way that work is organised in call centres across the three countries. Observing the call centre labour process in the USA, the UK and the Netherlands, it is clear that common technologies and systems are in place, there is little to distinguish between the configurations of workspace, and work content involves remarkably similar tasks, reflected in similar organisational methods.

However, as is increasingly acknowledged, call centres are not uniform and, as we have argued, the distinctions that exist between them can perhaps best be explicated through reference to a spectrum of quantity and quality (Taylor and Bain, 2001a). However, the distinctions that can be drawn between call centres according to these criteria transcend national boundaries, rather than existing as contrasting, nationally-based systems. To make this point concrete, a highly routinised, telephone directory inquiry service, prioritising strict quantitative measurements often of less than 30 seconds duration, is remarkably similar whether located in the USA, the UK or the Netherlands. At the same time, but at the other end of the quality/quantity spectrum, complex technical help desks will display much the same characteristics across national boundaries. One further important observation is that, despite differentiation on quantitative and qualitative criteria, the majority of call centres in all three countries are located towards the quantitative end of the spectrum. Thus, the imposition of a wide range of targets, reinforced by extensive call monitoring, are common features, alongside the simultaneous expansion of cross-selling as earlier forms of pure customer service give way to the imperative to sell a growing variety of services.

However, this is not to argue that there are no points of differentiation between countries and, for example, contrasting industrial relations contexts exist in the USA, the UK and the Netherlands. Inevitably, these broader frameworks will have a significant bearing on the nature of the employment relationship and the ways in which call centre work may be experienced. One reflection of these contextual factors is that the USA exhibits extremely low levels of trade union density in contrast to the relatively low percentages in both the UK and the Netherlands. We have argued elsewhere (Taylor and Bain, 2001a) that trade unions and collective organisation provide the only means through which real democratisation of the call centre environment can occur. Thus, where unions are sufficiently strong they have already displayed an ability (*albeit* unevenly) to negotiate and bargain with employers over the 'traditional' agenda of pay and conditions, but they also possess a largely unrealised potential to challenge and modify management's determination of the frontiers of control.

Here the comparative picture is complex and contradictory, with sectoral characteristics exercising a major influence. With two per cent of workers in the US financial sector in trade unions, the possibilities of moderating and mediating managerial *diktat* are extremely limited. By contrast, in the telecommunications sector in the USA, there are notable pockets of union strength and influence which are most manifest in the agreement between the CWA and Bell South, where the union successfully contains the exercise of call monitoring and disciplinary action. In the UK, despite high union density in British Telecom, strike action was required before management agreed to moderate stringent performance targets. In the Netherlands, the existence of a national sectoral agreement, covering 138,000 finance sector employees, had been successfully defended by FNV Bondgenoten, the union representing the industry's workforce. However, the withdrawal of the major banks from the agreement, from 2001, clearly poses a major challenge to call centre workers' conditions of employment. In all countries, the growth of outsourcing threatens to undermine the unions in two ways; first, because the overwhelming majority of these operations remain non-unionised and, second, competing largely on the basis of labour costs, they target in-house operations which are often unionised.

The fact that associations of call centre employers have been established is a significant development, even if their present role is extremely limited and does not extend to direct involvement in the conduct of the employment relationship. However, in the UK, it is clear that the CCA's Standard for Best Practice, for example, reflects serious concerns amongst their members about how to handle day-to-day workplace problems and issues. *De facto*, the CCA increasingly seems to be performing a regulatory and an industrial relations advisory role but, of course, this is still a far cry from systematic bargaining with employee representatives. Given the traditions and bargaining structures of the UK system, any such direct involvement by the CCA is difficult to imagine in the foreseeable future. However, it is not so difficult to conceive of the recently established association of Dutch outsourcing companies assuming a more central role in determining pay and conditions. Indeed, overtures to the Dutch industrial courts to recognise an outsourcing call centre 'sector' have already been made (EIRR, 2000b). Furthermore, had KLM proceeded to set up their new call centre without the existing industrial sector agreement as the industrial court accepted, then the question of the sectoral location of KLM staff would have been raised sharply. And, if the example of the big banks in breaking from the sectoral agreement were to be followed elsewhere, then the idea of separate arrangements for call centre workers would be significantly strengthened. More generally, the pattern, evident in all three countries, of employers initially meeting on a local or regional basis to discuss mutual problems, reflects the classical methods by which associations with much wider aims and responsibilities have developed historically (van Waarden, 1995).

Undoubtedly, the emergence of the call centre has also proved to represent a major organisational challenge for trade unions, with implications conceivably far beyond the parameters of the sector itself. In all countries, unions face both opportunities and problems in committing themselves financially and organisationally to undertake large-scale recruitment campaigns. While there have been some encouraging signs for the unions in terms of organising success, there are also a series of nationally-specific problems which have yet to be addressed.

In the USA, massive gaps exist between some well-organised sectors and companies on the one hand, and what can only be described as organisational deserts on the other. Deserts have a tendency to colonise previously verdant territory if left untended, while it takes a programme of conscious policy and action to re-generate previously barren ground and to produce new life. In the Netherlands, the existence of national legally-recognised agreements can be a double-edged sword for the unions. While possibly strengthening employees' rights in some directions, the extensive legal framework can conceivably lead to an over-reliance on formal regulation by the state at the expense of developing independent union activity. In the UK, the picture is mixed. On the one hand collective bargaining and trade union recognition exist in many sectors, yet on the other, there is no shortage of unorganised call centres from which unions have been excluded through employer opposition and/or continuing union inactivity.

Realising the undoubted potential in call centres would require of unions a commitment to recruitment and organisation on a scale not witnessed since the growth experienced by the movement internationally in the 1960s and 1970s (and earlier in the USA). An essential ingredient in any such mobilisation would appear to be the inclusion in the unions' bargaining agendas of issues directly and sharply experienced by workers at the point of production. Such campaigns would need to aim to give expression to the undoubted desire of the growing ranks of the workforce for a serious challenge to managerial prerogatives over the pace, intensity, monitoring and general organisation of work in the call centre.

References

Bain, P. and Taylor, P. (1999a), *Call Centres in Scotland: An Overview*, Glasgow, Scottish Low Pay Unit.
Bain, P. and Taylor, P. (1999b), *Employee Relations, Worker Attitudes and Trade Union Representation in Call Centres*, 17th International Labour Process Conference, University of London, March 1999.
Bain, P. and Taylor, P. (2000), 'Entrapped by the "electronic panopticon"? Worker resistance in the call centre', *New Technology, Work and Employment*, Vol. 15, pp. 2-18.
Bain, P. and Taylor, P. (2002), 'Ringing the Changes: trade union organisation in call centres in the UK finance sector', *Industrial Relations Journal*, Vol. 33.
Batt, R. (2000), 'Strategic segmentation in front-line services: matching customers, employees and human resource systems', *International Journal of Human Resource Management*, Vol. 11, pp. 540-561.
BIFU (1996), *Dialling the future? Phone banking and Insurance*, London.
Bristow, G., Munday, M. and Griapos, P. (2000), 'Call centre growth and location: corporate strategy and the spatial division of labour', *Environment and Planning A*, Vol. 32, pp. 519-538.
CCA (1999), *Statement by M. Stock*, Financial Sector Direct Staff Forum, Haywards Heath, 21 January.
CCA (2000a), *Sixth Annual Members Convention*, Glasgow, 14 November.
CCA (2000b), *Standard for Best Practice*, Glasgow.
Certification Officer (2000), *Annual Report of the Certification Officer 1999-2000*, London.
CWU (2000), *Call Centre Excellence*, London.
Datamonitor (1998), *Call Centres in Europe: Sizing by Call Centres and Agent Positions in 13 European Countries*, London.
Datamonitor (1999), *Opportunities in US and Canadian Call Centre Markets: The Definitive Vertical Analysis*, New York.
EIRR (2000a), *European Industrial Relations Review*, no. 313, March, London.
EIRR (2000b), *European Industrial Relations Review*, no. 320, October, London.
Finance Sector Unions (1999), *Seminar*, Bishop's Storford, 19 February.
FNV (1997), *The FNV in profile: general information on the Netherlands Trade Union Confederation*, Amsterdam.
IDS (1999), *IDS Report 798*, Incomes Data Services, London.
IDS (2000), *Pay and Conditions in Call Centres*, Incomes Data Services, London.
Hutchinson, S. et al. (2000), 'Evolving high commitment management and the experience of the RAC call centre', *Human Resource Management Journal*, Vol. 10, pp. 63-78.
Mitial (1996), *Telephone call centre in the British Isles*, London.
Mitial (1999), *Telephone call centre in the British Isles*, London.
Neff, T. (2000), *The Multimedia Contact Center: Corporate Façade or Human Face?*, The Fletcher School of Law and Diplomacy, Purdue University, Iowa.
Parle, J. (1999), Call Centre Manager, Halifax Direct, *Finance Sector Direct Staff Forum*, Halifax, 19 July.
Plowman, D.H. (1991), 'Management and industrial relations', in Adams, R.J. (ed.), *Comparative Industrial Relations*, Harper Collins, London.
Roncoroni, S. (2000), *Call Centre Association, Sixth Annual Members Convention*, Glasgow, 14 November.
SNT Group n.v. (2000), *Preliminary Prospectus*, Zoetermeer.
Taylor, P. and Bain, P. (1997), *Call Centres in Scotland: A Report for Scottish Enterprise*, Glasgow.

Taylor, P. and Bain, P. (1999), '"An assembly line in the head": work and employee relations in the call centre', *Industrial Relations Journal*, Vol. 30, pp. 101-117.
Taylor, P. and Bain, P. (2000), *Trade Unions and Call Centres*, Finance Sector Unions/MSF, London.
Taylor, P. and Bain, P. (2001a), 'Trade Unions, Workers' Rights and the Frontier of Control in UK Call Centres', *Economic and Industrial Democracy*, Vol. 22, pp. 39-66.
Taylor, P. and Bain, P. (2001b), *Call Centres in Scotland in 2000*, Glasgow, Rowan Tree Press.
Taylor, S. (1998), 'Emotional labour and the new workplace', in Thompson, P. and Warhurst, C. (eds.), *Workplaces of the Future*, London, Macmillan.
Van Waarden, F. (1995), 'Employers and employers' associations', in van Ruysseveldt, J., Huiskamp, R. and van Hoof, J. (eds.), *Comparative Industrial and Employment Relations*, London, Sage.
WERS (1998), *The 1998 Workplace Employee Relations Survey: first findings*, London, DTI.

Interviews

Abbott, S., President, CWA Local 3902, Birmingham AL, 27 April 2000.
Camp, D., Manager, Bell South Small Business Call Center, Birmingham AL, 15 June 2000.
De Rooy van Zuydewin, L., HRM Manager, ABN-AMRO Call Centre, Nijmegen, 9 March 2000.
Flynn, D., Manager, Southwest Airlines Phoenix Reservation Center, Phoenix, AZ, 6 June 2000.
Folts, A., Administrative Vice-President, Metropolitan Development Board, Birmingham AL, 20 June 2000.
McGrath, M., President, CWA Local 7026, Tucson AZ, 8 June 2000.
Nijenhuis, P., Manager, Randstad Callflex, Enschede, 6 March 2000.
Sprenger, W., FNV (work and organisation), Amsterdam, 22 February 2000.
STEC Groep, (P. van Geffen, director, and M. Molenaar, advisor), Nijmegen, 9 March 2000.

Chapter 4

Call Centres in Germany: Employment, Training and Job Design

Susanne Bittner, Marc Schietinger, Jochen Schroth and Claudia Weinkopf

Introduction

Throughout Europe, call centres are regarded as an area of economic activity experiencing strong and rapid growth. In Germany too, this mode of organising customer communications is displaying considerable dynamism. However, there are no reliable data on the exact number of call centres, the number of people employed in them or the structure of the industry. The reason for this is that call centres take a variety of different forms, provide a diversity of services and are to be found in virtually all industries. This notwithstanding, it is the aim of this chapter to provide a comprehensive overview of the German call centre scene.

To this end, we draw on the results of a survey of the literature on the current state of development of and future prospects for call centres in Germany (Bittner, Schietinger, Schroth and Weinkopf, 2000a) that was carried out as part of the 'Personnel management in call centres and the retail services' (FREQUENZ) research project.[1] The central objective of the project is to lay the foundation and develop criteria for the benchmarking of approaches to personnel management in call centres and the retail services. The project focuses in particular on the connections and interactions between personnel management and work organisation, on the one hand, and economic indicators, service quality and working and employment conditions, on the other. Case studies were carried out in a total of 18 call centres located throughout Germany. The sample contains a wide range of centres that differ considerably in size, organisational structure and

---

[1] The FREQUENZ research project is funded by the German Federal Ministry of Education and Research and is being conducted by the *Institut Arbeit und Technik* and B+S management consultants in Bonn in co-operation with 18 call centres and 5 companies in the retail services in the period from February 2000 to January 2002.

services provided. It includes, for example, a small in-house call centre in the chemical industry with just 12 agents that provides high-quality product advice as well as a large direct banking organisation with more than 1,000 employees. It also includes call centres operated by mail order companies, insurance companies and IT consultants as well as by telemarketing agencies operating in the outbound market. This chapter also draws on the findings of these case studies.

The chapter is structured as follows. The following section focuses on the structure and evolution of the German call centre 'sector' based on a review of all available previous studies. We examine the distribution of various forms of call centre, the number of jobs, the employment structure, the working and employment conditions of call centre agents and their remuneration as well as the qualifications and training of call centre workers. Most of the surveys cited in the course of this examination were conducted by management consultants, interest groups and market research institutes between 1996 and 1999. To the best of our knowledge, there have not been any major German investigations into the structure of the call centre 'sector', so that in many areas there are unfortunately no up-to-date figures available. Nor are there any comprehensive, systematic studies that capture the quantitative dimensions of the call centre 'sector' in its entirety, since the studies that do exist are characterised by their own specific epistemological interests. Furthermore, the methodologies adopted in these studies are often unclear, small sample sizes are the norm and none of them can be regarded as representative (Bittner, Schietinger, Schroth and Weinkopf, 2000a, p. 36). For this reason, the figures and data used in this section should be regarded as estimates.[2]

In the last section, our aim is to shed light on work organisation in German call centres based mainly on our own case study sample and research. Many call centres suffer from high turnover and absenteeism rates, with firms incurring considerable costs as a result. In our view, it is the form of work organisation that decides whether call centre operators are able to offer workers longer-term career prospects in a skilled occupation. We investigate both the opportunities for improving call centre agents' immediate working environment and the forms of structural and operational organisation typically encountered in call centres. We then turn to the question of how far the rigid division of labour that is such a prominent characteristic of work organisation in German call centres is unavoidable or whether there is scope for the introduction of more participatory forms of work organisation.

---

[2] This is why, whenever possible, we cite the results of several studies in order as far as possible to even out any distortions caused by data collection methods.

Structure and Evolution of the Call Centre 'Sector' in Germany

Recent years have seen strong increases in the number of call centres and call centre jobs in Germany, and these increases look set to continue over the next few years. One major problem with any attempt to quantify the number of call centres and call centre jobs, however, is that the available data amount to little more than a rough estimate. Forward-looking data are frequently produced merely by linear extrapolation from unreliable assumptions about growth, in which even the starting position is very uncertain, so that nobody knows the exact number of call centres currently in existence. As a result, the number of call centre jobs, and of those employed in them, is derived solely from assumptions.

Quantitative assessments of the growth of call centres start from the assumption that the number of call centres is likely to more than double between 1998 and 2003 from 1,600 to around 3,700, which equates to an average annual growth rate of 18 per cent (Datamonitor, cited in European Industrial Relations Review, 2000, p. 19). Currently, according to the Datamonitor estimate, there are just about 3,000 call centres in Germany.

In line with the growth in the number of call centres, strong rates of increase in the number of jobs in this sector are also forecast. Since call centres frequently have extended opening hours, with some even operating round the clock, and since the share of part-time workers is also relatively high, there is no simple one-to-one relationship between the number of jobs and the number of people employed (Table 4.1).

Table 4. 1   Number of Jobs and Employees in Call Centres

Year	Jobs	Employees
1996	Approx. 45,000	90,000 – 135,000
1997	Approx. 61,000	121,000 – 183,000
1998	Approx. 80,000	160,000 – 240,000
1999	Approx. 99,000	198,000 – 297,000
2000	Approx. 119,000	238,000 – 357,000
2001	Approx. 138,000	276,000 – 414,000

Source: Michalke 1999, p. 26.

In the investigations conducted to date, it is assumed that there are between two and three workers per job (for example, Michalke, 1999, p.26). If this were so, between 300,000 and 400,000 people would currently be employed in approximately 138,000 call centre jobs.

However, an increase in the number of jobs does not necessarily mean that the establishment of call centres has actually led to the creation of new employment relationships. (Michalke, 1999, p.26). In many cases, jobs are simply shifted to call centres from other departments in the course of internal restructuring exercises and filled with existing employees. Even the establishment of external call centres does not generally produce new jobs, since work volumes in the outsourcing companies can decline as a result.

In essence, call centres constitute a specific mode of organising the management and initiation of communication processes. Consequently, they take a variety of different forms and are found in many areas of economic activity. The majority of call centres currently in operation are part of already existing companies; consequently, it is too early to speak of call centres as an 'industry' in their own right. Several studies have sought to ascertain in which sectors they occur most frequently. Although the results of these studies are not directly comparable, they do, nevertheless, make it possible to identify some of the sectors with high concentrations of call centres (Table 4.2). The leader is undoubtedly the finance, insurance and banking sector, followed by the retail services and the information and communications sector. The manufacturing sector makes a significant impression only in the ProfiTel study (1998); concentrations in other sectors vary from study to study, which is probably attributable to different survey methods, among other factors.

In the case of call centres that are not part of larger companies but which operate as independent service providers, there are already discernible trends pointing to the formation of an independent industry, for example the founding of associations of common interest (*Deutscher Direktmarketingverband, Call Center Forum e.V.* etc.) and efforts by trade unions to negotiate specific collective agreements for these call centres. Various studies put the share of external service providers in Germany at between 30 and 40 per cent (GfK, 1998, p. 1; ProfiTel, 1999, p. 1; MMB, 1999, p. 9; Emnid 1998, p. 7).

The official German statistics on the service sector do not help to determine the structure and evolution of the call centre 'sector', even when a sectoral distribution of call centres is available. In-house call centres are not

---

[3] Another Datamonitor estimate (European Industrial Relations Review 2000, p. 20) suggested that the number of jobs in call centres had already reached 148,000 in the year 2000.

recorded separately but classified in the same category as the company operating them. The independent call centre operators are subsumed within the 'clerical services' category and cannot therefore be the object of statistical analysis in their own right.

Table 4.2 Sectoral Distribution of Call Centres According to Results of Various Studies (in per cent)

	Computer Fachwissen	ProfiTel*	GfK*
Financial services, banking, insurance	39.1	27	54.8
Information and communications	19.1	17	31.3
Retail Services	11.6	24	16.5
Media	7.2	12	26.3
Manufacturing	4.4	17	5.8
Transport/tourism	not included	9	16.0
Market research/marketing	not included	not included	34.0
Others	18.6	15	14.8

* in the *ProfiTel* and *GfK* studies, multiple entries were possible

Source: Own compilation based on Computer Fachwissen, 1998, p. 17; ProfiTel, 1998, p. 7; GfK, 1998, p. 2.

Examination of the regional distribution of the 3,000 or so call centres that currently exist in Germany reveals certain imbalances. According to the available information, the highest concentrations are found in the German federal state (Land/Länder) North Rhine-Westphalia and in the northern *Länder* of the former German Democratic Republic (*Mecklenburg-Vorpommern, Sachsen-Anhalt, Brandenburg*). Smaller *Länder*, such as the *Saarland* or the city-state of *Bremen*, have also taken steps to attract call centres (Kerst and Arzbächer 2000, p. 1). Accurate figures on the distribution of call centres by *Land* and region are not available.[4] Since the *Länder* with high concentrations of call centres are predominantly regions

---

[4] A publication on this subject by Tenzer (2001) is based on a survey of regional economic development organisations. However, since these organisations are probably not aware of all the call centres in their particular regions, the significance of these figures for the actual regional distribution may be rather limited.

with structural weaknesses or in the process of structural change, public authorities in those regions have provided high levels of financial support in order to attract call centres. 'Call centre campaigns' were initiated in virtually every state, with the aim of providing, among other things, information to potential investors on establishment grants, training opportunities for agents, suitable premises, technical equipment, and so on (for more detail on the workings and objectives of the call centre campaigns, Arzbächer, Holtgrewe and Kerst, in this volume). These regions were very successful in attracting call centres since, in addition to financial support, high unemployment meant that call centre operators were able to tap into a large pool of potential labour. Moreover, these *Länder* took measures at a very early stage to ensure that the new call centres would be able to operate round the clock. Many municipalities and regions, particularly in Eastern Germany, now regard the establishment of call centres as one of their main hopes for reducing the high levels of unemployment from which they suffer.

After this brief survey of the number of call centres, the number of jobs they offer, their sectoral affiliation and their regional distribution, we turn now to the structure of employment in call centres, employment and working conditions and training.

Employment Structure

Important factors in describing the structure of employment in call centres include the gender distribution, the share of full-time and part-time workers and the age and/or qualification structure. In these respects, call centres turn out to have certain specific characteristics that set them apart from other areas of economic activity. For example, call centres are generally regarded as having a highly feminised employment structure (Bittner, Schietinger, Schroth and Weinkopf, 2000a, pp. 40-41). There are various reasons for this, ranging from the large number of part-time jobs on offer and the relatively low pay to women's allegedly superior telephone manner. In fact, the various surveys put the share of women among call centre employees at between 53 and 70 per cent (Thieme and Ceyp, 1997, p. 47; MMB, 1999, p. 3). However, the share of women at the various levels of the management hierarchy varies considerably and declines as job status rises. Thus an analysis of the FREQUENZ research project showed that approximately 55 per cent of all call centre agents are female, while women account for only about 31 per cent of managerial staff (also Thieme and Ceyp, 1999, p. 56). Thus the structural imbalances between men and women that prevail in the world of work in general are also found in call centres. Nevertheless, the share of women at all levels of the management hierarchy is considerably higher than in the economy as a whole.

Table 4.3 Shares of Women by Hierarchical Level and Function

	Share of women	
Level/Function	Thieme and Ceyp	FREQUENZ
Agents	52.0 %	55.2 %
Team leaders	32.0 %	57.5 %
Management level	30.5 %	31.3 %
IT and technical staff	not included	14.6 %

Source: Own survey; Thieme and Ceyp 1999, p. 56.

The duration of individual working time is closely linked to the composition of the workforce. A high part-time rate is widely regarded as a typical characteristic of call centres, with the rate generally being put at between 40 and 50 per cent (ProfiTel, 1998, p. 15; GfK, 1998, p. 8; Biehler and Vogl, 1999, p. 9). However, there are considerable differences between the genders in this respect. Thus men working in call centres are much less likely than women to work part-time (for example, Thieme and Ceyp, 1999, p. 55). Part-time rates also differ considerably between call centres. Of the call centres involved in the FREQUENZ research project, some employ only full-timers, while others employ only part-timers, with the exception of managerial staff. The share of part-timers is strongly correlated with the nature of the service the call centre provides. Thus in call centres providing complex services and employing mainly skilled workers the part-time rate tends to be low, while the converse applies to centres providing simple standardised services.

The need to work with information technologies, the strong customer-orientation and the 'newness' of this kind of work are all grounds for assuming that call centre employees are predominantly young. This is all the more true since attributes such as flexibility and the ability to work under pressure are generally regarded as necessary for such work. And indeed, according to the available surveys, more than three quarters of call centre agents in Germany are under 40 years of age and as many as one third are under 30.

On the other hand, the qualificational level of call centre agents is on the whole considerably higher than is often assumed. Fewer than four per cent have no vocational qualifications at all (ProfiTel, 1998, p. 16). The majority have a vocational training qualification, and some even have university degrees (two per cent according to the FREQUENZ survey and nine per cent according to ProfiTel). Call centres are obviously benefiting predominantly from human capital that their employees have acquired in other sectors of the economy. Although the results of the FREQUENZ research project show that only a few call centres stipulate a completed course of vocational training as a requirement for new recruits, the 'typical' call centre agent in Germany has in fact already learnt a trade. The share of students, on the other hand, is lower than often assumed. The average figure for German call centres is about 30 per cent (ProfiTel 1998, p. 18) and many centres do not employ any students at all. Thus in more than half of the FREQUENZ call centres, there are no students at all in the workforce and only in two companies do they account for more than 30 per cent of total employment.

The Working and Employment Conditions of Call Centre Employees

Call centres have a somewhat mixed reputation in Germany as far as employment and working conditions are concerned. In the eyes of the outside world, they employ a young, flexible, semi-skilled workforce (TBS, 1999, p. 7). Moreover, many call centres have to cope with very high turnover rates which, according to the findings of various surveys (ProfiTel, 1998; Wiencke and Koke, 1999, p. 177; D'Alessio and Oberbeck, 1999, p. 168), average between 15 and more than 50 per cent. In individual cases (including one of the call centre companies involved in the FREQUENZ research project), average job tenure among agents is less than one year. In this section, we investigate some of the factors that influence employees' work situation.

Until now, customer advice services in the German insurance and banking industry, for example, have been accessible only at fixed and relatively restricted times. Many companies are now hoping that the establishment or use of call centres will enable them to extend their customer contact hours at relatively low cost. Clearly, this will have repercussions on employees' working times. Shift work is one of the characteristic features of call centre jobs (Isic, Dormann and Zapf, 1999, p. 204), which results in high demands being placed on employees' time flexibility. These demands are further intensified by the fact that, in some shift systems, work schedules are drawn up less than two weeks in advance, while in a number of call centres agents' working times even vary from day to day.

Although there are currently no representative data on operating and working times in German call centres, call centres are clearly playing a pioneering role in the extensive of customer contact times. In our estimation, however, call centres that are open round the clock are still the exception rather than the rule. Thus only 25 per cent of the FREQUENZ call centres, for example, actually provide a 24-hour service, and even in these centres night-time manning levels are generally low. However, the demands on employees' time flexibility could increase further as a result of the rising number of exemptions from German working time legislation that are being granted. Already, willingness to work shifts and weekends is frequently a basic precondition for employment in a call centre.

In addition to the time flexibility required of employees, call centre work is associated with other mental and physical demands that can give rise to considerable stress for the workforce (Biehler and Vogl, 1999, p. 13). Thus the 'voice with a smile in it', the considerable demands on workers' powers of empathy and tolerance of frustration, computer problems, the constant noise of the open-plan work area, a high level of performance and behaviour monitoring, continuous work on computer screens and, in some cases, the inadequate ergonomics of work stations are all factors which, combined, can prove exhausting for workers.

Remuneration also plays a key role in determining the work situation of call centre employees. The wage and salary range turns out to be very wide. Starting pay for agents in the FREQUENZ call centres, for example, was between 1,406 € and more than 3,068 € (gross full-time rates). This wide range reflects the differences in job content from centre to centre as well as differences in sectoral affiliation (Thieme and Ceyp, 1999, p. 40). However, other factors such as length of job tenure, age, qualificational levels and, not least, the performance-related bonus payments that are part of the pay package in many call centres all have a major influence on remuneration levels.

Furthermore, there are also considerable differences in remuneration between the various types of call centres. Thus an inquiry conducted by the German market research company GfK Group found that wages and salaries are considerably lower in external service providers than in in-house call centres (GfK, 1998, p. 12). In 1997, the average monthly earnings of an agent in full-time employment in an external service provider were 1,917 € gross, some 665 € lower than those in in-house call centres, where average gross monthly pay 2,275 €. The findings of the FREQUENZ project reveal similar trends. Thus starting salaries of more than 2,045 € are paid by all the in-house call centres, without exception.

The differences in remuneration levels, some of them very considerable, between in-house call centres and external service providers can be explained by, among other things, the differences in the collective agreement coverage of the two types of call centres. Unfortunately, there are no empirical data available on either the collective agreement coverage of call centres or the share of companies with works councils and staff committees. Estimates start from the assumption that in-house call centres account for about half of currently existing call centre jobs. If these are located in departments of large companies, then most of them will be covered by collective agreements and will also have a body representing employees' interests (Einblick, 1999, p. 5). However, since call centres are frequently set up by spinning off or establishing subsidiaries, which are often not covered by collective agreements, the share of jobs without regulated pay would seem to be increasing (Mirschel, 1999, p. 3). At the same time, independent telephone service providers, which are springing up, are also not covered by collective agreements. These new providers offer their services to other companies and in many cases do not fall within the scope of one of the traditional industries and cannot therefore be bound by any existing collective agreement (Meier, 1999, p. 2). The service-sector trade union ver.di (*Vereinigte Dienstleistungsgewerkschaft* – United Services Union), founded in March 2001 following the merger of five separate unions, is currently trying to coordinate trade union activity in call centres to counter this trend in a number of different ways (http://www2.verdi-net.de/projekte/index.php3 from 9 April 2001, on industrial relations in German call centres; Arzbächer, Holtgrewe and Kerst, in this volume).

The Training of Call Centre Agents

True to the motto 'everyone can use a telephone', the training needs of workers in German call centres were neglected for a long time (TBS, 1999, p. 29). However, the quality of the service provided by a call centre is not determined solely by organisation and technology, but stands and falls also with employees' performance and qualificational levels. The skills and qualifications required for call centre work can basically be divided into two categories: technical and extra-technical.

Extra-technical skills, such as social skills, good diction, the ability to present complex material in a readily accessible way, quick-wittedness and time flexibility, are generally regarded as basic requirements for call centre work. Depending on the nature of the services provided, however, technical skills are also important, although requirements in this respect vary considerably from call centre to call centre. Besides general product knowledge, IT and basic commercial knowledge are also required. In some high-skill areas, such as the insurance industry, a formal vocational qualification is often required. In other areas, such as routine telephone information services, the technical skill requirements are low.

The German dual system of vocational training does not yet provide any training for call centre agents. However, there are numerous training programmes offered by various training providers (Bittner, Schietinger, Schroth and Weinkopf, 2000a, p. 64). In order to cut through the rank growth of courses and qualifications, many chambers of industry and commerce (*Industrie- und Handelskammern* - IHK) have for a long time been working in close co-operation with call centre operators to offer training courses leading to the award of the IHK Call Centre Agents Certificate. The course lasts between six weeks and three months and is intended to give workers the basic skills required for working in call centres. The course is geared primarily to people who already have a vocational qualification and who are interested in changing occupation or are seeking to re-enter the labour market (MMB, 1999, p. 8). In addition to providing training in service and customer-oriented communication techniques, the focus of the course is on the acquisition of basic commercial skills and knowledge of modern IT systems. The programme also includes a work placement generally lasting between one and four weeks.

However, both the quality of and the need for these training programmes are disputed. The diverse activities and demands that characterise call centre work make it difficult to draw up uniform standards for training. While some call centre operators merely require a pleasant voice, others argue that additional training modules should be added to the courses provided by the chambers of industry and commerce (Brötz and Oberlindober, 1999, p. 8). The German trade unions, moreover, are demanding that employees should have the right to have a say in the determination of training needs and that individual training plans, which could be based on specific analyses of needs, should be drawn up for workers in all call centres (TBS, 1999, p. 31).

The call centre manager courses offered, for example, by the European Business School at Oestrich-Winkel are another attempt to establish and standardise training in call centres (Rudolf, 1999, p. 26). This private university offers aspiring call centre managers and those already in post an opportunity to follow a career development programme leading to the award of a certificate in call centre management. However, attempts to integrate training for call centre work into the German dual system of vocational training have not yet borne fruit. The *Bundesinstitut für Berufsbildung* (BIBB)[5] developed a training module to be incorporated into the

---

[5] The *Bundesinstitut für Berufsbildung* (Federal Institute for Vocational Training) is a state institution that is jointly responsible with employers and trade unions for managing and developing the German dual system of vocational training.

vocational training for office communications staff qualification, but a pilot project has not been started.

In practice, therefore, training for call centre workers mainly takes the form of in-house programmes, although the scope of the measures described in this section varies considerably from case to case. Although some call centres provide a whole range of different programmes, others rely largely on their employees' existing skills and place their trust in employees' ability to 'learn by doing'.

In many call centres, the induction of new recruits takes place solely in-house. It usually takes place through basic training courses run by group leaders, supervisors or trainers, by allocating new recruits to special training teams or through mentoring schemes. In call centres providing simple, standardised services, the induction period sometimes lasts only a few days; in others, it may last several months. Some call centres also have recourse to outside assistance during the induction period. Thus specific product training is sometimes provided by clients and certain modules, such as communication training programmes, may be contracted out to external training providers.

Although induction programmes give new recruits the basic skills they need for their work, one-off training programmes at the beginning of an employment relationships are not sufficient to ensure service quality and customer satisfaction on a permanent basis (Lütze, Schuler and Wecker 1999, p. 54). This is all the more the case since the range of services provided by many call centres tends to expand or change over time which, together with recent technical developments such as Internet telephony, leads to changed and/or increased skill requirements. It can be inferred from this that there is a growing need for further training programmes for call centre workers, a need which, like the induction of new recruits, is met by firms in different ways.

In this context, coaching measures and team discussions are relatively widespread in German call centres. The coaching is intended to help agents further develop their customer-oriented behaviour, heighten their sensitivity to customers' concerns and recognise their own strengths and weaknesses in call management. Team meetings offer agents an opportunity to exchange experiences, to discuss new work procedures, to put forward suggestions for improvements or 'simply to have a good moan'. In many call centres, team meetings also serve to promote group cohesion.

The importance attached to technical training programmes, on the other hand, varies considerably. Some call centres attach no particular importance to such measures, while others have put in place a relatively comprehensive range of activities. In these centres, some of the technical training provided takes the form of special product training courses, which are often project-related or operated as required. In the case of external service providers in particular, product training courses are provided not only internally but also by clients. Some call centres even have their own training departments, some of which also provide training for outside bodies. The training courses on offer range from stress management seminars through IT courses to sales training for outbound agents.

Table 4.4 Examples of the Training Received by Call Centre Agents in a German Bank

1. Initial training (duration approx. 3 months)	
a.) Basic call centre skills (marketing, technology, etc.)	(5 days)
b.) Service and customer-oriented communication skills	(8 days)
c.) Basic business principles (data protection, project management, etc.)	(4 days)
d.) Modern data processing (IT, data banks, Internet)	(7 days)
e.) Banking services – introduction and basic principles	(7 days)
f.) The bank's services and products	(3 days)
g.) Training on the job (IT, case studies, telephoning with mentor)	(12 days)
h.) Final examinations	• IHK call centre agent's certificate • Bank's own test
2. Further training	
a.) Regular coaching	• Once a month with team leaders • Once a quarter with in-house technical or communications trainer
b.) Team meetings	• Regularly every four weeks • 'Team day' once every six months (planning and organisation left to team)
c.) Advanced training seminars	• Specialist banking training (e.g. payment transactions, savings deposits) • Communications training (e.g. time management, voice and breathing) • Stress management training
3. Advanced training for aspiring team leaders	
After an internal job advertisement and selection procedure, training for aspiring team leaders is provided, leading to the award of the IHK certificate.	

Source: Own compilation.

One interesting training programme is that adopted by the telephone department of a major German banking group (Table 4.4). It combines internal training and further training with the training programmes offered by the chambers of commerce and industry (IHK). The main feature of this programme is that, once employees have been recruited by the group, they receive their basic training from the local chamber of commerce and industry, while technical and company-specific training is provided by the bank's own training department. On completion of their training, employees automatically receive the recognised IHK call centre agent's certificate. Considerable importance is also attached to further training. Thus agents undergo regular coaching and must attend six to eight further training seminars per year. There are also opportunities for agents to become team leaders by acquiring the appropriate IHK certificate.

We can conclude by emphasising the difficulty, indeed the impossibility, of painting a uniform picture of the training of call centre agents in Germany. Many call centre operators are clearly benefiting from the relatively high qualification levels of their workers. In addition, new recruits are expected to have numerous basic attributes, such as communication and IT skills and a high level of resistance to stress. Because of the absence of an occupational profile for call centre work and the diverse work histories and skill and qualificational profiles of call centre workers, call centre operators deal with the induction of new recruits and the further training of agents in a wide variety of different ways. In view of the increasing demands being made of workers in many cases, there are good grounds for believing that operators will have to extend and improve the training of agents. This would appear to be all the more urgent if there are to be more attempts to extend the range of tasks performed by call centre workers. We examine this topic in greater detail in the next section.

The Organisation of Work in German Call Centres

Employees' work situation is determined to a large extent by the organisation of work in call centres. As has already become clear, the demands on call centre workers are often very great, which is not the least of the reasons for the sometimes very high levels of labour turnover and sickness. Since it is very expensive and time-consuming for companies to be constantly recruiting and training new workers, the question of how to improve work organisation in call centres is a very pertinent one.

In practice, the strategies adopted to date have focused primarily on two different factors - on the one hand, the duration of working time and, on the other, improvements to the work environment. To date, the dominant approach has been the more 'passive' strategy of attempting to mitigate the specific stresses caused by call centre work by increasing the number of part-time jobs on offer. According to many call centre managers, it is impossible to do more than five or six hours' productive telephone work in a day (Michalke, 1999, p. 27; D'Alessio and Oberbeck, 1999, p. 169). This is one of the reasons, in addition to more flexible employee rostering, why the part-time rate in call centres is above average.

In the FREQUENZ call centres, for example, 43 per cent of workers are part-timers, although the part-time rates in the individual companies vary considerably (Figure 4.5). Part-time employment is particularly prevalent in call centres that provide simple, standardised services (e.g. telephone information, taking of orders, etc.).

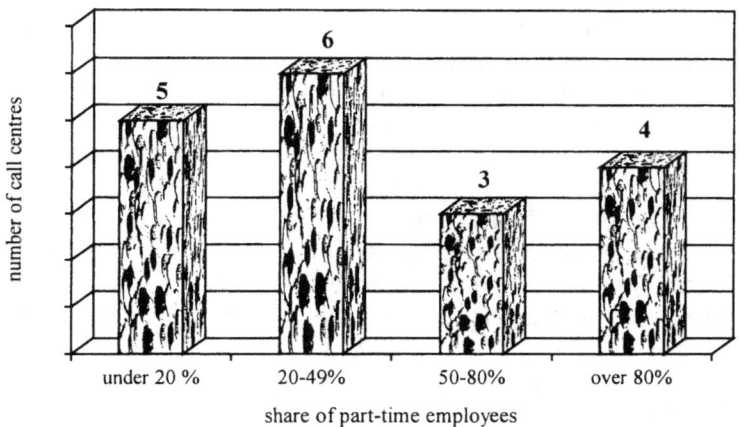

Figure 4.5   Share of Part-time Employment in the FREQUENZ Call Centres (n=18)
Source: Own survey.

Some companies have also tried to improve the work environment, particularly in terms of ergonomics. Thus the *Europäische Zentrum für Medienkompetenz (European Centre for Media Competence)*, in collaboration with the *Kooperationsbüro 'Multimedia + Arbeitswelt' (Cooperation Office: Multimedia + the Working World*), were commissioned by trade unions and employers to produce a checklist that lays down some important criteria for the ergonomic design of call centre work stations (Call Center Akademie, 1999). In addition to hardware norms governing such factors as screen size, keyboard design and headset, the criteria relate to work station layout, health and safety measures, breaks and working-time equalisation periods and are intended to prevent many of the potential adverse health effects of call centre work.

Furthermore, some companies have now recognised the importance of employees having permanent work stations. This can help to reduce the stresses and strains of work, as has been demonstrated, for example, by the investigation conducted by Isic (1999), which discovered that call centre agents with their own work stations display significantly fewer psychosomatic problems than those who work at different work stations each day.

These strategies can of course help to improve employees' immediate work situation. However, the trend towards more part-time employment is perhaps of dubious benefit in the longer term. In view of the sometimes very low hourly rates, the increase in part-time employment reduces the chances of obtaining a call centre job that pays a living wage.

In our view, greater attention must be paid in future to the organisation of work in call centres. This is because, in our estimation, work organisation is the point around which the future development of the call centre industry will crystallise. It is here that it will be decided, on the one hand, whether call centres will be an attractive area in which to work and are able to offer workers long-term employment prospects or, on the other, whether they will develop primarily into 'stopping-off places' for certain categories of workers, such as students. Factors such as service quality and the feedback of experiences acquired at the firm-client interface into other areas of companies' activities will also play a key role in this context.

Call centres tend to be characterised by a pronounced division of labour. This reflects the basic philosophy of extracting customer contacts from the case handling process, concentrating them in specific organisational units and dealing with them as far as possible solely by telephone. It is against this background that call centre work is often described as a form of 'neo-Taylorisation' of service activities (Bittner, Schietinger, Schroth, Weinkopf, 2000b; Halm, 2000; D'Alessio and Oberbeck, 1999).

In many cases, this is also reflected in the organisation of operations. Tasks are highly standardised, frequently monotonous (e.g. involving giving the same information or taking the same orders all the time) and with a short time allowed for completion.[6] In many call centres, moreover, there are scripts that prescribe the exact words to be used at each stage of the call. What is more, tasks are usually allocated externally via the ACD system or by supervisors or team managers. Individual calls are put through automatically to particular work stations, thereby virtually eliminating any need for co-operation among employees.

---

[6] On average across all sectors, calls to call centres last no longer than three minutes, so that many agents deal with several hundred calls in a day (ProfiTel, 1998, p. 20). In one FREQUENZ call centre the length of the average call is as low as 45 seconds.

All this is further compounded by the fact that call centre agents are usually allocated operational tasks, while team leaders and/or management are primarily responsible for planning and performance monitoring. In many cases, such monitoring is very rigid, since ACD technology allows employers to control every aspect of employees' performance (e.g., number and length of calls, frequency of breaks, length of post-processing time).[7]

However, neo-Taylorist forms of work organisation are by no means the only way of processing telephone inquiries rapidly and efficiently, particularly since they are the cause of many stress-creating factors, as has been shown by various studies carried out by occupational psychologists. Thus studies by Scherrer (2001) and Metz, Rohte and Degener (2000) have found that monotonous tasks and those allowing little scope for personal initiative and decision-making give rise to increased stress. This may well be one of the reasons for the high turnover rates and motivation problems among call centre workers. In order to avoid such difficulties, various strategies for modifying rigidly Taylorist work organisation systems are currently being discussed in Germany. The focus of all of them is the development of integrated forms of work organisation, that is to some extent a retreat from an over-rigid division of labour.

One approach that might best meet the demand for a less rigid mode of work organisation is the introduction of group work systems, such as semi-autonomous work groups in call centres. Proposals for such systems, which have been developed mainly by trade unions, all envisage employees working in teams that provide a 'complete' service relatively independently and with little outside monitoring or control. Each group would be responsible on an equal footing for task allocation, rostering and working time organisation, as well as for monitoring and quality control. Regular team meetings would ensure that there are constant exchanges of experience within the group (Mola and Zimmermann, 2001, p. 29). The hope is that employees' job satisfaction and commitment can be increased by giving

---

[7] However, works councils and staff committees in German firms (when they exist) have a legal entitlement to negotiate company or establishment agreements governing all relevant aspects of performance and behaviour monitoring. In the absence of any such agreement between management and the employee representative body, call centre technologies such as ACD and CTI systems, together with all associated software applications, may not be deployed (on the following, cf. Michalke, 1999, p. 38). It makes no difference whether the employer intends to use such systems for the purpose of monitoring performance and behaviour. According to the prevailing legal opinion in Germany, all that matters is whether the system is capable of being used for such a purpose. In any event, the secret monitoring, cutting into or recording of calls falls within the scope of German legislation on post and telecommunications confidentiality and is punishable in law.

agents greater scope for individual decision-making and through improved communications and co-operation.

However, such far-reaching approaches to group work have to date made virtually no inroads into German call centres. One of the reasons for this may well be that such approaches would require a reorganisation of the entire company. This is likely to be associated, at the outset at least, with additional costs and frictional losses. Moreover, such approaches generally require comprehensive generalist knowledge and a standard level of qualification for all call centre agents, in order that workers can cover for each other, for example. Furthermore, it should not be ignored that such forms of work organisation can create additional stresses and strains for employees, some of whom may not be willing, for example, to take on greater responsibility or to avail themselves of the various opportunities to assert their own interests.

A number of somewhat less ambitious approaches seek to enrich call centre work. More or less wide-ranging forms of approaches such as job enlargement, job enrichment and job rotation (Table 4.6) are already being instituted on a trial basis in some call centres.

Table 4.6   Approaches to Work Enrichment in Call Centres

Approach	Description
Job enlargement	Activities requiring the same level of competence are incorporated into the job.
Job enrichment	Activities that extend the competence range are incorporated into the job.
Job rotation	Employees take on or swap jobs in new or different areas on a temporary basis.

Source: Own compilation based on Mola and Zimmermann 2001, p. 7.

Job enlargement involves extending the scope of call centre agents' duties by combining telephone work with tasks requiring the same level of competence. For example, agents may deal not only with telephone inquiries, but also with inquiries made by fax, letter, e-mail or text message. If only because of the breathtaking pace of technological change in the call centre industry, such forms of job enrichment will become increasingly widespread in German call centres. Thus only in two FREQUENZ call centres are agents' responsibilities confined solely to telephone work. In more than half of the companies, on the other hand, agents deal with fax and e-mail inquiries as well as with telephone calls.

Other opportunities for job enlargement include inputting data into computer systems, taking part in training programmes, maintaining hardware and software, managing personal work documents, dispatching orders, writing down impressions of calls and initiating actions independently on the basis of information made available and objectives laid down (Mola and Zimmermann, 2001, p. 23). In this way, agents can take on a much wider range of duties, customer inquiries can be dealt with more flexibly and it also becomes possible to vary the demands made of employees in the course of their daily work. Job enlargement is also an appropriate means of implementing German regulations on screen work. These regulations stipulate that firms should organise screen work in such a way as to reduce the stresses and strains of such work, either by a change to other duties or by introducing regular paid breaks (Mola and Zimmermann, 2001, p. 22). However, job enlargement has to be supported by appropriate training measures. Not all call centre agents who are proficient at dealing with telephone calls are also able to draft letters without making mistakes.

In contrast to job enlargement, the main focus of *job enrichment* is the incorporation of higher-level tasks, such as planning, managerial or supervisory activities. The aim here is to give agents increased opportunities to act on their own initiative and take responsibility (Mola and Zimmermann, 2001, p. 24). Within the existing organisational structures, this may well lead to some degree of overlap between the competencies of call centre agents and those of team managers and supervisors. Implementation of such a strategy may, therefore, require further changes in work organisation and management structures.

Job enrichment is an approach that seeks to make better use of employees' human capital and to promote the specific strengths of individual workers. Thus in some firms, for example, call centre agents are involved in the development and implementation of proposals for improving scripts or help with statistical evaluations. In one of the FREQUENZ call centres, some experienced agents even operate the central ACD system on a part-time basis. In other FREQUENZ call centres, employees are responsible for the induction of new recruits as part of various mentoring schemes, are engaged in coaching or provide training for colleagues. Extending the range of employees' tasks and competences in this way can also provide the justification for higher pay levels.

Another approach to work enrichment is *job rotation*. This approach offers employees an opportunity to extend their operational area by changing jobs temporarily, thereby gaining the skills necessary to be considered for different jobs. Typical examples of the job rotation schemes that have been introduced in some FREQUENZ call centres are transfers between inbound and outbound telephone duties, work on a range of different projects and the combination of telephone duties with back-office case handling.

Thus job rotation gives agents an opportunity to look beyond the boundaries of their current sphere of activity, to familiarise themselves with work processes in other areas of the call centre and to have increased contact with colleagues. For their part, call centre operators benefit from increased potential for self-management at the operational level, greater individual responsibility for results and the development of an entrepreneurial attitude among agents. Moreover, as with job enrichment, such programmes make it easier for call centre operators to recruit potential managerial staff from within their own ranks (Mola and Zimmermann, 2001, p. 26). What is more, job rotation offers firms a means of reacting more efficiently to fluctuations in workloads over the course of the day or week by temporarily shifting personnel to other areas of activity. Thus workers in a large in-house call centre in the German tourist industry, for example, are lent to other departments during periods when few calls are coming in, so that after a brief induction period they can be called on during busy periods, for example when the new brochures are being produced. In this case, the call centre acts as an internal temporary work agency (Casdorff, 2000, p. 243).

A large German health insurance provider has gone down another route. Instead of transferring telephone services to a newly created call centre, use was made of the existing organisational structures. Twenty-four out of a total of 913 branches throughout Germany were networked to make the largest virtual call centre in Europe (Hildebrandt, 2000, p. 50). In this way, up to 1,100 clerical staff can be deployed as call centre agents. An intelligent routing system ensures that a call is almost always answered within about ten seconds in one of the branches scattered throughout Germany. One major advantage of this system is that the skilled clerical workers are able to remain at their workstations and to continue with their normal case processing activities. It is only at certain, pre-planned times that they are called on to undertake call centre duties, but without having to leave their own workstations. The even distribution of telephone duties among a large number of workers, together with the hybrid workstations that have been developed, mean that each individual has to deal with only a very small number of calls. From the company's point of view, the system has the major advantage of enabling the company to make use of existing skilled personnel rather than having to recruit and train call centre staff in the external labour market.

Conclusion

Our description of the structures and specificities of the German call centre industry has shown that it is very diverse and heterogeneous. It is not yet possible to say whether particular types of call centres will prevail in the future and what these types might be. Moreover, the case studies carried out in the course of the FREQUENZ research project show that, despite some discernible trends, there is no direct relationship between the particular characteristics and organisational forms of call centres, on the one hand, and personnel policy strategies, on the other. This suggests that, within certain limits, there is considerable scope for shaping the future development of the call centre industry in such a way as to serve the interests of employees and to improve service quality and productivity.

In our view, one key aspect is the question of further training. It is clear that the scope and intensity of the training effort has hitherto varied considerably from firm to firm. However, a supply of well-qualified and motivated agents, who identify with their company, is an important precondition for improving work processes and increasing productivity, service quality and customer satisfaction. To that extent, there are good grounds for paying (even) more attention to the continuing training of existing employees.

In our view, it is not possible to predict with any certainty whether the oft-cited trend towards the evolution of call centres into customer care centres will actually materialise to any great extent in Germany or whether there will be a greater polarisation in the future between highly standardised services, on the one hand, and more differentiated, high-skill services, on the other. However, in the interests of both employees and customers, it would seem desirable to increase task integration and to extend the activities of call centre agents in order to create 'hybrid jobs'. A further argument in favour of such an approach is that it must surely be in firms' interests to use the feedback produced at the customer-firm interface to inform their strategic decision-making (e.g. in the development of new products or the modification of existing ones). The use of agents with only a limited range of competencies does not seem to be the best way of organising the transmission of such information as efficiently and effectively as possible.

However, the future development of the industry will also be determined to some extent by the available labour supply. Those groups, such as students or returners to the labour market, that see call centre work as a transitional phase, are likely to have less interest in a form of work organisation that makes more demands on staff than other groups that value longer-term career prospects and more highly-skilled work. Provided that recruitment does not become any more problematic, there is little incentive for call centre operators to adopt the approaches to work enrichment outlined above to any great extent. However, many companies are already complaining of difficulties in recruiting suitable personnel. This could be a driving force in the further development and increased implementation of participatory forms of work organisation.

References

Biehler, H. and Vogl, G. (1999), 'Call Center: Zusatzleistungen sind nicht üblich', *WSI-Mitteilungen*, Vol. 4, pp. 261-267.
Bittner, S., Schietinger, M., Schroth, J. and Weinkopf, C. (2000a), '*Call Center – Entwicklungsstand und Perspektiven. Eine Literaturanalyse*', Projektbericht des Instituts Arbeit und Technik 2000-01, Gelsenkirchen.
Bittner, S., Schietinger, M., Schroth, J. and Weinkopf, C. (2000b), 'Call Center – Neue Taylorisierung oder innovative Dienstleistungsorganisation?', in Institut Arbeit und Technik (ed.), *Jahrbuch 1999/2000*, Gelsenkirchen, pp. 46-61.
Böse, B. and Flieger, E. (1999), *Call Center – Mittelpunkt der Kundenkommunikation*, Braunschweig, Vieweg.
Brötz, R. and Oberlindober, H. (1999), 'Call Center und Berufliche Bildung', *Gewerkschaftliche Bildungspolitik*, Vol. 5/6, pp. 5-9.
Call Center Akademie NRW (1999), *Checkliste für Call Center-Arbeitsplätze*, http://www.callcenterakademie.de/Berufsbild/Checkliste from 15 March 2000.
Casdorff, A. M. (2000), 'TUI Call Center – ohne Stress "Schöne Ferien!"', in Schuler, H. and Pabst, J. (eds.), *Personalentwicklung im Call Center der Zukunft: Fluktuation verhindern, Mitarbeiter langfristig binden*, Neuwied, Luchterhand, pp. 235-244.
Computer Fachwissen (1998), 'Call Center = Wachstumsmarkt', *Computer Fachwissen*, Vol. 4, p. 17.
D'Alessio, N. and Oberbeck, H. (1999), 'Call Center als organisatorischer Kristallisationspunkt von neuen Arbeitsbeziehungen, Beschäftigungsverhältnissen und einer neuen Dienstleistungskultur', *Jahrbuch Sozialwissenschaftliche Technikberichterstattung. Schwerpunkt Arbeitsmarkt 98/99*, Berlin, pp. 157-176.
Einblick (1999), 'Mit Boykott gegen Tarifflucht. Gewerkschaften und Call Center', *Einblick*, Vol. 22, p. 5.
Emnid (1998), Expertenbefragung, http://www.callcenterakademie.de/2/emnid/sld001a.htm from 26 May 1999.
European Industrial Relations Review (2000), 'Call centres in Europe: part one', *European Industrial Relations Review*, Issue 320, September, pp. 13-20.
Gesellschaft für Konsumforschung (GfK) (1998), 'Call Center Studie 1998: Marktstudie zur Entwicklung der Call Center–Branche in Deutschland', http://www.callcenter-akademie.de/06/f_ergebnisse/start.html from 28 March 2000.
Halm, T. (2000), 'Die Fabriken der New Economy', *Die Mitbestimmung*, Vol. 7, pp. 24-25.
Hildebrandt, K. (2000), 'Von der Steinzeit ins 21. Jahrhundert. Das größte virtuelle Call Center Europas – die integrierte Lösung der DAK', *TeleTalk*, Vol. 6, pp. 50-52.
Isic, A. (1999), 'Psychische Belastungen der Call Center-Arbeit', *Vortrag anlässlich des Pressegesprächs "Arbeit im Call Center: Arbeitsplatz der Zukunft mit Schattenseiten" der Redaktion "Computer-Fachwissen für Betriebs- und Personalräte" am 15.06.1999 in Frankfurt*, unpublished manuscript.

Isic, A., Dormann, C. and Zapf, D. (1999), 'Belastungen und Ressourcen an Call Center-Arbeitsplätzen', *Zeitschrift für Arbeitswissenschaften*, Vol. 3, pp. 202-208.
Kerst, C. and Arzbächer, S. (2000), 'Call Center im Ruhrgebiet – Eine Erfolgsstory mit Langzeitwirkung?', in Kommunalverband Ruhrgebiet (ed.), *Standorte. Jahrbuch Ruhrgebiet 2000*, Essen.
Lütze, B., Schuler, H. and Wecker, B. (1999), 'Implementierung von Coaching-Programmen', *Personalwirtschaft*, Vol. 7, pp. 54-57.
Meier, C. (1999), *Strategien zur Verbesserung der Arbeitsbedingungen in Call Centern aus gewerkschaftlicher Sicht*, Vortrag anlässlich des Pressegesprächs 'Arbeit im Call Center: Arbeitsplatz der Zukunft mit Schattenseiten' der Redaktion 'Computer-Fachwissen für Betriebs- und Personalräte' am 15.6.1999 in Frankfurt, unpublished manuscript.
Metz, A., Rothe, H. and Degener, M. (2000), *Belastungsprofile von Beschäftigten in Call Centers*, http://www.psych.uni-potsdam.de/work/pubs-d.html from 27 February 2001.
Michalke, F. (1999), 'Handlungsanleitung für Betriebs- und Personalräte', *Gewerkschaftliche Praxis*, Vol. 1-2, pp. 22-46.
Michel Medienforschung und Beratung (MMB) (1999), *Qualifikationsanforderungen in der Call Center Branche – Status quo und Perspektiven. Eine Untersuchung im Auftrag des Projektträgers des Bundesministeriums für Wirtschaft und Technologie*, Bonn.
Mirschel, V. (1999), 'Citibank-Konflikt. Weltweit erster Callcenter-Streik', *login and find out*, Vol. 2, p. 3.
Mola, E. and Zimmermann, E. (2001), 'Arbeitsorganisation im Call Center – Chancen einer menschenzentrierten Arbeitsgestaltung', in *Arbeitsorganisation im Call Center: Teamarbeit mit qualifizierten Beschäftigten. Veranstaltungsdokumentation der Hans-Böckler-Stiftung, des Kooperationsbüros Multimedia und Arbeitswelt und der TBS beim DGB NRW e.V.*, pp. 6-40.
ProfiTel (1998), *Benchmark-Studie Call Center Markt Deutschland 1998*, Hamburg.
Rudolf, B. (1999), 'Diplom für Call Center-Manager', *Call Center profi*, Vol. 5, pp. 26-27.
Scherrer, K. (2001), 'Dauerarbeitsplatz Call Center: Gesundheitsförderliche Arbeitsgestaltung senkt Fluktuation und Krankenstand', in Badura, B., Litsch, M. and Vetter, C. (eds.), *Fehlzeiten-Report 2000. Zukünftige Arbeitswelten: Gesundheitsschutz und Gesundheitsmanagement*, Berlin, Springer, pp. 61-79.
Technologieberatungsstelle (TBS) beim DGB Landesbezirk NRW e.V. (1999), 'Call Center. Handlungshilfen zur Gestaltung von Call Centern und Regelung automatischer Anrufverteilsysteme (ACD)', *Reihe Arbeit, Gesundheit, Umwelt, Technik*, Vol. 40, Oberhausen.
Tenzer, D. (2001), 'Spieglein, Spieglein an der Wand – wo ist der beste Standort im Land?', *TeleTalk*, Vol. 4, pp. 56-67.
Thieme, J. and Ceyp, M. (1997), *Großer Call Center Gehalts- und Karrierevergleich*, Hannover, telepublic.
Thieme, J. and Ceyp, M. (1999), *Großer Call Center Gehalts- und Karrierevergleich*, Hannover, telepublic.
Wiencke, W. and Koke, D. (1999), *Call Center Praxis. Den telefonischen Kundenservice erfolgreich organisieren*, Stuttgart, Schäffer-Pöschel.

Chapter 5

Call Centres as Organisational Crystallisation of New Labour Relations, Working Conditions and a New Service Culture?

Nestor D'Alessio and Herbert Oberbeck*

Introduction

Some observers consider the expansion of call centres a sign of innovation in service industries. Municipalities and regions thus endorse and promote the establishment of call centres under the heading of 'modern economic policy and employment promotion', and public funding for the support of incoming firms is provided generously. Even the labour unions tentatively applaud, as in the logic of traditional interest politics, call centres might after all have a certain short-term potential as grounds for recruiting new members.

Whatever the judgement about this trend toward more and more jobs in call centres might be, in part it is nothing more than the mere shift of office jobs that have existed for a long time already. We cannot make out in the trend a sign of innovative and promising business strategies on the part of service enterprises. The contrary appears to be the case instead. Taylorist labour policy is celebrating a merry comeback and the increasing service quality for customers that is so often proclaimed can hardly ever be proven to have become a reality.

This development is not inevitable though. The establishment of call centres can, and in some cases do indeed pursue other goals, such as strengthening interactive and communicative processes of exchange between the company and its customers, in order to increase the quality of information and advice (Finger 2001, p. 7). This, however, is unlikely to be

---

* The text was translated by Margitta Mätzke.

accomplished under the regime of Taylorist labour policy. In the following we draw on the findings from a small number of case studies as well as the results put forward in the relevant published sources, in order to contribute to the development of a conceptual framework for analysing the nature of work, employment, and service quality one can observe in German call centres today. Besides this, we point to questions for further research in this under-researched terrain of working life.

Call Centres as Organisational Principle

What do we mean at all, when we refer to a call centre? Is it a modern form of a telephone centre, or is it an integrated service centre, from which services are being designed in a new fashion both qualitatively and quantitatively?

To begin with, new technological developments and new forms of using the information and communication technologies have facilitated the establishment of call centres. Without going into the technical details, the central aspect of this is the connection between telecommunication and electronic data-processing on the basis of digital transmission technologies. CTI- (Computer Telephone Integration) interfaces, as they are called, bring together telephone conversations with information about customers and products stored in databases. This builds the basis on which telephone interactions between customers and producers can be further intensified and services can be shifted to technology; in the case of call centres, the telephone. To put it differently: service relationships are 'mediatised' even further.

For some time already customers' and firms' ability to reach one another by phone for advice and consultation has been contributing to a situation in which interaction between firms and customers takes place without direct personal contact. Originally this was considered to supplement the network of branch offices or the field service. Communication by phone meanwhile makes visiting the firm or the customer, respectively, superfluous, and at first this does indeed save time for both the customer and the firm. There used to be limits to this kind of expansion of service provision over the phone, however, and these were not only technological in nature.

This expansion of customer service over the phone was premised on standardised products and services, and all industries have experienced standardisation of products and services more or less intensely during the past 40 years. In many areas this made the service relationship much more straightforward. Although personal contact in the process of service provision did not become completely obsolete, the intensity of advice and assistance in a service relationship was markedly reduced.

As customers became more and more assertive in dealing with firms, this process became more and more easy, and the overall volume of telephone contact between firms and their customers increased. Today many people who started making their first experiences with financial services or travel agents in the 1960s, are capable and willing to specify their wishes over the phone with only a minimal amount of assistance and to insist on competent processing of their request. The breakthrough we are currently experiencing in the amount of communication over the phone for purposes of advice, assistance, and sales can only be explained with reference to this long and creeping transformation of the interface between firms and customers, which had prepared the ground for the present breakthrough. It started with the use of the first computers and depended on the standardisation of service relationships.

The transition from the traditional telephone centre to today's call centre as organisational principle also promises to ease some of the strain that the overload of telephone transactions poses to firms. The cost-saving potential of the information and communication technologies can only unfold, however, if customers accept the new technologies. Even though the social and cultural prerequisites for this are much further developed today than they were less than one or two decades ago, transferring services to the telephone on a large scale still entails a new quality of services, and the success of such a transfer is, to a crucial extent, a function of the accessibility of call centres and of the problem solving capacity that they can furnish.

Call centres are praised as original organisational concepts, because they are available beyond normal business hours, very often 24 hours a day. Planned as a strategy for building closer relationships with customers, this strategy only produces the desired effect when the times that customers are put on hold and the time customers need to get what they want are drastically reduced. Customers who are offered extended business hours, but do not get through to the call centre or need excessively long phone-calls to get their wishes attended to, will experience phone contact as an additional burden, rather than a relief. This would destroy the strategy of closer customer relations that many firms pursue by establishing call centres.

One must also underscore the following point. Establishing and organising call centres is informed by a philosophy of rationalisation, as it has dominated business strategies in many service industries. The goals of this philosophy can be outlined as standardisation, 'mediatisation', and automatisation. The exclusive focus on these goals, we submit, closes off rather than develops innovation potentials in many service industries. In the last ten years a considerable amount of resources have already been lost because of this preoccupation with rationalisation (Oberbeck, 2001).

Standardisation and de-personalisation of service relationships entails that firms and organisations rely on technological measures and systems for determining customer profiles. Instructions for the behaviour of service representatives derived from these profiles increasingly pre-form the relationship with the customers, which more and more assume the character of service *transactions* (Oberbeck, 2001). In many services, customers and service providers interact with one another in only brief encounters, but there is no real exchange of information. Customer questions and wishes must either fit into the predetermined structures, or they remain unattended. This is the reality in many call centres, particularly in the financial service industries, which are particularly active in the area of call centres. It ultimately leads to a situation in which companies and organisations in the service sector lose a lot of their problem-solving capacity. That is, service providers are not responsive to all customer needs and interests anymore. For this reason we consider the bias toward rationalisation on the part of call centre operators to be the main reason for the fact that as of now customer evaluations of service quality are predominantly negative.[1]

We should reiterate that establishing call centres could in principle also be part of a very different kind of business and organisational strategy. Particularly in a number of industrial segments call centres are taking on more qualified sorts of advising in areas such as the handling or the repair of certain more complex products. In these segments firms experience the development of information technology as a chance for restructuring the production and service networks in their firms (Neumann, 2000). The crucial future question will be whether there are structural characteristics specific to certain corporate functions or industries where the tasks and the organisational forms of call centres must be defined more broadly or more narrowly.

Moreover, another question is whether it might not be only certain types of products and services that lend themselves to being provided by call centres. If this were the case, it would entail that certain other services cannot be furnished through the medium of the telephone. Regardless of these questions about uniformity or differentiation in the character of newly established call centres, there are many already existing – the telephone information service, for instance, is one of the oldest call centres and was established at a time when the term call centre did not yet exist – and for

---

[1] This negative outcome is, among others, the conclusion of a study by the Institute for Market and Communication Research in Hürth (see Süddeutsche, 2001; Financial Times Deutschland, 2001, p. 10).

these already existing call centres, structures and operating procedures appear to be highly homogeneous.

Working Conditions and Labour Relations

The precondition for human resource planning in call centres is an analysis of typical distributions of calls. Such distributions help organise shift patterns. In addition distribution curves are generated to reflect the patterns of calls broken down by certain types of services, and this is used to further refine the planning of manpower requirements.

Supervisors can steer the workload of their employees to a certain degree by manually routing the calls. The basis of this flexible personnel disposition, however, is shifts with their respective working time and fixed-term provisions, organised in such a way that they fulfil the operative requirements. These in turn depend on the frequency of calls and on the employees' ability to cope with strain. These functional requirements give rise to employment patterns and labour relations, in which full-time and part-time employees, people with fixed term contracts and permanent employees work together in varying combinations, leading to highly uneven levels of compensation.

Eight of the nine call centres that we examined at the end of the 1990s[2] are internal call centres established by savings banks, insurance companies, or automobile clubs. Between ten and forty employees work at these call centres. 81 per cent of the employees have permanent work contracts, and 66 per cent are women. 68 per cent are full-time employees, and these people work between 37.5 and 39 hours per week. The weekly working time of the part-time employees varies between 20 and 30 hours. In three cases we found contracts of low-wage part-time work,[3] and employees with such contracts work eight hours per week. Ten per cent of the employees are students, and 85 per cent of the part-time employees are women.

The external call centre working on behalf of other firms has other patterns of employment. Its tasks include information service, taking orders, ticket service, assistance with products, and carrying out follow-up cam-

---

[2] A systematic study, which would allow statements about working conditions and labor relations at call centers on a sound empirical basis does not exist, and the material presented here does not claim to be representative. It merely summarizes and presents the findings of a small survey among works councilors at nine call centers. It is intended to provide a framework for analysis and to help identify the different constellations of working conditions, labor relations, and employment patterns in the industry.

[3] In Germany a special regulation exempts companies from the requirement to pay most social contributions below a specified weekly hour average.

paigns. Seventy people are employed in this call centre, and only 57 per cent of them work under permanent employment contracts. Fifty-eight per cent of the employees are women. Only 32 per cent of the staff are full-time employed, with 38 hours per week, while the part-time employees work between 18 and 20 hours per week. Fifty-five per cent of all people working at this call centre are students, and 61 per cent of the part-time workers are women.

These data from our cases indicate that women's work, part-time work, and fixed-term contracts are central components of employment patterns at all call centres, but at the same time the differences between call centres are very obvious too. Internal call centres, which concentrate on specialised and regularly occurring tasks, have lower proportions of both part-time workers and fixed-term contracts than do call centres that work on behalf of other firms.

While the internal call centres usually organise work in two shifts, which enables them to extend their business hours to mornings and afternoons, the external provider in our sample is open 24 hours a day, with six different, partly overlapping shifts. The explanation for the varying flexibility in working hours appears to be the different skill requirements that come with the broad range of business activities in which the external provider is involved.

We also found differences between the internal and the external providers with regard to fixed term contracts and collective bargaining coverage. The employees at internal call centres were all covered by the collective bargaining agreement valid for their respective industry, but in the external provider there is no collective bargaining agreement.

One issue that is often the focus of discussions about call centres is the amount of fluctuation among employees. One frequent argument is, for instance, that due to the stressful nature of the work and the lack of career perspectives, employees of call centres cannot or will not remain in that occupation for longer than two years. In a benchmarking study including about 100 call centres, conducted by the University of Hamburg in co-operation with the US-Centre for Customer Driven Quality at Purdue University, Indiana, and the Profitel Call-Centre Consulting GmbH Hamburg, about 70 per cent of the call centres surveyed reported that they are facing the challenge of fluctuation rates of more than 50 per cent. (Frankfurter Allgemeine Zeitung, 1 August 1998).[4] Against this backdrop the working conditions of the service representatives are critical. A few of the call cen-

---

[4] The period of time that people work in German call centers is an average of one to two years. In more specialized call centers it is more than three years. In the US the average period of time worked at call centers is between six moths and one year (Michel, 1998).

tres in our sample take this strain into account by not placing their employees at the phones for more than six hours at a time. For full-time employees this means that they carry out tasks in the back-office area after this time. In that sense this limitation of the employees' ability to work under pressure is another reason why part-time work is a central variable in the planning of shift patterns.

Data such as these underscore the great variety of working conditions and employment patterns in the call centre industry and they can hardly be reduced to a few straightforward findings. The work requirements are such that they must facilitate a flexible disposition over workers, which in the short run creates employment opportunities for certain social groups with their particular employment needs. This does not imply, however, as to whether one can derive long-term employment opportunities from this. To put it differently, in view of the high occupational strain, the question of whether or not additional jobs evolve and for whom they are attractive must remain open for the time being. Maybe call centre jobs are only attractive to people who are looking for part-time jobs and do not plan on doing the job for the rest of their lives.

Apart from students, who have an obvious interest in part-time work and flexible employment contracts, it is a question of whether there are other groups in society for whom call centre jobs would be the right kind of work and who these people are. The answers from our respondents suggest that besides the potential call centre employees among the students, the working conditions also match the needs of single mothers, retired people who would like to earn some additional money, or women who want to work shorter hours for family reasons. Men and women with interrupted working careers and who are looking for a starting point to re-enter the labour market apparently find an occupation at call centres attractive as well.[5]

Pressure and Strain on the Service Representatives

One can define work at a call centre as 'computer-controlled work', the beginnings of which we described more than 15 years ago in the book 'The Future of White Collar Workers' (Baethge and Oberbeck, 1986). Back then we took front-office occupations in banks and savings banks as an example. In this kind of work we then identified the restrictive standardisation of the

---

[5] Such employment patterns and labor relations for the people at the phone lines are considered completely irrelevant in certain areas of the computer industry. These areas consist of call centers that are specialized on valuable assistance with the technology. Among these employees, work at the call center is considered the stepping stone for employment under better conditions in one of the firms assisted by the call center.

personal service relationship between customers and bank employees and analysed it as a trend toward Taylorist organisation of service occupations.[6] By now this appears to have evolved to a new level under the influence of the development and spread of call centres as an organisations principle.

Answering the phone calls is controlled by interfaces presented to the service employee on the computer screen. The result of this standardisation of work processes is that the time needed to provide the service could be reduced drastically. This can be considered as easing the burden on the employees, because it provides them with all the necessary information automatically, without them having to leave their workplaces. However, the flipside of it is that calls can be allocated automatically, so that work can be organised in a prescribed tempo. In that sense the long-standing management-goal, to limit (and reduce) the time needed to assist customers by introducing computer 'assisted' forms of work, is becoming a reality in the wake of the control-potential inherent in the new-technology.

While in our brief survey we found processing times between two and a half and four minutes per call, the benchmarking study cited above mentions an average of three minutes for the processing of one call, but plus 2.68 minutes after each phone call for finishing up the case.

The times for both processing and finishing up calls are set by management, and deviations from the norm are recorded by the system, so that the performance of the employees can be monitored. Particular company agreements and company-specific practices determine how this kind of monitoring employee performance is then used. In the call centres we studied there are company internal collective bargaining agreements in place which ensure that such analyses of employee performance are created only on the level of work teams, without the possibility of identifying individual employees. The people we talked to referred to the practices at other call centres, though, in which the performance of individual employees is monitored. The pressure emanating from this potential to completely monitor the performance of individual employees is all too evident if managers use (which does not always happen) such performance summaries as a basis for meetings with their teams, even if it is wrapped in the jargon of coaching and called well-meaning support.

Besides this potential for automatic recording and analysing the calls, there is the possibility for supervisors to monitor the phone interaction manually. Many call centres justify the practice of monitoring by pointing

---

[6] Fifteen years ago this type of white collar work was not predominant among the white collar occupations. The prevalent type of work at that time was computer assisted clerical work, which provided employees with greater room for maneuver for both the analysis of existing business relationships and for advisory sessions with new customers.

out training purposes. Supposedly the intention is to improve the conversation-techniques of the staff at the phone lines. Here too it is to a large extent up to the supervisors, whether or not such training guidelines amount to direct pressure for the employees.

Call centres offer fixed-term contracts partly because the duration of projects is limited, but also because fixed-term contracts serve the purpose of helping in the recruitment of permanent staff, as they are considered as a trial period of sorts. Call centre managers use this trial period to filter out those people who are suitable for a job that is very monotonous with regard to work pressure. At the same time, our respondents mentioned, that fixed-term contracts are used to discipline the service representatives and to increase their performance. Mere hints at the possibility that a contract will not be extended are enough to increase performance.

Due to the technological developments in the area of communication technology, supervisors and managers of call centres have a large toolbox of control instruments at their disposal. When used for the purpose of rationalisation, these tools provide not only the means for near to comprehensive human resource planning, they also facilitate a compression of performance requirements. In view of the variety of practices in the field of labour policy that exists in the industry, one should not make generalisations about the actual use of the potential for control and the room for manoeuvre that remains in staff placement and performance. One can still say a lot, though. The work in call centres tends to be timed and organised under flat hierarchies where superiors have far-reaching possibilities for monitoring and control.[7] The potential for control that can be used for increasing work pressure, however, does not say much about the *actual* strain under which the employees are working. Suppose the ergonomic minimal standards with regard to equipment, premises, noise, air conditioning, and lighting are kept, which is not always the case (see Menzler-Trott, 1997), then we still do not know much about the pressure emanating from the monotony of the standardised work at the computer screen and the tight timeframe for each customer.

There is still another kind of strain affecting the service representatives to a particular degree. Unlike the synchronised work at the assembly line, in which workers have to discipline primarily their body, the employees in call centres must discipline their behaviour in the physical and the mental and emotional respect. Service quality is defined not only in terms of acces-

---

[7] Unlike industrial work at the assembly-line, the work in call centers in not synchronized and linked. The nearly uninterrupted flow of communication is comparable to assembly-line work, though. Thus Taylor and Bain (1999) called the work process in call centers an 'assembly line in the head' (p. 7).

sibility or the duration of assistance, but always also in terms of the social skills of the service representatives. The predominant aspects of these social skills are friendliness and powers of persuasion. Behind this slightly euphemistic description of social skills, however, looms emotional work, whose exertion absorbs the entire personality, as A.R. Hochschild (1990) has demonstrated. Being nice in a conversation is no spontaneous act of emotion any more, but instead a normed sentiment that is part of work performance and demanded by one's employer.[8]

This creates a tension between inner emotions and behaviour on the surface, which may not be unknown as a phenomenon in society, but which can still cause a stressful situation at work when it needs to be systematically upheld over the entire workday.[9]

This is particularly pronounced when the work activities have to be repeated in tight timeframes. An additional factor is that in many cases the actual contact with the customers must be repeated in a relatively tight structure of instructions, in order to gain the desired rationalisation effects. What used to be the sign of good customer service, the autonomous interaction with people, tends to be completely destroyed by this.

In the context of an increasing role of psychology and deliberate management in designing work contexts, which is spreading in the wake of the spread of the service society and the accompanying emphasis on selling and presenting oneself and one's business, the manipulation of emotions is becoming a core issue not only in training, but also in managing work teams. In a few, appropriately organised and professional cases, one important topic concerns learning skills that can make emotional work less burdensome. How far this can contribute to actually easing the strain on service representatives is one of the open questions that warrant further research.

How to Organise Training?

While labour unionists tend to express their concerns in the traditional language of occupations, that correspond to certain skill requirements and training courses, other actors, like call centre managers or representatives

---

[8] Hochschild defines emotional work as '... management of one's feelings, geared toward creating a publicly perceptible expression of the face and the body; emotional work is sold for a wage and thus has an exchange value. The expression management of one's feelings refers to the same acts of emotional manipulation as in the private realm, in which they have the character of a use value for this reason'. (Hochschild, 1990, p. 30)

[9] In our research we have met service representatives who were unable to answer their phones at home during the first two hours after a four-hour shift.

of training facilities tend to be more unassuming, and merely talk about an adjustment-training. A participant of a professional conference put this point as follows: 'With the call centre we in fact only have a certain medium through which the service is conveyed. The skills must be brought by our service representatives themselves' (Becker-Redschow 1998, p. 43).

For the trade unions, the public debate about vocational training for call centres is part of an overall strategy of intervention, aiming at gaining some influence in a segment in which many firms are not covered by collective bargaining agreements. And while training facilities have an inherent interest in vocational training, call centre managers are interested in not only having qualified staff, but also lowering the fluctuation rates by offering training opportunities.

The call centres in our sample require vocational training in business, banking, or the insurance industry, but not all applicants who fulfil this requirement are considered suitable candidates. Social skills like service orientation and communicative skills are also required, if not even more importantly vocational skills.[10] However, can social skills be taught in workshops? Confronted with this question, experts answer with yes. The precondition is a certain disposition, however, which enables people to do the necessary emotional work. 'The main point – the main problem is that I need staff members who are capable for services and willing to provide that infamous communication with customers, communicative competence, and the like. These are simply things that must evolve over time. In training sessions that is of course not always easy. You must get at the personality of people who might have had very different ideas before' (Becker-Redshow, 1998, p. 39).

That training can contribute to developing and modifying predispositions, but cannot create them from scratch, appears to be a widespread opinion in the industry.

> 'We recently had a workshop ... at which we asked call centre managers, how they select their employees, and they told us: We see that at first glance. They only need to come through the door and open their mouth, then I already know whether he or she is capable or not ... An important thing is that somebody is open, they can take a setback or two, since such things always happen, however good the products are, in every service firm, whether it is in the department

---

[10] A glance at the substance of training courses for employees of call centers, offered by private educational organizations in cooperation with the labor offices in several federal German States confirms that in addition to teaching basic computer skills and an introduction to the business processes and work organization of call centers, the emphasis is on general skills like telephone training, communicative techniques, and the management of complaints on the phone.

store at the cashier or in the bank. They will always have to deal with complaints, and the service representative in the call centre who is so concerned about this that he or she cannot act reasonably any more when the next customer calls is certainly not in the right place. These are skills that one must presume that they are already present in the person who applies for the job... in their essence these skills must already be there.' (Michel, 1998, p. 41)

Without doubt, learning communication and sales techniques on the phone can contribute to lowering the amount of emotional pressure on service representatives and help increase the quality of service. That can be considered beneficial for the employees in call centres, to the extent that it might even foster motivation and lower fluctuation. The burden that comes with the timed and tightly controlled work process, however, is not completely removed by this.

Costs, Compensation, Rents from Regulation, and Wage Subsidies

Roughly 60 per cent of all costs of call centres are personnel costs, while 10 to 15 per cent are for the technology (Schnorr, 1999). These numbers indicate that call centres are a very labour intensive segment, and thus the rationalisation of work plays a central role in its organisational development. And as already explained, it is precisely technology itself, with its varied possibilities for analysing the flow of communication and the performance of employees, that provides the tools for efficiently employing the staff members and thus saving personnel costs.

Lowering payroll costs is not only accomplished through rationalisation, though, but also by siphoning off what can be describe as rents of regulation (Albach, 1989). This means that call centre providers that work on behalf of other firms or, as in the case of direct banks, are off-shoots of parent-companies, are all active in a legal space that is not regulated by collective bargaining agreements, so that employees are shifted from a tightly regulated area of working life into a less tightly regulated one: a process that labour unions criticise as flight from collective bargaining. With regard to compensation this means that extra benefits regulated in collective bargaining agreements, such as Christmas bonus or holiday pay are abolished or that for a similar kind of work people earn less if they work in a call centre (Biehler and Vogl, 1999).

In our research we found gross hourly wages that ranged from 7.66 € (call centre provider) to 11.25 € (Direktbank) without extra benefits in the area of call centres. In comparison, the gross hourly wage of call centre employees covered by the collectively bargained framework agreement of the banking and insurance industry ranged from 13.30 to 14.30 €.[11] These are data that not only point toward the need for regulation, but also toward a serious degree of polarisation in the world of call centres.[12]

In our interviews some people expressed concerns that wages in the area of call centres not covered by collective bargaining agreements will decline even further, driven by price competition from new market entrants. Even the closing down of some call centres is not ruled out. In this respect locational competition between municipalities and Bundesländer appears to play a significant role. At a conference about the industry, for instance, there were reports about a call centre with around 100 employees in Düsseldorf that had to close down, because its business shifted to Mecklenburg-Vorpommern, where full-time jobs in that area are subsidised by about 435 € per month (Deutsche, 1998). To what extent this is an exceptional case must remain an open question at this point. However, one should not rule out the possibility that creating subsidised jobs in this area not only increases rents of regulation, but also may lead to the destruction of jobs that already existed elsewhere.

Conclusions

In view of saturated markets that have become consumer markets innovative business strategies are in demand, particularly those that are geared toward customer satisfaction and price reductions. In this situation many firms not only use call centres to further rationalise the interface between firms and customers. They also experiment with new forms of sales, assistance, and marketing strategies. This trend is further nurtured by innova-

---

[11] In a survey about the structure of wages and salaries in call centers, which the authors themselves consider not representative, the average gross income of full-time service representatives is estimated at 1,892 € per month (Thieme and Ceyp, 1997). One can assume that this average reflects the fact that 60 per cent of the call centers are in industries like the insurance business, financial services, and communications, in which service representatives are in part covered by framework agreements or, as in the communication industry where higher rates are being paid.

[12] By pointing out that services must be provided at market prices, some people in the chemical industry call for separate collective agreements for the services provided within the large companies. This kind of discussion is geared toward lowering payroll costs (Express, 1999). Should such a plan become the reality and spread throughout the industry, then one could not exclude the possibility that separate collective agreements will be demanded for the service representatives of call centers in banks and insurance companies as well, with the argument that costs outside the banks and insurance companies would be lower. In this case cost savings would not be realized by means of outsourcing and rents of regulation, but by means of directly negotiating with the labor unions in the contact of a framework agreement.

tions in the area of information and communication technologies as well as by falling telephone costs and by the prospect that a more efficient implementation of the new strategies will yield both cost savings and higher customer loyalty. It is particularly this promise that appears to be the driving force behind the dramatic development of this area.

By the year 2001 there will be an estimated 150,000 jobs in the segment of call centres, and this implies an employment growth, as only part of these jobs will be filled with full-time employees (ibv, 1998). These projected numbers of jobs, one must concede, cannot all be considered employment growth, as the establishment of internal call centres with staff already in the firm does not yield any additional jobs. These cases are merely instances of organisational restructuring within firms. Nevertheless, one can expect the call centre industry to bring an overall employment growth. This net growth will probably be the result of trends in opposite directions, in which the destruction of existing jobs and the creation of new ones are occurring simultaneously, and the latter overcompensates the former.[13]

The particular characteristic of the new jobs that emerge in call centres is not so much the fact that they do not provide job security. The significant aspect is rather, that a lot of the people working in these jobs do not envision a long-term perspective in the job. In other words: the emerging jobs are characterised by a comparatively high rotation in and out of such work.

At the same time one should not disregard the fact that the emerging jobs do offer attractive employment opportunities for certain groups of the population: students or women who are looking for part-time work for family reasons, retired people who would like to boost their income, but also men and women who are in the process of re-entering the labour market.

We have characterised the work process in call centres as work under the conditions of a tight time frame and strict controls (in the sense of Taylorist principles) and we pointed out the stress-factors that this kind of work incurs for the service representatives. Such a characterisation should not lead to the impression that all work in call centres is unskilled work. According to our findings, service representatives all have had business training or training in banking or insurance occupations; this kind of training is a requirement for applications in the industry. The question of whether the staff in call centres consider themselves overqualified for their

---

[13] The establishment of direct banks has contributed to the expansion of call centers in the area of financial services. There are, however, estimations that only four to five of them will survive (Halfman, 1997). This would mean that jobs in this area are in danger in the medium term.

jobs and, if they do, how this sentiment influences their work motivation must remain open in this article.

In closing, a brief remark about service quality: the fact that work in call centres is tightly controlled should not necessarily lead one to conclude that this negatively affects the quality of the services. Service quality depends, among other things, on whether or not standardisation and 'informationisation' of services is done in such a way that they facilitate short and effective communication between customers and service representatives. In addition, the way in which the work process is organised, and how call centre managers attend to the stress situation in which service representatives constantly find themselves, both play a significant role in determining service quality. As of now the restrictive solutions appear to outnumber the innovative ones, so that the surveys among customers about service quality produce predominantly negative answers. Overall, we are very doubtful whether this can be changed fundamentally in the context of a call centre conception that is still biased towards cost savings and rationalisation. What is probably needed here, as in many other service industries, is the resurgence of personal services, taking place in direct interaction.[14]

References

Albach, H. (1989), *Dienstleistungen in der modernen Industriegesellschaft*, München, Beck.
Baderschneider, H., Lemke, A. and Menzler-Trott, E. (1999), 'Call-Center Systeme', in Menzler-Trott, E. (ed.), *Call-Center Management. Ein Leitfaden für Unternehmen zum effizienten Kundendialog*, München, Beck, pp. 177-224.
Baethge, M. and Oberbeck, H. (1986), *Zukunft der Angestellten*, Frankfurt/M, Campus.
Becker-Redschaw, R. (1998), 'Diskussionsbeitrag', in DGB (ed.), *Call Center zwischen Mc-Jobs und qualifizierter Dienstleistung. Fachtagung zu Beschäftigungsperspektive, Qualifikation und Arbeitsbedingungen in Call Centern*, Bremen, pp. 38-39.
Biehler, H. and Vogl, G. (1999), 'Call Center: Zusatzleistungen sind nicht üblich', *WSI Mitteilungen*, Nr. 4, pp. 261-267.
CoPers (1998), *Computer Fachwissen*, Nr. 4, p. 8.
Deutsche, A. (1998), 'Diskussionsbeitrag', in DGB (ed.), *Call Center zwischen Mc-Jobs und qualifizierter Dienstleistung. Fachtagung zu Beschäftigungsperspektive, Qualifikation und Arbeitsbedingungen in Call Centern*, Bremen, pp. 33-35.
Express (1999), *Kein Anschluß unter dieser...*, Nr. 2, p. 9.
Express (1999), *Verhandlungen über Billigtarifvertrag*, Nr. 4, p. 9.
Financial Times Deutschland (2001), *Callcenter haben eine lange Leitung*, 24. April, p. 10.
Finger, L. (2001), *Einsatzpotentiale von Call Centern als Instrument des Beziehungsmanagements unter besonderer Berücksichtigung zentraler Entscheidungs-, Gestaltungs- und Problemfelder*, unpublished manuscript, Braunschweig.
Frankfurter Allgemeine Zeitung (1998), *Deutsche Call Center im Leistungsvergleich*, 10.08.1998, http://www.callcenter-benchmark.de/bpresse4.htm.

---

[14] For this point, see in greater detail Oberbeck (2001).

Gutek, B.A. (1995), *The Dynamics of Service. Reflections on the Changing Nature of Customer/Provider Interactions*, San Francisco, Jossey-Bass.

Halfman, M. (1997), 'Vier bis fünf Direktbanken werden im Markt überleben', *Blick durch die Wirtschaft*, 31.10.1997, p. 4.

Hochschild, A.R. (1990), *Das gekaufte Herz. Zur Kommerzialisierung der Gefühle*, Frankfurt/M, Campus.

Ibv (1998), 'Arbeitsplatz Call Centre. Ein neuer Wirtschaftszweig boomt', in *Informationen für die Beratungs- und Vermittlungsdienste der Bundesanstalt für Arbeit*, Heft Nr. 39, Nürnberg, Bundesanstalt für Arbeit.

Menzler-Trott, E. (1997), 'Call Center. Reorganisation tut Not', *Computer Fachwissen*, Nr. 11, pp. 9-10.

Michel, L. (1998), 'Diskussionsbeitrag', in DGB (ed.), *Call Center zwischen McJobs und Qualifizierter Dienstleistung. Fachtagung zu Beschäftigungsperspektive, Qualifikation und Arbeitsbedingungen in Call Centern*, Bremen, pp. 39-42.

Neumann, J. (2000), 'IT verändert die Welt. Der Einfluss der Informationstechnologie auf die Transformation von Unternehmen und Geschäftseinheiten', in Klitzke, U., Betz, H. and Möreke, M. (ed.), *Vom Klassenkampf zum Co-Management? Perspektiven gewerkschaftlicher Betriebspolitik*, Hamburg, VSA, pp. 39-46.

Oberbeck, H. (2001), 'Zum Verhältnis von Dienstleistungsqualität und Dienstleistungsbeschäftigung', in Baethge, M. and Wilkens, I. (eds.), *Die große Hoffnung für das 21. Jahrhundert? Perspektiven und Strategien für die Entwicklung der Dienstleistungsbeschäftigung*, Opladen, Leske und Budrich, pp. 71-83.

Schnorr, G. (1999), 'Der Rahmenplan. Ein effektives Instrument', in Menzler-Trott, E. (ed.), *Call-Center Management. Ein Leitfaden für Unternehmen zum effizienten Kundendialog*, München, Beck, pp. 305-369.

Süddeutsche Zeitung No. 192, 22. August 2001, p. 27.

Taylor, P. and Bain, P. (1999), 'An assembly line in the Head: work and employee relations in the call centre', *Industrial Relations Journal*, Vol. 30(2), pp. 101-117.

Thieme, J. and Ceyp, M. (1997), *Großer Call Center Gehalts- und Karrierevergleich*, Hannover, Telepublic-Verlag.

PART II
RATIONALISATION, SKILLS AND CONTROL

Chapter 6

Skill Formation in Call Centres

Paul Thompson and George Callaghan

Service work continues to extend its share of total employment and interactive services, such as that carried out in call centres, constitute one of the fastest growing categories within that. The rise of call centres has generated a considerable debate, particularly in the UK, with emphasis on the nature of the labour process and managerial regimes. Less explicit emphasis has been placed on workforce skills. However it is possible to identify a general contrast between optimistic scenarios associated with the new service management literature and bleaker pictures of routinisation painted by radical critics.

The new service management literature (Schneider and Bowen, 1999) tends to emphasise general trends in service work, but the essential themes are largely consistent with the official call centre industry image of empowered, highly skilled, and committed employees, delivering customised, quality service. In contrast, radical critics, noting highly scripted job tasks and closely monitored performance, draw parallels to assembly lines and information age factories. Poynter extracts the most unambiguous conclusions from such work. Call centres and other new forms of service work embody practices once the preserve of manual employees, routinising and deskilling professional work: 'A form of organisation that was once the preserve of manual labour has rapidly diffused within industries that were previously associated with white collar workers and the exercise of "mental" labour' (2000, p. 151).

Such views have been criticised for focusing on the 'management-worker dyad', while neglecting the mediating role of the customer contained within *interactive* service work (Korczynski, 2001). Actually, most critical researchers recognise the differences from classic manual and white-collar work regimes. Most significantly the labour and product of call centre work is relatively intangible. Though this is not specific to factory work, the emphasis is almost exclusively on the quality of communication. Call centre work is a good example of interactive service sector work, which Leidner (1993) defines as work involving face-to-face or voice to voice interaction with customers. In such work particular attitudes and feelings – sometimes summed up in the term emotional labour – are combined with product knowledge in order to maximise the quality and quantity of output, often measured in terms of customer satisfaction (S. Taylor, 1998).

The intermediary role of the customer is regarded as a central defining feature by some researchers, allowing them to develop a middle ground position that emphasises contrasting strategies or logics. Batt (1999) sees a tension between serving and selling, and contrasts mass production strategies that maximise sales and minimise costs with 'relationship management' that seeks to maximise sales by providing good service. Each invokes different patterns of skill and work organisation. Korczynski (2001) refers to a 'dual logic' of efficiency and bureaucratic standardisation versus customer-oriented service quality. This deep-seated contradiction is reconciled in the development of customer-oriented bureaucracies, whose features vary according to sector and segment. Echoing his work with Frenkel (Frenkel et al, 1998), Korczynski argues that though variations exist, there is a trend towards a middle category of service work, away from cost minimisation and emphasising service quality.

One way of assessing these claims and the characteristic practices in the industry is by focusing on the actual processes of skill formation. Traditionally, social scientists have tended to focus largely on inputs into this process, notably labour market and training institutions, qualifications and formal skill hierarchies. This may, of course, still be pertinent in situations where call centres are operating in dense institutional frameworks that condition their labour strategies; or in company/sectoral circumstances where there is a positive association between traditional skills and new job requirements. One example is provided in Batt's case study of a US telecom's operation. The skill requirements for a customer service representative (CSR) are customer interaction skills, keyboard skills, knowledge of procedures, products services and legal regulations, technical proficiency in programming languages and databases. This reflects both the varied and complex demands of the job, and an 'institutional context' where, 'the historic HR practices of the Bell system had created a highly skilled work force with tremendous tacit knowledge of the customers, the tele-communications infrastructure, and the use of information systems' (1999, p. 557).

However, it is not obvious how generalisable such conditions are. The traditional signifiers of skill formation are largely absent or inverted in much of the UK call centre industry. For example, a recent study in Scotland (Watson et al., 2000) showed that 22 per cent of telephone sales staff possessed a degree compared to 7 per cent of clerical workers and 3 per cent of sales. In their case studies, the figure was even higher at almost 40 per cent (though this included management grades). Yet even the most generous interpretation of call centre work would find it hard to see a connection between such qualifications and the nature of work or opportunity structures. Indeed it is highly likely that in many call centres, graduates will be working alongside co-workers with no qualifications at all. As one of our interviewees put it referring to one call centre location, 'the hairdresser in Hemel Hempstead can do the same job as someone who's worked for the bank for twelve years' (Manager 1).

Something different is going on, and it is not wholly new. In economies such as the UK, with thin institutional frameworks and largely local, voluntaristic labour strategies, an increasing number of manufacturing companies have turned towards recruiting 'green' labour, showing little interest in formal qualifications or technical skills (Thompson et al, 1995). This has been a particular preference of Japanese companies in the UK, who focus on developing enterprise-level skills that they can specify and reward according to their own criteria. The call centre industry in the UK has been able to develop a similar enterprise orientation, drawing on local labour markets, and attempting to fashion it in its chosen image. This parallels general trends in service work, 'The aims are to select staff with the required attitudinal and behavioural characteristics, induct them into a quality culture and, equally important, but often neglected, retain their services... selection often focuses on attitudes to flexibility and customer service rather than skill or qualification levels ' (Redman and Mathews, 1998, p. 60). Korczynski (2001; and in this volume) argues that the whole recruitment approach in call centres is based on selecting people with the right 'customer focus', developing these values in training and performance appraisal.

It is also increasingly recognised that there has been a general shift towards 'extra-functional' skills to cope with new organisational requirements (Flecker and Hofbauer, 1998), or as part of the growth of teamwork (Thompson and Wallace, 1996). Such trends have considerable significance for processes of skill and competence formation and therefore for selection. As Crouch et al note, 'These changes lead employers to seek in new recruits both a continuing ability to learn and what they usually call "social skills", which might mean anything from ability to co-ordinate and secure co-operation, through ability to communicate effectively, to simple willingness to obey orders' (1999, p. 222). Call centres, and service work more generally, are at the forefront of such shifts. Whereas such skills are a *part* of the profile of manufacturing work, in interactive services social skills and competencies are the main part (Thompson, Warhurst and Callaghan, 2001). Indeed, according to the industry, such qualities constitute the primary source of competitive advantage.

Given that traditional indicators are unreliable, the role of selection, recruitment and training in identifying and shaping social competencies is moved to the centre of the stage. Yet, there are few critical studies in this area. This is surprising given that call centres are putting considerable emphasis on attempting to identify potential employees who are predisposed to become effective customer service representatives. This is discussed more extensively elsewhere (Callaghan and Thompson, 2002), but recruitment, selection and training processes are also good indicators of assumptions and practices concerning skills and their utilisation. This forms the basis of our empirical material.

The Case Study: Methods and Context

The research for this paper is based on a case study of 'Telebank'. Located in Central Scotland in a new, purpose built building, it is one of four dedicated UK call centres used by a large bank. Data was gathered through a combination of semi-structured interviews with fourteen managers, non-participant observation of recruitment and training processes and analysis of secondary company literature. This material is supplemented with data drawn from 24 semi-structured interviews with customer service representatives (CSRs). The 24 were drawn from two teams of 12 from different work areas.

Given the focus on skill formation in this chapter, it is useful to outline some of the basic conditions of work and employment. Telebank has five hundred CSRs dealing with around twenty thousand incoming calls a day. Eighty per cent of these CSRs are full time, working 35 hours a week within the bank opening hours of 8.00 a.m. - 10.00 p.m., Monday to Sunday. The full time shift pattern involves 6.5 hours of work per day, with one hour for lunch and two 15 minute breaks (although both the rest periods can be exchanged for overtime). The remaining twenty per cent of staff are described as 'key-time' (part time) employees, working a variety of shifts. The organisational structure is flat, with three basic categories - CSR, team leader and call centre manager. The wage rate, of £11,500, is reached in three stages, with trainees starting on eighty per cent and working up to one hundred percent over their three month probationary period.

There is very little task variety and discretion over the pace or type of work. Eighty per cent of calls consist of three routine types of requests for account information or actions to manipulate the accounts. The remaining 20 per cent are partially dealt with by CSRs before being passed on to colleagues elsewhere in the bank for further action; 'Something that you have to think about comes along probably about three times a day. Everything else is quite straightforward. Maybe there are things you have to refer to your material for, but you know where to find it and doesn't make you think' (CSR 14). As this quote illustrates, the depth of product and organisational knowledge required in the job is also limited. Such knowledge is procedural and located within IT systems; 'the rep doesn't make the decision about where it (the query) goes, the product code determines where it goes'. (Manager 1). This can be seen in the terms used – 'cookery cards' for routine information and 'added ingredients' for anything more complex.

> 'When I came in here I had no idea about the banking system, but it's easy to pick up. You have a bunch of information to refer to... You have a cookery card, you look up your card and it tells you what to do. You can read it off to the customer what information you need.' (CSR 1)

The dominant element in the control system is technical. Work is machine paced and extensively monitored. Within this environment CSRs take around 120 calls per day. Each call lasts around 3 minutes 30 seconds and CRS are put under continual pressure to keep within talk time targets (160 seconds); minimising post call or 'wrap up' time to around 20 seconds. Each of these categories is electronically recorded and measured. However, this is supplemented by both bureaucratic and normative controls (see Callaghan and Thompson, 2001 for more details). The former is structured through the scripting of interactions with customers through company manuals and the use of core standards of behaviour that in turn shape feedback and appraisal procedures. The latter is reproduced through two mechanisms. First the division of CSRs into teams, whose primary purpose is to offset task individualism through extra-functional forms of social interaction. Second, and a major focal point later in this chapter, normative regulation is attempted through forms of emotional management and self-management.

Identifying Skills, Recruitment and Selection

A sub-set of questions in our interviews with managers and CSRs focused on perceptions of skill. By establishing common themes across the two sets of interviews we were able to evaluate the gaps and inconsistencies between managerial objectives and employee experience. Telebank management believes that they require a particular mix of skills. This is less based on technical abilities (such as keyboard skills), but social competencies, that are more difficult to identify yet crucial to Telebank's labour process.

While some levels of product and systems knowledge are pre-requisites for the job; personality and communication skills are seen by management as the crucial differentiating qualities, given that, 'If one bank invents a new savings product and market it tomorrow, the rest would have it on Friday' (Manager 5). The same manager observes that while keyboard and technical skills can be taught, 'Customer Service. That's not a skill. That's in you. It's the attitude towards customer service'. As we shall see later, the company does try and shape attitudes and enhance social competencies, but the recruitment and selection process is undoubtedly used to screen-in those pre-disposed to display the desired attitudes and behaviours.

> 'The vast majority of these people in customer service centres, we are talking 99 per cent plus, are not bankers, they've been recruited because of their personalities and communication skills.' (Manager 6)

Within the general view of management that 'we recruit attitude', specific emphasis is placed upon positivity, energy and enthusiasm:

> 'To fit into the category you need to be first of all, very, very enthusiastic. You need to really want to do it, because it's a tough 6 weeks training. You need to be positive, the whole company is geared towards a positive attitude, again a can-do approach, not "I've never done that before, but yes, let's give it a bash, let's try it".' (Manager 4)

The other characteristic that emerged was sense of humour. This is not simply a quality of the autonomous, individual personality. CSRs have to know when to deploy this humour, be able to read the conversation and decide when it is appropriate to engage in banter: 'It depends on the customers, the more experience they (the CSR) have the best they can judge the type of customer they've got on line'.

This is an example of how it is not enough to simply possess 'personality', CSRs must know how to communicate this. More broadly, communication competencies include verbal tone, pitch, fluency and energy and enthusiasm. These constitute a cluster of technical and emotional competencies ranging from body language to language itself.

> 'If I'm not hearing energy and enthusiasm, what I'm looking for is energy drop. Energy drop is where you've got someone who's started a sentence, sounded quite bright, and then it drops off. And also looking for sentence shape, are they melodic, are they using good pitch, or are they monotonous, have they got the one tone they always speak at. Are they too musical, do they give a little squeak at the end of the sentence?' (Manager 7)

With these factors in mind, we can focus more explicitly on the process of recruitment. Applicants pass through the following filters:

1. Application pack: containing a sheet headed 'What we are looking for', which gives prominence to 'attitude'. This is defined as 'sense of humour; flexibility; receptive to change; realistic expectations of career progression; confidence; positive; respect for other peoples values; understanding customers priorities; sociability and common sense'. Women returners are targeted through the comment 'running a house and raising children requires many of the skills we are looking for!'
2. Application form: requiring self-assessment of two categories - previous work experience and personal qualities. For the first of these applicants are asked to rank (on a scale from 1-3) how much they enjoy certain tasks, for example 'dealing with customers', while the second category asks applicants whether they agree or disagree with a list of statements - for example 'enjoy speaking to people' and 'listen carefully to others'. Recruiters score each form, giving weight to customer service and/or outlook.
3. Telephone interview: this lasts for around 20 minutes and assesses basic English, fluency, grammar, rapport, enthusiasm and voice tone/pitch. This again is scored.
4. Role play: applicants act as a travel agent and, after studying holiday details (flight times, hotel details), take two calls from a 'customer' and are (statistically) assessed on their ability to extract and impart information.
5. Formal interview: this is conducted by two interviewers and is based around a series of set questions. Interviewers complete a skills profile containing 12 categories where the emphasis is on customer service.

Getting a job at Telebank is not easy; only seven out of a hundred applicants successfully get through the multistage recruitment process. What sort of people are recruited? We shadowed a team of 17 employees during training (15 women and 2 men), and their previous jobs were often service related (see table 1).

One obvious feature is the predominance of female employees. As argued elsewhere in this volume (see chapter by Belt), there is a strong association between the social competencies prioritised in call centre work and broader interactive service work, and assigned 'natural' female characteristics. However, in contrast to Belt's case studies we found that female and male managers alike resisted any attempt to link skills and gender characteristics. They pointed to the growing percentage of men in the centre and argued that, 'The job itself – the guys are just as happy doing it as the girls are'. If pressed, managers tended to use labour market rather than labour process rationales; notably that the company goal of flexibility through a workforce that is at least 50 per cent part-time would most likely be met through predominantly female recruitment. A minority accepted a traditional association between women and social skills, but believed that the recruitment net would also pick up suitable men: 'Very, very much so, but then we would hope to pick that up at interviews, male and female' (Manager 10).

Table 6.1 Previous Jobs of 17 Employees

Sewing machinist	Women returner	Travel agent
Assistant bakery manageress	Call centre worker	Office worker in property company
Practice manager in a dental surgery	Insurance clerk	Women returner
Manufacturing worker (T.V's)	Women returner	Sales manager
Manufacturing worker (T.V's)	Bank cashier	Call centre worker
Women returner	Check out assistant	

Skill Utilisation and Training

Groups of new recruits get six weeks full-time training. For the first four weeks they are based in a separate training room and then move to a dedicated area on the ground floor (known as the 'paddling pool') to begin taking calls. Trainees are taught about the technical equipment and given some information on basic banking, products and systems. The focal point is to ensure competency in navigating around systems and the procedural knowledge necessary to deal with queries.

The main emphasis, however, is on communication skills. During this time trainees are taught how to vary their voice and manage conversations to ensure every caller gets the same level of customer service. Trainees are told they need not only master specific techniques (such as controlling the conversation) but also must learn how to manage themselves; customers should not be able to tell if CSRs are unhappy. Together these begin to give trainees an awareness and influence over the regulation and management of feelings.

Training in products and systems is complemented by training in communication: managing a conversation (techniques of conversational control) and managing yourself (control over one's energy and enthusiasm). A 'conversation cycle' is used to teach trainees to 'build rapport' with the customer. While 'rapport' evokes images of empathy, the actual focus is on specific techniques of managing the information flow through question prompts and situationally appropriate answers:

> 'If someone says I want to order some money, I'm going to Australia to see my daughter, "Oh, wonderful". They then need to retain that information so at the end of the call they say, "Have a really good time".' (Manager 7)

Some CSRs are understandably puzzled at the balance of priorities in training; 'The conversation cycle, when I first came here I'd never heard in my life. I think I would rather have more training with the systems than concentrate on how we are supposed to have a conversation with a person' (CSR 2). The other procedure is known as the eight elements of conversation, including using the first person, stating intention and giving attention. Together with techniques developed in 'rapport sessions', such as varying voice pitch and tone, these are used as tools to guide interactions and maintain an emotional distance. Thus, in addition to managing the conversation CSRs are taught to manage themselves.

The training period is also used to institutionalise workers into the social and organisational framework, including the nineteen 'core standards of behaviour' referred to earlier. Interestingly, training is often used to emphasise tough facts about the work - workers are not trusted to use their own autonomy, can expect lots of repetitive calls and that they will be continually monitored. A powerful example of this 'scene setting' is the first day pep talk given to trainees by the call centre manager when he said 'I won't hesitate to sack someone who doesn't provide customer service' and that 'we can monitor when you fart'.

That is not to say that emphasis on quality is absent. Quality is more likely to be handled through 'call coaching', which begins in dedicated training rooms and then moves to real calls. Under-performing CSRs can be sent back to the training area to improve their skills. During a conversation with one such CSR we were told that he had been taken off the phones to work on his tone, which went down when he didn't know the answer to the customer's question. A Development Room is also provided for coaching and learning purposes.

Having discussed the form and formation of skills through recruitment and training, we want to explore two key and contested areas, bringing in the voice of employees to a larger extent than so far.

The Skills Gap

One issue that emerges from the case study is a skills gap, at least in terms of rival perceptions. Managers, as we have seen, tend to talk up the need for 'personality', 'passion' for customer service, and communication skills. For employees, the most consistent themes to emerge from the question, 'what kind of skills do you think are necessary to do this job?' were patience, tolerance, level-headednesss, sense of humour, listening, flexibility and emotional self-management. Interviews with CSRs did reveal some continuity with management on perceptions of skill requirements. In particular, there is common ground that social rather than technical competencies and knowledge are primary. But the emphasis was often different. CSRs were much more likely to associate job requirements with surviving stressful and repetitive work, rather than applying a particular set of personality characteristics to the enthusiastic pursuit of customer service:

> 'You have to be patient, first of all. Often you get irate people coming on the calls, you've got to be able to listen to them, and not patronise them. You've got to be quite patient and take in everything they say.' (CSR 10)

> 'You've got be very tolerant, I think. You have to be able to take a deep breath, the customer is always right, kind of thing. But it's very repetitive. I've been here for six months now and it's very mundane – just waiting for the next beep!' (CSR 8)

> 'Communication skills, you really need to talk to people. A good sense of humour. You need to be able to take abuse, because you do get abuse. The majority are fine. It just doesn't affect me, I would get more upset if someone talked down to me than swore.' (CSR17).

However, the difference between management and employees may be less than it appears. The following quote makes clear that management are fully aware of the characteristics of the labour process at the low-end of the financial services market:

> 'At the end of the day, a call centre job is boring, it's call after call, day after day, week after week, month after month. There is very little variety. Now for someone to be able to cope with that, the challenge there is, each customer is different and therefore you have to treat each customer differently, that's where the challenge comes. You have to be tenacious and you've got to have energy, and that energy has got to last if you're a full-timer say from 9–5pm at the same constant level of energy. You have a passionate belief in customer service and all that entails.' (Manager 6)

The somewhat self-deluded rhetoric about passionately believing in customer service is concretely embodied in training to developing 'rapport'. CSRs do value techniques of conversational control, consistent with the need to survive stressful and repetitive work. But genuine empathy and rapport requires time and discretion, qualities that are heavily constrained by the nature and extent of surveillance. Monitoring of calls is undertaken by the 'Research Department' and by Team Leaders; the subsequent statistics are graded as a basis for feedback and discipline. For example, out of every 10,000 calls the target is that only three should produce complaints. Not surprisingly, adverse reaction to 'the stats' was a familiar feature of CSR interviews, and this constitutes a second feature of the skill perception gap. Contrasts with expectations at recruitment interview and in training were noted by employees:

> 'I thought that each customer was supposed to have individual needs, so you've got to give them time.. But it's 'we need to bring those down, let's look at bringing your stats in line with everybody else's'. It's on top of you all the time... Basically, at the moment I feel like a machine. The personal touches have gone and they need to bring them back. But then you've always got the stats at the back of your mind.' (CSR 12)

Nevertheless, CSRs can and do distinguish coaching from surveillance and monitoring:

> 'It's really good having a one to one with someone who's listened to your calls. You never just get negative feedback. I might be a bit biased that way, because I left McDonalds because we didn't get any feedback. It was just "you did that wrong".' (CSR 5)

The balance between coaching and control varies within sections, due to the attitude of team leader, and at different times, according to the pressure on the workflow. Some CSRs were sceptical of the use of practices such as the Development Room; 'I've never used it, or been encouraged to use it. It's never been mentioned. Once you come out of training that's it' (CSR 5).

Emotions and their Management

As we have seen, one of the most important call centre skills is the ability to manage emotions. The concept of emotional labour is helpful here - employees must work on their emotions in order, for example, to present a pleasing voice to the customer. This concept was popularised by

Hochschild (1983) in her work into the labour process of cabin crew, and has been explored in a number of other studies (James, 1989; Ogbanna and Wilkinson, 1990; Filby, 1992; Wharton, 1996; S. Taylor, 1998 and Bolton, 2000). Hochschild argues that if this is done consistently and in a concentrated way workers can move beyond 'surface acting' and actually change their own emotions, a process known as 'deep acting'.

The capacity to manage feelings is clearly important in call centre work but, interestingly it is not explicitly searched for during recruitment and is only indirectly referred to in training. And, while managers frequently referred to the need for CSRs to 'change themselves', they proved highly resistant to the notion that employees may be 'acting', whether surface or deep. The following quote is typical:

> 'I don't think it is putting on an act. What we have is a very good training programme where we train people on their communication skills and how to answer a call and handle that call to the customer's satisfaction. For someone to do the job here and to do it well, they've got to believe in the customer service aspect. To do that job full time would require more than putting on an act, I think. It requires that commitment and wanting to do it.' (Manager 13)

We can see here the management find it difficult to move beyond a rationale that they have recruited a particular kind of person predisposed to provide effective service. Management also find it difficult to reconcile the idea that workers are employed for their 'bubbly' personalities but are then taught techniques that help them manipulate these personalities to suit customer requirements. During recruitment and training management seem to use the proxy of 'people skills' for emotional labour, and the evidence looked for is in what can be seen on the surface, such as body language.

> 'All of us, in the nicest possible way, are icebergs. We only see the tip of the iceberg, which is behaviour. What we don't see as individuals are things like the emotional state, the experiences you've had, general state of mind; we don't know what your beliefs are, stuff like that. All you can do initially is to look at the behaviour to gain an insight into the stuff down here. The things you are looking at is what's going on in their face ...' (Manager 7)

Once in training the focus shifts away from characteristics of personality and moves to developing techniques that allow workers to apply their personality in different work situations. Evidence of non-compliance or poor performance, such as 'energy drop', are treated as technical issues rather than the genuine constraints in delivering manageable emotions in circumstances where, 'We know the job is boring and you don't know whether the next call is going to be Mr Angry or Mr Nice' (Manager 1).

Just as there is a gap in management rationales, the traditional concept of emotional labour is insufficient to understand the complex and contested terrain. Bolton (2000) has developed Hochschild's conceptual framework through a fuller exploration of the way workers manage their own emotions. She argues that workers do not simply provide passive emotional labour but rather are active and skilled emotion managers, with the possibility of conflict with managerial objectives. While some managers are reluctant to talk openly about the need for workers to act, CSRs readily discuss emotional management and the need to act: 'I work until 7 o'clock at night, and it's the last thing you want to do, be bubbly on the phone, you can't be bothered. So there is a bit of pretence behind it sometimes' (CSR 9). In some cases, employee responses mirror managerial goals.

> 'You've got to be very much a people person. Handling the public, emotions, be very customer focused, you bring your emotions into it, you've got to empathise and sympathise with someone, you can't let your emotions in and let yourself get angry on the phone.' (CSR 3)

However, while CSRs are aware of the need to vary their face, the actual responses are themselves extremely varied, with little evidence of deep acting. Many put minimal emotional effort into the work:

> 'My way of handling it is coming in and saying to myself "I do my shift from 2-10, it's not a career, it's a job. I answer the phone and that's it". By not looking for anything more than that, that's my way of handling it. When I first came in, it thought it was maybe just me, but speaking to other people it's the same.' (CSR 8)

> 'There is one part of your brain that does go into repetitive mode just so you can deal with the repetition over and over again.' (CSR 4)

This 'satisficing' strategy is linked to the types of 'endurance' skills identified earlier as primary by CSRs. Others wish to determine the emotional effort bargain on their own terms, for example, displaying emotional labour as a 'gift' to customers even when that means calls go on longer than management would like; 'We have our regulars that call... And they'll call once or twice in the night and sit and talk for a wee while, they just want a bit of company. I just feel you can't cut them off' (CSR 11). Others relieve the pressure by simple forms of misbehaviour such making fun of the customer, 'They can't see us so we can actually take the mickey out of them while they're trying to speak to us' (CSR 1).

The emotional effort bargain thus constitutes a hidden and contested dimension of skill formation. Nor does it necessarily stop at the workplace gate:

> 'It takes about an hour to totally unwind, not thinking about this place at all. I find I'm saying the phrases they want us to say in here, at home, because it's become part of my vocabulary. Oh, I can do that for you! All these positive phrases.' (CSR19)

CSRs continually stated that these pressures contribute to the high levels of turnover and absenteeism in call centres (Deery, Iverson and Walsh, 2000). In Telebank turnover was more than 20 per cent and many managers believed that this was a necessary price to pay for the kind of work required, despite the fact that it costs at least £3,000 to recruit and train each new employee.

Discussion and Conclusions

As we have demonstrated, the official skill story tells us little. We would re-conceptualise skill formation as follows. The recruitment and selection process is indeed used, though in a fairly basic manner, to identify, through experience or predisposition, the existence of social competencies functional to service interactions; 'Basically they're looking for the potential to mould' (CSR 13). Training and subsequent control systems are then used to make those competencies appropriate to the particular workflow. However, use of the term deskilling (Poynter, 2000) obscures more than it illuminates. It underestimates the extent to which interactive service work is distinct from rather than a debased version of previous white collar occupations such as those in banking; and it fails to recognise that emotional labour does not fit neatly into the classic manual/mental divide.

Critical research needs to pay more attention to the actual constitution of competencies in a call centre setting. An exception to the neglect is Becker (2000) in his case study of a Japanese mail order company. This had a clear hierarchy of CSR, unit leader, supervisor and general manager. He reports that two factors shaped competency requirements – the dominant role of information technology determines the 'what' of the process, while routinised scripts, reinforced by training determine the 'how'. Anything that does not fit in has to be referred to the supervisor. The skills of the CSR are, therefore, of a basic human character that is ubiquitous in their everyday lives. Unit leaders also do not require any significant formal knowledge or technical skills. Experienced telephone operators who have been promoted, they are a repository of tacit knowledge, and need to develop judgement skills. Discretion is, however, the province of supervisors, who have knowledge and connections across the various divisions, facilitated by Intranet access. Their main skill lies in problem solving. In other words the skills of unit leaders and supervisors are predicated on the planned routinisation of the CSR role. There was little opportunity for further skill enhancement, though there is some possibility of limited career progression.

How typical is this? In call centres such as Telebank there are clear, objective constraints in the opportunity structure. Given low complexity work and flat structures, the most generous interpretation that could be put on the situation of CSRs is that they are developing or enhancing a set of generic, transferable social skills that makes them more employable in other call centres or service settings. That may not stop a more widespread use of training to certify such skills. There are internal and external pressures on the industry to invest in worker training, for example by codifying social skills, which would give workers a qualification. Telebank operates a system of National Vocational Qualifications in Customer Care. For example, after the end of the 6 week training period, CSRs can get recognition for the 'talk' stage:

> 'NVQs are actually ongoing, so it's while they are out in their teams. The NVQ will have a couple of assessors that literally go in and assess their calls they've been coached on and they get their NVQ that way. They don't have tests or anything like that.' (Manager 3)

What this quote unfortunately indicates is that the current British system of vocational and educational training, by basing qualifications on the demonstration of existing competencies, reinforces the current low skill equilibrium (Grugulis, 1999; Crouch et al, 1999).

We are conscious of the fact that the constitution of skills and competencies is not uniform in the industry, let alone in service work more generally. While the workplace hierarchy is limited, it is also possible that skill and career development could take place within the broader financial services group of which Telebank is part.

By improving workers' broader product and business process knowledge, it is possible that CSR work could provide increased levels of customer service and improved selling opportunities - while also doing more interesting and rewarding work. Telebank are continually assessing the existing technical division of labour and some managers believe that new technology will allow greater specialisation and flexibility, 'So you can have generalists and specialists all sitting in the same room, but a mortgage person may only get a few calls a day on mortgages, the rest of the day they take general calls' (Manager 1).

However, the same manager noted that, 'The main dilemma facing call centres at the moment is the increase in call volumes. Call volumes have gone up 22 per cent this year and they went up 18 per cent last year'. This emphasis on keeping the set up largely the same as a means of coping with increased volumes was confirmed in our discussions with the Call Centre Executive of the company.

Telebank is typical of a type, but not all types. In their comparison of two quite different call centres in Scotland, Watson et al (2000) noted that both were drawing on a labour pool that included many younger, well-qualified people. A large proportion had no notion of a career in any traditional sense, Yet at 'M' a far greater proportion viewed their jobs as part of a career than at 'T'. This is hardly surprising, as 'M' is embedded in a market segment of the financial services industry that allows some of its CSRs to acquire formal knowledge, qualifications and mobility within the company. In contrast, 'T', though containing some high value operations, is basically an outsourced centre supplying services to a variety of clients. Like Telebank, the transferable, generic skill pathway was more likely.

In considering the future of skill requirements in the industry, there are those who foresee the disappearance or marginalisation of routine roles under the impact of automation or other initiatives. There has been talk of internet banking or interactive voice response and speech recognition software making call centre work and workers redundant. But initial signs show that there is still a need for human interaction. This continued demand for person to person communication is connected to cost and flexibility, with the industry press reporting that a telephone call is cheaper and more effective than an e-mail or interactive chat session (Call Centre Technology, 2000 a, b). On the phone customers can ask for what they want immediately, rather than having to negotiate lots of telephone keypad prompts, and there is also space to explore any ambiguities in customer requirements. Such call centre strengths have led to claims that the number of CSRs will continue to grow (Market Assessment International, 1999).

Given these constraints, public policy, at least in the UK, cannot focus wholly on skill enhancement. Trade unions and local economic development departments are already beginning to develop agendas to ensure decent pay, regular breaks, ergonomic workstations, negotiated use of recording equipment, and on site occupational health (Unison, 2001). It's difficult, however, to be optimistic about the chances for positive developments without such external pressure. Most of the call centre industry in the UK and in many other contexts, has been developed as a way to increase productivity through economies of scale. The organisational mind set, facilitated by innovative technologies has from the beginning been used to simplify and routinise tasks, and establish tight control and surveillance mechanisms. No matter what technological developments are introduced, unless there is a fundamental shift in the way work is organised, it is unlikely jobs done in the customer contact centres of the future are going to require greater skills, or be any more rewarding, than much of the call centre work of the present.

References

Batt, R. (1999), 'Work Organization, Technology and Performance in Customer Service and Sales', *Industrial and Labour Relations Review*, Vol. 52(4), pp. 539-564.
Becker, M.C. (2000), *The Constitution of Competence in a Call Centre: An Empirical Contribution of a Theory of Competencies*, unpublished paper, Judge Institute of Management, Cambridge University.
Bolton, S. (2000), 'Emotions Here, Emotions There, Emotional Organisations Everywhere', *Critical Perspectives on Accounting*, Vol. 11, pp. 155-171.
Callaghan, G. and Thompson, P. (2001), 'Edwards Revisited: Technical Control and Worker Agency in Call Centres', *Economic and Industrial Democracy*, Vol. 22, pp. 13-37.
Callaghan, G. and Thompson, P. (2002), 'We Recruit Attitude: The Selection and Shaping of Call Centre labour', *Journal of Management Studies*, March, pp. 233-254.
Call Centre Technology (2000a), 'Listening to a customer's voice', *Call Centre Technology*, Vol. 5(5), p. 13.
Call Centre Technology (2000b), 'Relying on a Call-Back System', *Call Centre Technology*, Vol. 5(6), p. 9.
Crouch, C., Finegold, D. and Sako, M. (1999), *Are Skills the Answer? The Political Economy of Skill Creation in Advanced Industrial Countries*, Oxford University Press.
Datamonitor (1996), *Call Centres in Europe 1996-2001: Vertical Market Opportunities*. Datamonitor, London.
Deery, S., Iverson, R. and Walsh, J. (2000), *Work Relationships in Telephone Call Centres: Understanding Emotional Exhaustion and Employee Withdrawal*, paper to International Industrial Relations Association Conference, Tokyo, May-June.
Filby, M. (1992), 'The Figures, the Personality and the Bums: Service Work and Sexuality'. *Work, Employment and Society*, Vol. 6(1), pp. 23-42.
Flecker, J. and Hofbauer, J. (1998), 'Capitalising on Subjectivity: The "New Model Worker" and the Importance of Being Useful', in Thompson, P. and Warhurst, C. (eds.), *Workplaces of the Future*, London: Macmillan, pp. 109-123.
Frenkel, S., Korczynski, M., Shire, K. and Tam, M. (1998), 'Beyond Bureaucracy? Work Organisation in Call Centres', *The International Journal of Human Resource Management*, Vol. 9(6), pp. 957-979.
Grugulis, I. (1999), *The Learning Organisation Revisited*, paper presented to the 17th International Labour Process Conference, Royal Holloway, University of London.
Hochschild, A.R. (1983), *The Managed Heart: The Commercialisation of Human Feeling*. Berkely, University of California Press.
IDS (1999), *Pay and Conditions in Call Centres*, London.

James, N. (1989), 'Emotional Labour: Skill and Work in the Social Regulation of Feelings', *The Sociological Review*, Vol. 37(1), pp. 15-42.

Korczynski, M., Frenkel, S., Shire, K and Tam, M. (1999), *Customers in Control? Front Line Work and the Role of the Customer in Management Control*, paper presented at the 17th International Labour Process Conference, Royal Holloway, University of London.

Korczynski, M. (2001), *Human Resource Management and Service Work: The Fragile Social Order*, London, Palgrave.

Leidner, R., (1993), *Fast Food, Fast Talk: Service Work and the Routinization of Everyday Life*. Berkeley, University of California Press.

Macdonald, C.L. and Sirianni, C. (eds.) (1996), *Working in the Service Society*, Philadelphia, Temple University Press.

Market Assessment International (1999), *Call Centres 1999*, Middlesex, Market Assessment International.

Mitial (1999), *Call Centres in Europe*, London.

Poynter, G. (2000), '"Thank You for Calling": The Ideology of Work in the Service Economy', *Soundings*, Vol. 14, Spring, pp. 151-160.

Redman, T. and Mathews, B.P. (1998), 'Service Quality and Human Resource Management: A Review and Research Agenda', *Personnel Review*, Vol. 27(1), pp. 57-77.

Schneider, B. and Bowen, D.E. (1999), 'Understanding Customer Delight and Outrage', *Sloan Management Review*, Vol. 41(1), pp. 35-45.

Taylor, P., Mulvey, G., Hyman, J. and Bain, P. (2000), *Work Organisation, Control and the Experience of Work in Call Centres*, paper to the 15th Annual Employment Research Unit Conference 'Work Futures', Cardiff University, September.

Taylor, S. (1998), 'Emotional Labour and the New Workplace', in Thompson, P. and Warhurst, C. (eds.). *Workplaces of the Future*. London, Macmillan, pp. 84-103.

Thompson, P. and Wallace, T. (1996), 'Redesigning Production Through Teamworking', *International Journal of Operations and Production Management, Special Issue on Lean Production and Work Organisation*, Vol. 16(2), pp. 103-118.

Thompson, P., Warhurst, C. and Callaghan, G. (2001), 'Ignorant Theory and Knowledgeable Workers: Interrogating the Connections Between Knowledge, Skills and Services', *Journal of Management Studies*, Vol. 38(7), pp. 923-942.

Unison (2001), *Unison's Guide to Making Call Centres a Better Place to Work*, London, Unison.

Watson, A., Bunzel, D., Lockyer, C.J. and Scholarios, D. (2000), *Changing Constructions of Career, Commitment and Identity: The Call Centre Experience*, paper to the 15th Annual Employment Research Unit Conference: 'Work Futures', Cardiff University, September.

Wharton, A.S. (1996), 'The Consequences of Emotional Labour', in Macdonald, C.M. and Sirianni, C. (eds.), *Working in the Service Society*, Philadelphia, Temple University Press.

Chapter 7

Capitalising on Femininity: Gender and the Utilisation of Social Skills in Telephone Call Centres

Vicki Belt

Introduction

It is well known that major changes have taken place in the sphere of work and employment in advanced industrial economies over the past two decades. A fundamental feature of this change has been the continued decline of manufacturing employment and the increase in the number of jobs in the service sector, to the extent that the service industries now dominate employment in many countries (Marshall and Wood, 1995; Macdonald and Sirianni, 1996; Poynter, 2000). It has also been widely observed that this broad process of economic restructuring has been accompanied with a cluster of strategies used at the level of the organisation, as employers increasingly attempt to become more 'customer focused' in order to achieve competitive advantage in global markets (see Macdonald and Sirianni, 1996). These strategies include the introduction of new employment practices, organisational structures, information and communications technologies, production systems and management techniques (Poynter, 2000).

These processes of economic and organisational restructuring have not been gender-neutral. Rather, they are closely associated with a movement towards what has been widely referred to as the 'feminisation' of the labour force (Bradley et al., 2000). Women have entered into paid employment in growing numbers in recent years, providing the bulk of the labour power behind the expansion of the service industries in many countries (Steiger and Wardell, 1995; Bradley, 1997, 1999; McDowell, 1997, 1999; Bradley et al., 2000). The reasons for this feminisation are of course highly complex. It has been observed, however, that the trend is closely linked to the rise in importance of what has been termed 'social labour' (Woodfield,

1998). Social labour is central to many jobs in the service industries, and this is particularly so in so-called 'interactive service occupations', or jobs in which employees spend the vast majority of their working time in direct face-to-face or voice-to-voice contact with customers or clients (see Leidner, 1991; Macdonald and Sirianni, 1996). With the growth of these occupations, employers are placing increasing emphasis on the possession of a range of social skills and personality attributes rather than technical or mechanical skills when recruiting workers. These skills and attributes are then further developed through specialised training programmes designed to ensure that workers are able to consciously draw upon them in order to influence the quality of the service being delivered (Thompson et al., 2000). It is in this context that Hochschild (1983) has influentially highlighted the way in which service workers are increasingly required to use their emotions during the service encounter, performing 'emotional labour' in order to contribute to the process of capital accumulation (Taylor, 1998).

Several authors have noted that women predominate in many jobs that involve social labour, especially that which has an emotional labour content (Hochschild, 1993; Noon and Blyton, 1997; Taylor, 1998; Taylor and Tyler, 2000). It has been argued that the over-representation of women in such work has occurred partly as a consequence of the fact that women are perceived to be particularly well-equipped with the kinds of social skills and qualities now required by employers. As Furedi has explained:

'It is sometimes suggested that women are... more in tune with the demands of the service economy... It appears that supposedly feminine traits such as sensitivity, tact, flexibility and caring have become the virtues of the postmodern era.' (Furedi, 1995, pp. 11-12)

In theory, these developments could represent an important shift in the established gender order, challenging existing and long-entrenched patterns of female disadvantage in the world of work. However, the body of academic literature that has been produced over recent years on women's work and employment emphasises *continuities* in terms of gender inequality rather than change. Numerous authors have warned that although women's labour is increasingly in demand in the service economy, this does *not* mean that the position of the majority of women in the world of work has improved. It has been argued that although women have entered into the labour market in growing numbers in recent years, occupational segregation persists, and women are overwhelmingly concentrated in low-grade servic*ing* occupations in advanced industrial economies (Lash and Urry, 1994; McDowell, 1997; Stanworth, 2000; Wigfield, 2001). Further, it has been argued that many of the low-grade service jobs in which women predominate are marked by processes of rationalisation, industrialisation, and deskilling (Steiger and Wardell, 1995). As Marshall and Richardson have explained in relation to developments in the financial services sector, many firms are now in the process of 'reorganising the labour process relating to front-office jobs at the customer interface' (1996, p. 1855). It is well documented that new information and communications technologies (ICTs) are increasingly used in order to Taylorise the service encounter, with employers for example using monitoring and scripting technologies in order to standardise and routinise the work process and ensure compliance to organisational procedures (see Leidner, 1993; Taylor, 1998; Poynter, 2000; Thompson et al., 2000). The indication appears to be that women have entered the labour force in growing numbers in recent years precisely at the same time as these trends have taken place, and the numbers of low-grade, routine service jobs have increased.

These developments raise important questions about the nature and quality of women's employment in the service economy. In particular, exactly *how* are employers drawing upon women's assumed skills in social labour, and to what extent can women actually utilise and develop these skills given the widely reported trends towards the industrialisation of service work? Also, to what degree are the social skills used by women in interactive service work valued, acknowledged and rewarded given the long established historical tendency to view the social skills used by women in the workplace as an innate 'talents' rather than acquired skills (Noon and Blyton, 1997)? Relatively little in-depth empirical research has been carried out to date that focuses on these issues. It is important that this research gap is addressed, because, as Stanworth (2000) has rightly argued, 'detailed sectoral and occupational studies' are required if we are to fully understand the outcomes and implications of recent restructuring processes for women, as well as other social groups. This paper makes a contribution to the debate by focusing on the specific case of women's employment in call centre work.

Perceptions of Skill and Call Centre Work

Call centres are particularly good sites in which to explore the kinds of questions outlined above about women, work and skill in the service economy. Significant employers of female labour,[1] it has been suggested that

---

[1] Several studies have estimated that women make up around 70 per cent of the call centre workforce in a number of different national and local labour market contexts (see for example Richardson and Marshall, 1996; Mitial, 1998; Buchanan and Kochschulte, 1999; Breathnach, 2000).

call centre employers are capitalising upon women's perceived social skills, particularly their ability to 'smile down the phone' to customers (Marshall and Richardson, 1996). However, many commentators have also pointed to the highly routine, standardised and repetitive nature of call centre work.

The dramatic growth in the number of call centres in Europe has provoked considerable discussion within the media, as well as in the business and academic communities over the last few years. Taylor and Bain (1999) have observed that the extent of this discussion in the United Kingdom (where call centre growth has been particularly pronounced) has been such that call centres perhaps received greater attention in the media than any other area of British industry during the late 1990s. Two very different images of call centre work are discernible in this discourse (Frenkel et al., 1998; Bain and Taylor, 2000). Firstly, the earliest representations of call centres were often very positive in tone. Call centre operations were presented as new, high-tech working environments in which favourable working conditions and highly skilled, knowledge-intensive and flexible work were the norm. As Bain and Taylor (2000) have noted, this image was largely created by management consultants and reinforced by call centre employers. In addition, local economic development agencies, many of whom have been keen to attract footloose call centre employers to invest in their regions in order to create much needed new employment opportunities (Richardson et al., 2000), were also key contributors to this positive imagery.

More recently, however, this optimistic scenario has been replaced by a second, distinctly negative picture. It is this negative imagery that has arguably had the most influence upon public consciousness. Much of the criticism that has been made of call centres over the last few years has focused on the highly distinctive technologies and management systems that are used in these new organisational settings. Concerned with the ways in which ICTs are used in call centres to both routinise work processes and heavily monitor employees, media commentators have produced some rather dramatic descriptions of call centre work (see for example, Arkin, 1997; Beckett, 1998; Turner, 1998; Stanford, 1999). Call centres have frequently been compared to assembly lines and referred to as 'customer service factories' because of the repetitive nature of the job and the lack of control that agents have over the pace of the work. Industrial metaphors have also been used by academic authors, most notably by Fernie and Metcalf (1997) who referred to call centres as 'the new sweatshops'. Although Fernie and Metcalf's portrayal of call centre work has been widely criticised, other academic authors have also emphasised the similarities between call centres and factory environments. Taylor and Bain (1999) for example argue that call centres represent significant developments in the intensification and Taylorisation of white-collar work. They assert that the constant flow of work in call centres means that agents experience the labour process as an 'assembly line in the head'. As a consequence of the circulation of these kinds of images, Holman and Fernie have noted that call centres now 'conjure up an image of oppressive, stifling working conditions, constant surveillance, poor job satisfaction' (2001, p. 1).

Influenced by recent criticisms of call centre work, Stanworth (2000) has recently speculated that call centres appear to represent the latest manifestation of a long-established trend in women's employment that has seen women pulled into deskilled occupations. Several feminist theorists have argued that women have historically been recruited by employers to jobs that are in the process of being degraded as a result of technological change (Game and Pringle, 1984; Cockburn, 1985; Bradley, 1986, 1989). However, claims about the deskilled nature of call centre work sit rather uncomfortably beside literature that has argued that call centre employees are regarded as a 'key strategic resource', and are expected to act as the public face or 'ambassadors' for their companies (Frenkel et al., 1999). A number of recent studies of call centre work have shown for example that as well as being measured in quantitative terms on factors such as the length and timing of telephone calls, employers also use a number of 'soft' criteria in order to assess employee performance. These are based on factors such as the agent's telephone manner and politeness to the customer (Bain and Taylor, 1999). In this context, authors have emphasised the ways in which employers actively draw upon and shape the *social skills* and competencies of call centre agents in order to ensure the provision of high quality service (Thompson et al., 2000). In their case study of a call centre in the airline industry, Taylor and Tyler (2000) have recently argued that *women* workers are assumed by managers to be particularly suited to the work as they are thought to 'naturally' possess the appropriate social skills and competencies required to perform emotional labour successfully.

This paper is concerned with these two competing images of call centre work – as routine and deskilled, and as dependent on the social competencies of (mainly female) employees. In particular, it aims to identify the ways in which employers attempt to draw upon women's assumed social skills, and the degree to which these skills can be utilised given the highly routinised nature of the work. It also briefly explores the extent to which the social skills used by call centre employees are valued and recognised.

Research Methodology

In order to examine these issues, this paper draws on evidence gathered through non-participant observation and semi-structured interviews carried out in eleven different call centre organisations.[2] These case study organisations were located in four contrasting industry sectors, namely retail financial services, information technology, mail order, and the 'third-party' or the outsourced call centre sector in the United Kingdom and Ireland - two of the countries at the forefront of call centre development in Europe. The four sectors were deliberately chosen in order to emphasise the diversity of call centre work. I shall now briefly explain in more detail why each sector was selected for study.

Retail financial services: This sector was chosen as a research focus as it is the second largest call centre market in Europe, and the largest in the United Kingdom. In 1997 it was estimated that financial services call centres accounted for 27 per cent of the total UK call centre market, with around 45,000 agent positions in the sector (Datamonitor, 1998). More recent reports suggest that this remains the case, with around one quarter of all UK call centres based in financial services industry (IDS, 2000). In addition, the financial services sector was chosen as a research focus because it has traditionally employed a large number of female workers, but is also known for its patriarchal management culture and marked occupational sex-segregation (Halford et al., 1997).

Information technology: Although employment in call centres in the information technology sector is much less significant in numerical terms than that in the financial services, the growth of call centres in this sector is significant in other ways. The emergence of technical 'help-desks' in areas such as software support has created a number of new jobs in the call centre industry that tend to be considerably better paid than in those found in other sectors. In addition, as it is well known, the IT industry as a whole has traditionally been male-dominated, and in line with this men tend to be better represented in these call centres than they are in other sectors (Webster, 1996).

Mail order: As Jones (1999) has noted, mail order companies began to establish telephone ordering call centres in the 1980s, and by so doing made a significant, yet often overlooked, contribution in pioneering the 'call centre revolution'. It is on this basis that this sector was chosen for study. Furthermore, mail order companies have traditionally employed large numbers of female employees, and serve a largely female customer

---

[2] Six of these organizational case studies were carried out by the author as a part of a research project funded by the European Commission (Belt et al., 1999).

base. The indications are that women continue to make up the vast amount of the workforce in mail order call centres, with a large proportion of these women working on a part-time basis.

Outsourced call centres: These organisations undertake call centre work on behalf of other firms, and are sometimes referred to as 'telemarketing bureaus'. Outsourcing companies will usually carry out teleservice functions in their own call centre offices, using their own employees. Most have a number of different 'campaigns' running simultaneously, with different teams of agents working on each. The main reason for selecting this sector was the fact that very little research has been carried out on outsourced call centres to date. In addition, the nature of the work is somewhat different in these settings than it is in 'in-house' call centres. Agents work for a client that is 'distant' from them, and often carry out a wider variety of work tasks for a number of different companies. Secondly, due to the impermanent nature of the work, many outsourced organisations employ large numbers of temporary staff.

In order to explore the issues with which this paper is concerned, it is necessary not only to examine the attitudes and practices of call centre employers, but also to pay central attention to the perceptions and experiences of female *employees*. In line with this, in each of the case study call centres the call centre manager, the human resources or personnel manager, and at least two female supervisors and three female agents were interviewed. In total, 85 one-to-one interviews were carried out, varying in length from 45 minutes to two hours and 30 minutes. Most of these interviews were conducted with women, but in some cases it was necessary to interview male managers (in those organisations in which the call centre manager or human resources manager was male). In addition, seven group interviews were undertaken with female call centre agents, each lasting for approximately one hour and 30 minutes. The same semi-structured interview schedules were used in all of the organisations.

In the interviews with managers contextual information was collected about each call centre in terms of the nature of the employee profile, organisational structure, work organisation and types of technological systems in place. In addition, information was collected on recruitment and selection processes, skill requirements, training provision and career progression. Specific questions about equal opportunities and women's position in the organisation were raised under each of these headings. The interviews conducted with the female supervisors and call centre agents tended to be less structured than those carried out with the managers and were generally more conversational in style. As a consequence, the interviews explored a broad range of issues. The themes discussed centred on the nature of the work performed and the specific skills involved, as well women's experiences of training and their attitudes towards their jobs, careers and their employers. Interviewees were also asked to reflect in general on the role of women within their organisations. The general approach taken was to focus on these key themes whilst allowing respondents the space to raise their own issues relating to their own work experiences.

In addition to the interviews, informal non-participant observation was also carried out within the organisations. This observation was approached in a flexible manner, and took two key forms. Firstly, informal observation of the work process was undertaken, with time spent 'listening in' to telephone conversations between agents and customers as they took place. This was done by sitting beside the call centre agent and wearing a headset. Secondly, in some of the call centres time was spent observing formal classroom-based training programmes. Finally, the paper also draws upon information gathered from semi-structured interviews with 35 call centre industry 'experts' (including trade union representatives, professional associations, training providers and management consultants) and analysis of specialist call centre literature in the form of industry magazines, IT brochures and training materials.

Call Centres and the Sexual Division of Labour

Before moving on to discuss the research findings on the utilisation of women's perceived social skills, it is first necessary to provide information on the sexual division of labour in each of the case study call centres.

Unfortunately, official and reliable data on the composition of the call centre workforce in European countries does not yet exist. However, as I have already noted, several research reports have indicated that women make up the majority of call centre workers, reportedly accounting for around seventy per cent of call centre employees in local and national labour markets in the UK and Ireland. My research findings, however, indicate that this average figure masks a good deal of variation. Table 7.1 below presents information on the gender composition of the workforce in each of the case study call centres. As the table shows, women were the predominant sex in numerical terms in all but one of the organisations. The proportion of female employees ranged considerably, however, between the sectors in which the case study call centres were located. The mail order sector was the most female-dominated of the four target sectors. Here women made up 89 and 86 per cent of the total workforce in the two call centres studied. The financial services call centres were also heavily female dominated, with women in these organisations constituting at the lowest 70 per cent, and at the highest 80 per cent of employees. In the outsourced call centres women were slightly less dominant, making up between 62 and 68 per cent of employees. Finally, the gender composition of the computer services call centres was more evenly balanced. Indeed, in one of the computer services organisations, women were actually in a *minority*, making up just 46 per cent of employees.

Furthermore, there were also marked gender differences across task and product areas *within* the call centres. Men outnumbered women in the specialised technical support roles in the computer services call centres, and women were concentrated in the customer-service roles. In the mail order and financial services call centres (where as we have seen women were most highly represented), most of the jobs were concerned with inbound

Table 7.1   Employee Profiles in the Case Study Call Centres

	Total Number of Call Centre Employees	Percentage of Females
Financial Services Call Centres		
FINANCE1	1,037	80 %
FINANCE2	429	76 %
FINANCE3	1,060	70 %
FINANCE4	434	79 %
Mail Order Call Centres		
MAIL1	1,781	89 %
MAIL2	810	86 %
Outsourced Call Centres		
OUTSOURCED1	250	65 %
OUTSOURCED2	630	62 %
OUTSOURCED3	105	68 %
Computer Services Call Centres		
TECHNO1	400	59 %
TECHNO2	1,200	46 %

Source: Data provided by case study companies.

customer service-related functions, with a small amount of telesales activity. In the outsourced call centres a much higher proportion of the work involved selling, although there were also differences here between functions in terms of gender, with women more likely to be found dealing with inbound calls. There were also marked differences between women and men in terms of the kinds of products dealt with in the outsourced call centres. In OUTSOURCED3 for example, all of the employees working on a campaign for a car company were male, whilst there was an all-female team dealing with incoming calls on a contraceptive product.

It is important to acknowledge, therefore, when discussing the gender composition of the call centre workforce that although women make up the majority of employees in general, they do not dominate employment in all sectors and across all task areas. However, in spite of these variations, women's labour power has clearly been central to the growth of the call centre industry.

Feminist theorists have long argued that employers do *not* view women and men workers as undifferentiated and substitutable groups (Liff, 1986). Rather, as Bradley has argued, 'Female labour is both *viewed* differently and *used* differently by employers and managers' (Bradley, 1986, p. 71, my emphasis). The remainder of this paper goes on to explore the specific ways in which women's perceived social skills and competencies are currently being viewed and used in the context of the call centre industry.

Recruiting Social Skills

Recruitment is viewed as a critical issue by call centre employers, and has been the subject of numerous articles in industry journals (including titles such as *Call Centre Europe* for example), as well as many conferences and seminars over the last few years. This is in part related to the fact that call centres are labour-intensive work environments in which staff costs make up a large proportion of total running costs (Bristow et al., 2000), and the high levels of labour turnover found in the industry as a whole. Indeed, recruitment of appropriate employees was an issue that was regarded as highly important by the managers interviewed in this study, and all of the call centres had spent a substantial amount of time and money on developing highly specialised recruitment and selection procedures. Typically, these recruitment processes consisted of a number of key stages for candidates. These were the completion of an application form, a telephone interview, and attendance at an assessment centre and/or a face-to-face interview (usually involving some form of role-playing exercise). In addition, some of the organisations used personality testing as a method of selecting suitable candidates. In some cases the recruitment procedures used were even more stringent. For example, one of the case study call centres required potential recruits to attend a training session for one week during which their suitability for employment was assessed, and at the end of which candidates received a job offer or rejection. In addition, in some of the organisations, the induction training course was used as a kind of 'trial period' at the end of which those candidates perceived to be unsuitable could be dismissed.

In all of the call centres, these recruitment and selection procedures were specifically designed in order to correctly identify people with appropriate social competencies and associated personality characteristics and attitudes. Importantly, these requirements were on the whole remarkably consistent between the case study organisations. With the exception of the technical support roles in the call centres information technology sector, these social competencies and personality traits were valued far more highly than the possession of formal qualifications, or any other relevant factors such as computing skills and technical or industry knowledge and experience. In relation to the issue of employers' requirements at recruitment, then, the following comment was typical:

'We're not looking for a good educational background necessarily, that's secondary, it doesn't really matter. We're looking for individuals that have the right people skills, are prepared to take responsibility and have the right personalities.' (Female Manager, Outsourced Call Centre, OUTSOURCED3)

When they were asked to specify the kinds social skills and competencies that they sought when recruiting employees, the managers in all of the case study organisations stressed that the possession of what was widely referred to as 'customer focus' was crucial. This term is used to refer to an employee's general attitude towards customers, as well as their ability to empathise with them. Managers frequently stated that it was vital that individuals with a 'caring attitude' towards customers were recruited. In addition, a key priority in terms of recruitment was to identify workers with high levels of self-confidence and what were repeatedly referred to as 'bubbly' or lively personalities, with the ability to build relationships or 'rapport' with customers.

In addition, the importance of recruiting sociable people with good teamworking and teambuilding skills was also emphasised. Call centre employees in all of the case study call centres were grouped into 'teams'. These teams usually consisted of around 12-15 members, with each team overseen by a team leader, whose key role is to motivate, supervise and train staff. It has been noted elsewhere that teamworking in the call centre environment does not involve employees working collectively on a range of tasks and sharing decision-making with other group members (see Belt et al., 1999). However, a strong emphasis does tend to be placed on building a sense of collectivity and 'team spirit' amongst employees in call centres. In the case study call centres employers actively encouraged interaction between employees in a variety of ways, including paying for regular team-based nights out, having regular team meetings and encouraging a sense of 'friendly competition' between teams within the workplace. As one manager for example stated:

> 'We create social events which keeps communication growing. Each team is a little community, and we can support that. People spend a lot of time together, they are bound to become close, and we support that through social functions and teambuilding and that kind of stuff.' (Female Manager, Outsourced Call Centre, OUTSOURCED2)

The primary responsibility for developing and maintaining the sense of team spirit in the call centre environment falls primarily upon the shoulders of the team leader. It was widely agreed that it was a vital requirement that team leaders possess strong 'people skills', particularly the ability to understand, communicate with, motivate, coach and provide support to others, in order to perform in their jobs effectively.

Managers asserted, therefore, that the possession of social skills and competencies, particularly, customer focus and teamworking related skills were highly important when selecting potential employees. Interestingly, however, these social skills were regarded as less important for the jobs in technical support functions in the information technology call centres, where, as I have already outlined, men made up the bulk of the workforce. In these roles, technical knowledge, qualifications and previous experience, as well as an interest in computers were deemed more significant. In fact, it was admitted by some managers that the people filling these roles were *unlikely* to possess good social skills because they were generally 'techies', and it was assumed that technically-minded people did not typically possess good interpersonal skills. Outside of the technical support roles, however, there was an assumption amongst managers that women were more likely than men to hold the types of social skills required in the call centre environment. This perception was also shared by most of the agents and team leaders interviewed. In particular, women were generally seen as better able to handle the interactive aspects of the job, and particularly skilled at empathising and building rapport with customers. The following comments were typical in this respect:

'Girls are just more bright and bubbly on the phone, and it definitely works in this job the brighter and bubblier you are.' (Female Team Leader, Outsourced Call Centre, OUTSOURCED3)

'Women on the phone are much more conversational, there's generally more of a rapport. Generally men are much more to the point, they just want to get the job done.' (Female Supervisor, Outsourced Call Centre, OUTSOURCED3)

Indeed, a number of interviewees indicated that they viewed women as somehow 'naturally' possessing these types of skills:

'I think that most of the call centre industry started in terms of customer service, and traditionally women are better at listening, they're better at empathising, they're better - I mean our *brains* function in such a way that we can take a much more holistic overview of a situation.' (Female Human Resources Manager, Outsourced Call Centre, OUTSOURCED1)

In addition, there was also a general perception that women were more likely than men to possess highly sought-after teamworking and team-building skills. Male employees were frequently said to be 'too competitive and individualistic' to work successfully as an integral part of a team, or as a team leader. By contrast, women were assumed to be especially suited to team leader roles, as the following two interviewees explained:

'I do think there's advantages in being in this business if you're female, because in general females are better at communicating, and its all about communicating, making people feel part of the team and making them feel like they belong.' (Female Team Leader, Financial Services Call Centre, FINANCE4)

'Women have got more understanding, more empathy and they can understand people, and they are the kind of skills that you need in a call centre with the coaching and all that. Maybe that's just a traditional thing, but with managing the staff, the women seem to just get on with it.' (Male Manager, Financial Services Call Centre, FINANCE4)

Indeed, there was evidence that women, especially more mature women returning to the workforce after bringing up families, were being specifically targeted by call centre employers for their perceived team leadership skills, a practice which has also been observed in other areas of service work (Kerfoot and Knights, 1994). Managers explicitly stated their preference for older women employees for team leader roles on a number of occasions. Again, many interviewees stated that they believed these kinds of social skills came 'naturally' to women, and were closely associated with their traditional caring role within the family:

'It's a natural instinct for women, looking after people. Men are more aggressive, more likely to take people to task first rather than encourage them.' (Female Team Leader, Information Technology Call Centre, TECHNO2)

Work Routinisation and the Utilisation of Social Skills

I have argued so far that call centre employers place considerable emphasis on the importance of the possession of a range of social skills and personality characteristics when recruiting employees. I have also asserted that there is an assumption amongst managers (and most workers) that women are especially likely to possess these social skills. However, as I have already noted, it is also the case that one of the key characteristics of call centre work organisation, which is acknowledged by call centre employers as well as by commentators and consultants in the industry, is the predominance of uniform and repetitive work tasks. This raises questions about the extent to which women are actually able to utilise their assumed social skills in their everyday work.

All of the case study call centres were marked by the highly routinised forms of work organisation that have been highlighted by other authors. Agents spent all of their working hours on the telephone, and most dealt with a narrow range of tasks and products. It is notable, however, that the work was least routine, and monitoring and control practices least stringently used in the male-dominated technical support roles in the information technology call centres. When asked about their experiences of working in the call centre environment, many agents claimed that they found their work repetitive and frequently stressful. This was particularly pronounced amongst those working in the mail order and financial services call centres, where the work was the most standardised, and women were most highly represented in the workforce. However, agents in all of the organisations studied talked of the lack of stimulation involved in their jobs, and the often 'robotic' nature of the work. Many identified similarities between the call centre environment and the factory assembly-line. Agents were particularly frustrated because they felt that the standardised and repetitive nature of the work meant that they could not fully use the range of social skills and competencies that they felt that they possessed. Giving good quality customer service emerged as the key source of job satisfaction for agents, and a desire to provide this was a main reason why many had applied for their jobs in the first place. However, agents felt that the emphasis placed upon efficiency and the speed and timing of the calls made it extremely difficult to provide good customer service, which it was widely agreed, was time-consuming. Some of the agents interviewed actually doubted whether their employers were in fact interested in delivering high quality customer service at all, as the following quotations indicate:

> 'It's a case of getting through as many calls as you possibly can, sometimes you haven't always got the time to spend enough on each call... you have to check how many calls you've had and how long you've been in what we call 'not ready', and how long you've actually been logged into the system. That means that sometimes you just can't give the best quality that you possibly could.' (Female Agent, Financial Services Call Centre, FINANCE2)

> 'The company doesn't give a toss about the quality – it's the quantity they want.' (Female Agent, Financial Services Call Centre, FINANCE3)

The managers interviewed were aware of the presence of these sentiments amongst agents. At the same time, however, they also acknowledged that recruitment and selection processes were not only designed in order to identify people with customer focus and teambuilding skills, but *also* to select people with the ability to deal with repetitive and time-pressurised work. Managers admitted that workers were actively sought for their ability to maintain a 'positive attitude' with customers regardless of the pressures placed upon them by the routine nature of the work and the near constant flow of calls, as two managers explained:

> 'What they are doing on the phone, it's not rocket science, and at the end of the day it can become repetitive over time, so we have to make sure that they've got the right personalities to cope with that.' (Male Manager, Financial Services Call Centre, FINANCE4)

> 'In the interviews we're looking for somebody that would have 'get up and go', we tend to be very fast-moving so we are looking for the people with the pace to deal with a bit of pressure, because we recognise that it is a case of, you know, you complete a call and two seconds later there's another call, so we're looking for someone who can deal with that.' (Male Manager, Financial Services Call Centre, FINANCE3)

There was an assumption amongst interviewees that women were especially likely to have the kind personality that is suited to the repetitive, yet highly pressurised work that characterises call centres. It was claimed, for example, that women were generally more able than men to handle routine work, and 'stick at the job' for longer than men:

> 'I find that the girls do the work better, they stay on-line and like what they are meant to do... where as I think the men are constantly coming off-line to try

and do other things.' (Female Team Leader, Information Technology Call Centre, TECHNO1)

A number of respondents felt that in general men did not tend to cope as well as women did with the pressures involved in the work:

'The people I've employed before, hundreds and hundreds of people that I've literally recruited and trained myself, a very, very small percentage - probably less than ten per cent - have been males. And that's not because I haven't given them the opportunities, because I have. In actual fact, in a short space of time it's the males that tend to come to me saying that they just can't hack it at the end of the day.' (Female Human Resources Manager, Outsourced Call Centre, OUTSOURCED1)

These findings indicate that call centre employers hold gendered assumptions about the abilities of women and men to perform highly controlled, repetitive and routine job tasks, tending to conform to a long-held view that women are more suited than men to routine work (Cockburn, 1985). The persistence of this perception raises questions about the ways in which female call centre agents are actually able to utilise the social skills and competencies that managers claim are central in call centre work. In fact, when they were questioned about the social skills they used in their jobs, the women workers interviewed tended to emphasise the importance of skills in resilience and self-control rather than those in customer focus and teamworking and teambuilding. These kinds of skills were deemed necessary by agents and team leaders in order to ensure that customers are handled professionally whilst under strict time pressures. The following kinds of comments for example were frequently made about the work carried out by the agents:

'You need a thick skin, without a doubt... You also need to be definitely bright and bubbly and very hard to knock down. You really need to be *very* determined.' (Female Team Leader, Outsourced Call Centre, OUTSOURCED3)

'The hardest thing is like going from a really horrible customer and then like "beep" and you've got somebody really nice on, so you'll have somebody that's really horrible on one minute and then the next minute you've got to start again with someone who's completely normal. You feel like you are a kind of punch-bag, you know, you get hit but you pop back up and carry on.' (Female Agent, Financial Services Call Centre, FINANCE1)

Team leaders also emphasised the importance of being resilient in the face of pressure in their work:

'I'm constantly looking to make sure that everything is where it should be and everyone is where they should be. My telephone rings incessantly, and you are just batting phonecalls about all over the place... it can be horrendous' (Female Team Leader, Mail Order Call Centre, MAIL2)

The evidence indicates that in spite of claims about the importance of 'customer focus' and teambuilding, the realities of the labour process mean that call centre employers centrally rely upon women's abilities to develop 'coping skills' in the context of a monotonous yet highly demanding work environment. Here, the ways in which women actively develop supportive work cultures is particularly important. In one of the mail order call centres for example, a number of women had been recruited who had previously come from a factory background, and their abilities in what one manager referred to as 'bringing some banter into the work' were highly praised. Further, women's actions in providing emotional support to their colleagues at difficult times were also frequently referred to, as one supervisor explained:

'You'll see women running around in tears quite regularly and the team leader will have to put their arm around them and sort them out.' (Male Manager, Financial Services Call Centre, FINANCE1)

In addition, there was also evidence that call centre employers rely on women's capacity to actively utilise stereotypical notions of femininity in order to deal with difficult customers and direct and control conversations. Some of the women interviewed were clearly aware of the fact that they deliberately enacted conventional gender stereotypes whilst at work, consciously using their 'femininity' in order to 'calm down' angry customers, or even 'persuade' male customers into buying products. One team leader for example stated that she felt that some of the women had purposely developed 'a flirty way of selling', and another agent explained:

'I know that particularly if I'm calling to America and I get a man, then I will use my feminine Irish accent. We do think for ourselves and think what would these people like, and then use our different skills... You know if you get a man, you will actually bring your voice down and hypnotise them into taking what you want them to take. There is a key difference between the sexes in that way, and the women would act differently to some callers.' (Female Agent, Outsourced Call Centre, OUTSOURCED3)

Indeed, when this issue was pursued, many of the managers also acknowledged that women deliberately performed stereotypical feminine roles in this way, and this type of behaviour was widely encouraged and developed through training programmes. As one manager stated:

> 'I think that women use their feminine skills to their advantage when they are selling. I don't think they have to overcome the natural reservations people have to men, and that's a real advantage I think on the telephone.' (Male Manager, Financial Services Call Centre, FINANCE1)

Skill Recognition in Call Centres

So far I have argued that call centre employers capitalise upon femininity by relying upon women's abilities to develop ways of coping with routinised work processes and highly pressurised customer interaction. As Woodfield (1998) and others have argued, female social skill contributions in the workplace have been ignored and undervalued in the past, and this is in part related to the fact that they have been viewed as 'natural' feminine talents, rather than acquired skills. As such they tend to be viewed as neither recognisable nor remunerable. Whilst on the one hand perceptions about women's 'natural' social competencies persist in the context of call centre work, at the same time, it is also the case that workers and managers alike on the whole tended to describe the work as 'skilled'. Many of the women interviewed were keen to stress that they had spent a long time developing and refining the skills used in their everyday work, and stressed the difficulties involved in doing their jobs well. Importantly, there was a sense of confidence amongst most of the agents interviewed about the social skills that they had developed, particularly in techniques of conversational control, which was in part generated through training programmes provided by employers. As the following quotations indicate, there was evidence that the process of training had raised consciousness amongst female employees about the social skills that they possessed:

> 'They are given training which has a bias towards communication, they're given the various techniques and are taught to be more perceptive and aware of other people's communication with them... it just builds a confident team of people, people that are not inhibited.' (Female Human Resources Director, Outsourced Call Centre, OUTSOURCED1)

> 'You may be a housewife and have brought up a family for 10 or 15 years - but they don't realise the skills they have. We try to get people to understand that and build on that.' (Female Team Leader, Mail Order Call Centre, MAIL1)

However, in spite of this there was also a widely held view that the expertise involved in the work is somewhat 'invisible' to those *outside* the call centre setting, both within wider society, and elsewhere within parent organisations. Managers spoke of the separation between the call centre and the rest of the organisation (a division which was sometimes exacerbated by geographical distance). In FINANCE3 for example, agents were particularly negative about this. One agent stated that she felt that the managers elsewhere in the organisation looked upon call centre employees as 'the lowly ranks'. Another agent similarly claimed that she felt that the skills involved in her job were overlooked by senior management:

> 'It would be nice if the company recognised that what we do is a tough job... it would be nice to sit down with the management and feel free to say my job's hard and nobody recognises it's hard.' (Female Agent, Financial Services Call Centre, FINANCE3)

The relatively low status of call centres is also reflected in wage levels in the industry. Information on the levels of pay and rewards received by call centre employees in the two countries studied is somewhat limited, although reasonably detailed information is available for the UK. Here, in spite of the demands of call centre employers in terms of skill requirements, and the rigorous selection processes used, average salaries for call centre employees fall well below national averages (TUC, 2001), with the average starting salary for customer service advisors in 2000 at £11,150 (IDS, 2000). It should be stressed, however, that pay levels varied considerably between sectors. In the case study call centres, salaries were significantly higher in the information technology call centres (for the sales and technical support roles), where men were predominant. The differences in this respect were not inconsiderable, with pay levels for technical support staff around a third higher than for those in the female-dominated customer service roles. The evidence indicates therefore that although women's perceived social skills are central in call centre work, they continue to be poorly rewarded in financial terms.

Conclusion

This paper has examined some of the ways in which women workers are viewed and used by call centre employers. I have argued that managers and most workers tend to assume that women are especially likely to possess the particular kinds of social skills (particularly in 'customer focus' and 'teamworking'), that are viewed as centrally important in most areas of call centre work. However, the highly routine and controlled nature of work organisation in call centres acts to severely constrain the ways in which women are able to utilise and further develop these social skills.

One of the most striking characteristics of call centre work is that managerial approaches that emphasise the importance of the provision of high quality customer service are used side-by-side with Tayloristic working practices. The existence of this situation means that employers place rather contradictory demands on employees, expecting individuals to provide 'good service' to customers, whilst at the same time handling repetitive, controlled, and frequently pressurised work. In fact, this paper has argued that call centre employers consider *women* as particularly good employees in part precisely because they assume that they are more capable than men of handling these demands. This situation means that women can only use their social skills in restricted ways, with workers emphasising the importance of abilities in resilience, self-control as well as 'coping skills'.

Call centre employers centrally rely upon women using these social competencies, and as such they could be said to be capitalising on 'the skills women have by virtue of having lived their lives as women' (Davies and Rosser 1986: 109). However, in spite of this, it remains the case that as in other female-dominated areas of work, the skills used by women in call centres are not rewarded well in financial terms. Related to this, the expertise women do develop and utilise in their work is largely 'invisible' to those outside the call centre environment, and the job widely considered to be low in esteem and status.

However, it should also be acknowledged that my research points to some positive developments in terms of women and skill development in call centres. In particular, there is evidence that many women working in call centres are developing a conscious knowledge of the value of their social skills. Indeed, it appears that employers are actively encouraging their employees to recognise their 'feminine' social competencies as important skills by providing training programmes specifically designed in order to raise personal awareness and self-confidence. An interesting issue for future research would focus on whether women call centre employees are be able to use this sense of self-confidence positively in order to improve their working lives and position within both the call centre industry and in the labour market more generally.

References

Austin Knight and Calcom (1997), *Call Centre Practice Not Theory: The First National Survey of Call Centre Management and Staff Attitudes*, Austin Knight UK Ltd., London.
Arkin, A. (1997), 'Hold the Phone', *People Management*, 6th February, pp. 22-27.
Bain, P. and Taylor, P. (1999), *Employee Relations, Worker Attitudes and Trade Union Representation in Call Centres*, 17th Annual Labour Process Conference, Royal Holloway College, University of London, 29-31st March.
Bain, P. and Taylor, P. (2000), 'Entrapped by the "Electronic Panopticon"? Worker Resistance in the Call Centre', *New Technology, Work and Employment*, Vol. 15(1), pp. 2-18.
Beckett, A. (1998), 'Hello Jim Speaking. How May I Help You?', *The Guardian*, 9th November, pp. 2-3.
Belt, V., Richardson, R., Webster, J., Tijdens, K. and van Klaveren, M. (1999), *Work Opportunities for Women in the Information Society: Call Centre Teleworking*, final report for the Information Society Project Office (DGIII and DGXIII), European Commission, Brussels.
Bradley, H. (1986), 'Technological Change, Management Strategies, and the Development of Gender-based Job Segregation in the Labour Process', in Knights, D. and Willmott, H. (eds.), *Gender and the Labour Process*, Aldershot ,Gower Publishing, pp. 54-73.
Bradley, H. (1989), *Men's Work, Women's Work*, Cambridge, Polity Press.
Bradley, H. (1997), 'Gender and Change in Employment: Feminisation and its Effects', in Brown, R. (ed.), *The Changing Shape of Work*, Basingstoke, Macmillan Press, pp. 87-102.
Bradley, H., Erickson, M., Stephenson, C. and Williams, S. (2000), *Myths at Work*, Cambridge, Polity Press.
Breathnach, P. (2000), 'Globalisation, Information Technology and the Emergence of Niche Transnational Cities: The Growth of the Call Centre Sector in Dublin', *Geoforum*, Vol. 31, pp. 477-485.
Bristow, G., Munday, M. and Gripaios, P. (2000), 'Call Centre Growth and Location: Corporate Strategy and the Spatial Division of Labour', *Environment and Planning*, Vol. 32(3), pp. 519-538.
Buchanan, R. and Koch-Schulte, S. (1999), *Gender on the Line: Technology, Restructuring and the Reorganisation of Work in the Call Centre Industry*, Ottawa, Status of Women Canada.
Cockburn, C. (1985), *Machinery of Dominance: Women, Men and Technological Know-how*, London, Pluto Press.
Datamonitor (1998), *Call Centres in Europe: Sizing by all Call Centres and Agent Positions in 13 Countries*, London, Datamonitor.
Davies, C. and Rosser, J. (1986), 'Gendered, Jobs in the Health Service: A Problem for Labour Process Analysis', in Knights, D. and Willmott, H. (eds.), *Gender and the Labour Process*, Aldershot, Gower Publishing, pp. 94-116.
Fernie, S. and Metcalf, D. (1997), *(Not) Hanging on the Telephone: Payment Systems in the New Sweatshops*, Working Paper 891, London School of Economics.
Frenkel, S., Tam, M., Korczynski, M. and Shire, K. (1998), 'Beyond Bureaucracy? Work Organisation in Call Centres', *International Journal of Human Resource Management*, Vol. 9(6), pp. 957-979.
Frenkel, S., Tam, M., Korczynski, M. and Shire, K. (1999), *On the Front-Line: Organization of Work in the Information Economy*, Ithaka, Cornell University Press.
Furedi, F. (1995), 'Is it a Girl's World?', *Living Marxism*, May, pp. 10-13.
Game, A. and Pringle, R. (1984), *Gender at Work*, London, Pluto Press.

Halford, S., Savage, M. and Witz, A. (1997), *Gender, Careers and Organisations: Current Developments in Banking, Nursing and Local Government*, Basingstoke, Macmillan Press.

Hochschild, A. (1983), *The Managed Heart: Commercialisation of Human Feeling*, Berkeley, University of California Press.

Holman, D. and Fernie, S. (2000), 'Can I Help You? Call Centres and Job Satisfaction', *Centrepiece Magazine*, Spring, London School of Economics, http://www.centrepiecemagazine.com/spring00/call_centres.htm.

Incomes Data Services (1997), *Pay and Conditions in Call Centres 1997*, London, Incomes Data Services.

Incomes Data Services (2000), *Pay and Conditions in Call Centres 2000*, London, Incomes Data Services.

Jones, B. (1999), *From Mail Order to Telephone Order: The Call Centre Revolution*, unpublished paper, Department of Industrial Technology, University of Bradford.

Kerfoot, D. and Knights, D. (1994), 'The Gendered Terrains of Paternalism', in Wright, S. (ed.), *Anthropology of Organisations*, London, Routledge, pp. 124-139.

Lash, S. and Urry, J. (1994), *Economies of Signs and Space*, London, Sage.

Leidner, R. (1991), 'Selling Hamburgers, Selling Insurance: Gender, Work and Identity', *Gender and Society*, Vol. 5, pp. 154-77.

Leidner, R. (1993), *Fast Food, Fast Talk: Service Work and the Routinisation of Everyday Life*, Berkeley, University of California Press.

Liff, S. (1986), 'Technical Change and Occupational Sex-typing', in Knights, D. and Willmott, H. (eds.), *Gender and the Labour Process*, Aldershot, Gower Publishing, pp. 74-93.

Macdonald, C.L. and Sirianni, C. (1996), 'The Service Society and the Changing Experience of Work', in Macdonald, C.L. and Sirianni, C. (eds.), *Working in the Service Society*, Philadelphia, Temple University Press, pp. 1-26.

Marshall, J.N. and Wood, P. (1995), *Services and Space*, London, Longman.

Marshall J.N. and Richardson, R. (1996), 'The Impact of "Telemediated" Services on Corporate Structures: The Example of "Branchless" Retail Banking in Britain', *Environment and Planning A*, Vol. 28, pp. 1843-1858.

McDowell, L. (1997), *Capital Culture: Gender at Work in the City*, Oxford, Blackwell.

Mitial (1998), *European Location Study: Call Centres in the UK, Republic of Ireland, Belgium and the Netherlands*, Wrexham, Mitial.

Noon, M. and Blyton, P. (1997), *The Realities of Work*, Basingstoke, MacMillan.

Organisation for Economic Co-operation and Development (1998), *The Future of Female-Dominated Occupations*, OECD Publications, Paris.

Poynter, G. (2000), *Restructuring in the Service Industries: Management Reform and Workplace Relations in the UK Service Sector*, London, Mansell.

Richardson, R., Belt, V. and Marshall, J.N. (2000), 'Taking Calls to Newcastle: The Regional Implications of the Growth in Call Centres', *Regional Studies*, Vol. 34(4), pp. 357-369.

Stanford, P. (1999), 'The Numbers Game', *Independent Magazine*, 2nd January, pp. 14-16.

Stanworth, C. (2000), 'Women and Work in the Information Age', *Gender, Work and Organisation*, Vol. 7(1), pp. 20-32.

Steiger, T.L. and Wardell, M. (1995), 'Gender and Employment in the Service Sector', *Social Problems*, Vol. 42(1), pp. 92-123.

Taylor, S. (1998), 'Emotional Labour and the New Workplace', in Thompson, P. and Warhurst, C. (eds.), *Workplaces of the Future*, London, Macmillan, pp. 84-103.

Taylor, P. and Bain, P. (1999), '"An Assembly Line in the Head": Work and Employee Relations in the Call Centre', *Industrial Relations Journal*, Vol. 30(2), pp. 101-117.

Taylor, S. and Tyler, M. (2000), 'Emotional Labour and Sexual Difference in the Airline Industry', *Work, Employment and Society*, Vol. 14(1), pp. 77-95.

Thompson, P., Warhurst, C. and Callaghan, G. (2000), 'Human Capital or Capitalising on Humanity? Knowledge, Skills and Competencies in Interactive Service Work', in Prichard, C. et al. (eds.), *Managing Knowledge: Critical Investigations of Work and Learning*, Basingstoke, Macmillan, pp. 122-139.

Trades Union Congress (2001), *It's Your Call: TUC Call Centres Campaign Report*, February 2001, London, TUC.

Turner, A (1998), 'Sound and Fury of the Call Centre Boom', *The Times*, 3rd June.

Webster, J. (1996), *Shaping Women's Work: Gender, Employment and Information Technology*, London, Longman.

Wigfield, A. (2001), *Post-Fordism, Gender and Work*, Aldershot, Ashgate.

Woodfield, R. (1998), *Working Women and Social Labour*, RUSEL Working Paper No. 33, Department of Politics, University of Exeter.

Chapter 8

Call Centres and the Contradictions of the Flexible Bureaucracy

Carsten Dose[1]

The speed and pervasiveness with which Call Centres have spread in the service and other sectors and beyond in many countries has been most impressive. That this was possible, hints at more basic changes in the service sector. If we tentatively interpret call centres as an indicator for the direction of such changes, contradictory findings concerning service quality and the kind of workplaces offered need to be accounted for. There are opposing accounts about whether service quality in general has become better or worse through the introduction of call centres. Some see higher levels of customer orientation being achieved, such arguments echoing standard critiques of the bureaucratic organisation and its supposed marginalisation of the customer. Other accounts point to a loss of customer orientation, based on a personal relationship between service workers and their customers (Gutek, 1995). Also, call centre workplaces are being shaped by seemingly contradictory trends: standardisation, regimentation and close surveillance on the one hand and enlarged discretion, increasingly complex tasks, challenging and rewarding assignments on the other. New bad jobs emerge in some sectors of call centre work, while in others, investments of ideas and money are made to provide good forms of work (Rieder, Matuschek and Anderson, in this volume). These latter findings seem to disqualify accounts of neo-taylorist developments or an ensuing downward spiral of regimented work organisation and bad service quality. But even the positive accounts do not lend support for an optimistic scenario of mutual gains, with good working conditions accompanying better customer orientation and service quality (Horstmann and Oberbeck, 1996).

In the German context, these contradictory observations lead to yet another question: Can we expect a continuation of the German model of white collar work, implying qualified employees, reasonably good and stable working conditions and reliable service quality (Lane, 1992; Muller, 1997)? Or do call centres signal a break from this model and in this case possibly

---

[1] The author would like to thank Karen Shire for helpful comments on this manuscript.

tell us something about general features of a new rationalisation model, that would be of importance beyond call centre work?

In this paper, I will first outline some specialities of white collar work in Germany. I will then argue, that remarkably stable arrangements concerning service work are drawing to an end. A case study of a large-scale rationalisation process concerning the back-office functions of a large private bank will then be presented. In the changing organisation of work at the bank studied, the establishment of a call centre played an important role. In an effort to better understand the logic behind developments in the case study, the concept of the flexible bureaucracy is introduced and it is contended, that the concept contributes to the understanding of the rationalisation of administrative work now underway. More specifically, it is argued that work processes in the flexible bureaucracy are shaped by contradictory management strategies: standardisation and formalisation in order to strengthen management's capacities for strategic decision making, but also the strengthening of opportunities for reflexive decision making. The consequences of such rationalisation processes for customers and workers alike are, as will be shown, inherently mixed. It is the general aim of this paper, to discuss call centres in the context of previous rationalisation strategies as well as in the context of complementary work processes. This approach promises to produce important insights into the rationalisation of work in the service sector.

Service Sector Rationalisation in Germany

From the early 1980s onwards, several empirical studies independently pointed to the fact, that companies broke away from Taylorist rationalisation strategies for administrative work processes (Littek, Heisig and Gondek, 1992). Accounts of future developments, inspired by Braverman's pessimistic account of developments to come (Kadritzke, 1982) were clearly falsified by these developments. Companies, it seemed, were frustrated with the shortcomings of highly fragmented work processes, unskilled labour and the associated deficiencies in flexibility and efficiency. Littek and Heisig (1995) reported, that 'nearly all experts and employees whom (they) interviewed in those days remembered, reflected, or agonised over the adverse effects of the Taylorist experiments which they experienced. Most managers reported their insight that strategies of fragmentation and de-skilling of qualified white-collar work had produced disadvantages for the level of performance' (ibid., p. 381).

These authors interpreted these findings as a return to a specific and long-standing German model of service sector rationalisation. What they saw as the 'Taylorist experiment' had been mainly caused by a severe shortage of qualified workers since the late 1960s, forcing companies into strategies of task fragmentation and de-skilling (Littek and Heisig, 1995). Others, and most importantly Baethge and Oberbeck (1986) interpreted developments as the rise of a new rationalisation model on its own right. Recently German scholars are unanimous, that recent changes are different to former Taylorist rationalisation strategies. I discuss these characteristics through the example of the German banking sector.

The German arrangements were summarised by Baethge and Oberbeck (1986) with the concept of integrative work organisation. This concept suggested, that task-fragmentation had come under pressure and that tasks which had been fragmented were becoming increasingly integrated, both horizontally and vertically, with more complex forms of work on the rise. The rationale behind this development in the eyes of the authors was that the efficiency gains of task fragmentation had been exhausted and that only more complex, 'systemic' approaches toward work organisation could ensure both efficiency and flexibility in relation to customer and general market demands. The authors limited this optimistic outlook to those tasks that were close to the customer, while assuming continued task-fragmentation and possibly de-skilling for those in the back-offices. The ideal type work place in the integrative work organisation was characterised by vocational training, clear responsibility towards a specified group of customers in the hands of one employee and enlarged discretion.

There is strong evidence, that work processes, according to this concept provided flexibility concerning customers' wishes and could even be very efficient. But today this concept of integrative work organisation has come under pressure. First, the concept does not allow for a strengthening of centralised steering capacities of organisations and secondly, it does not enable the sort of reflexive decision making at the level of the work process, which may help companies to adequately react towards changing market demands.

Empirical Findings

Below, I shall present empirical evidence from a case-study, dealing with the restructuring of the back-office departments belonging to the retail banking division of one of the top five German private commercial banks. The reorganisation described here involved about 1,500 workers. The key change was to set up six regional units to succeed the former structure of 21 dispersed departments. All evidence is based on interviews conducted in 1999 and early 2000. A total of 26 interviews were conducted with ordinary white-collar-workers (*Sachbearbeiter*), call centre-agents, team supervisors, management and specialist staff and work council members. Interviews were held in two of the six newly reorganised units.

The back-office was concerned with administrative tasks related to financial services for retail customers. Take as an example a customer, who had just signed an application for a new credit card in the branch. This form was transferred to the back-office where the application was checked, data entered into the system, new internal accounts set up and the necessary data forwarded to the credit card company. Other back-office tasks dealt with savings and loans, current accounts, shares and funds, credit-cards, but also with answering requests from public administrations like the tax office.

To understand the rationalisation process in question, a look back at different steps of the reorganisation of the back-office over the past decade may be helpful. Starting in the late 1980s and in an effort to focus branches completely on selling financial products, back-office administrative functions had been taken out of the branches and concentrated in specialised regional back-office-departments. By 1991, this gradual process had resulted in what one could call an ideal type example of integrative work organisation for the back-office, based in 21 regional departments: nearly all tasks necessary to support the branches were integrated into single workplaces. The so-called 'all-round-branch-supporter' was responsible for all the assistance needed from the back-office by his or her one or two branches. In the back-office, workers were thus dealing with internal customers. Why it is justified to talk about branch workers as customers of back-office workers (and not as their colleagues) will become clearer below.

The wide range of responsibilities was a challenge for the back-office workers. They had to have a comprehensive understanding of products offered and their processing in the bank and its partner organisations (e.g. credit card companies). Not surprisingly for Germany, most workers had vocational training, with a majority of them having apprenticed in a bank. Workers were combined in teams, which provided on-the-job training for new colleagues, support in case of difficult assignments and in case of vacation or sick-leave. Supervisors exercised control through their personal presence within the team, counter-checking important tasks or liasing with branch staff in case of complaints.

This concept was – and still is – seen to be very successful by both workers and lower management. Its two main strengths were high quality support for the branches and quality work for employees. High quality support for the branches rested on the development of a relationship of mutual dependency and obligation towards each other. Due to the stable relationship, mutual trust could be built up and in return formed the basis upon which flexible co-operation was practised. At times, this also implied compromising the official standard procedures. For example, if a form was not signed, back-office-staff proceeded anyway on the understanding, that the colleagues in the branch would sign it later and return it quickly. An exceptionally high workload was often handled by back-office-staff without complaint, hoping for patience in times, when they would not be able to work as quickly as usual. Thus, the integrative work organisation provided opportunities to build up customer-worker coalitions (Frenkel et al., 1999, p. 17). Many employees expressed satisfaction with this sort of work practice because of the high amount of responsibility they were given for defined tasks, the chance for continuous learning, leading to improved chances in the internal labour market, and the variety of tasks, ranging from routine to complex. They experienced close personal contact to their colleagues in the branches and the regular feed-back they received as very rewarding.

But despite these advantages, in 1997, the board of directors opted for sweeping changes to back-office departments, that were carried out in autumn 1998. The whole reorganisation process was centrally planned and executed without much prior discussion with workers, lower or even middle management in the regional back-office departments. The new concept was based on the concept of establishing a transaction-bank, offering back-office services to other parts of the bank. In adherence to this concept, back-offices were taken out of regional structures and put into a division of their own.

The next reorganisation step, was to centralise back-office departments. The former number of 21 units was reduced to six. These back-office units were run as profit-centres. Branches from now on had to pay for back-office services. Establishing larger units put to an end the integrated one-person branch-support and reintroduced task-fragmentation. In each of the six back-office units, direct contact with the employees in the branches was centralised into a small call-centre (see figure 8.1).

More complex tasks and everything that necessarily involved paper was dealt with outside the call centre, in functionally specialised teams responsible for current-accounts, credit-cards, small businesses and the like. With the call centre serving the outside customers in the branches, these teams might be termed a back-office in the back-office. There were two types of teams, differing in skill levels required: 'specialised production' (*Sonderfertigung*) and 'mass production'[2] (*Serienfertigung*) for complex and simple

---

[2] These terms alluding to production work were not chosen by accident. Rather, they show that in the German context manufacturing activities are again seen as a model of

products respectively, with some specialised teams performing supportive tasks like archiving. Call centre staff made up around 15 per cent of the total workforce in the back-office units; about 55 per cent worked in the specialised teams and 30 per cent in the standardised teams. Nearly all employees in the call centre and in the specialised production teams had undergone vocational training, most of the mass production teams had not. Subsequently, these three different types of teams, the call centre team, the specialised and the mass production teams will be discussed in more detail with an analysis of the organisational logic behind the reorganisation strategy following suit.

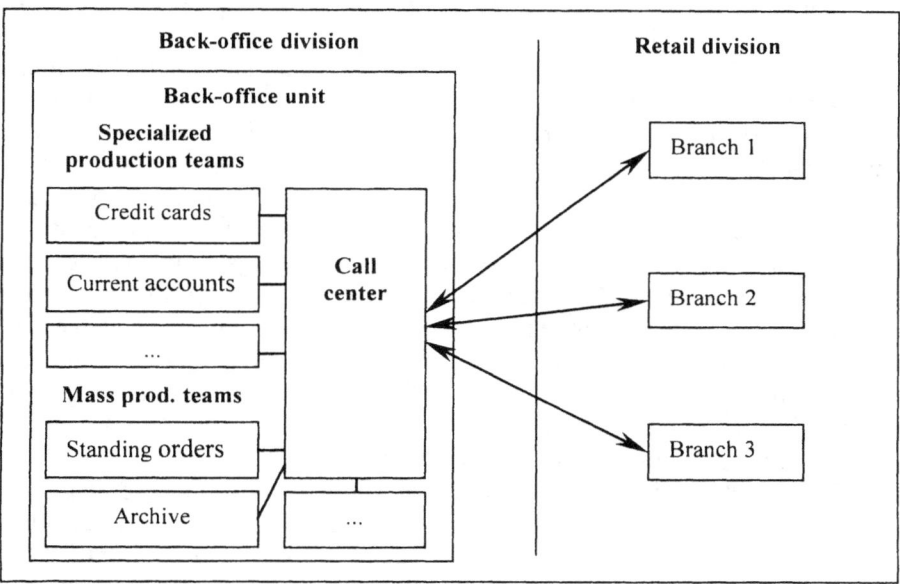

Figure 8.1 Organizational Structure of the Newly Established Back-office Units

Working in the Call Centre

As a result of this reorganisation, communication between the back-office unit and its branches was concentrated in the call centre. Agents' responsi-

---

efficiency – also for service sector work. Also they signal, that the privileges of white collar workers in general and of working in a bank in particular might be gone for good – at least in the back-offices.

bility was twofold. They carried out all tasks, which did not need to be documented on paper. Additionally, they were supposed to answer branch-staff's questions on products, standard procedures, problems, how to proceed in exceptional cases etc. As the company was also reducing the skill level of branch staff, the advising function of the call centre became of increasing importance for maintaining quality standards. The call centre remained the only place where knowledge about the complete range of products and processes was required and developed. With time, most queries became routine, but there were enough unusual inquiries to require call agents to constantly expand their professional knowledge.

Work in the call centre was deemed very attractive. This was due to better pay but also to the chance for using and developing one's own competencies and skills. Call agents were secured a good position on the internal labour market of the bank. And initially, workers were attracted to the chance of participating in establishing a new organisational unit. There was hardly any fluctuation. All this gave management the opportunity to select the best from the above mentioned 'all-round branch supporters'. Not surprisingly therefore, employees in the call centre were communicative, oriented towards participation and motivated to engage themselves on behalf of the company. Accordingly, management pursued a co-operative approach, aimed at strengthening these intrinsic motivations. Changes in the relation between branch staff and back-office staff were obvious. No longer were they based on long-standing personal acquaintance and a shared history of co-operation. This comes down to what Gutek (1995) calls the change from relations to encounters.

While such a shift surely has its downside, the call centre had clear advantages for its internal customers from the branches: Good service quality, helping branch staff to get things done quickly from 8.00 a.m. until 8.00 p.m. and very competent service in complex cases, which went beyond what could have been expected from the typical all-round-supporter. Consequently, the call centre received recognition for its contribution in the new reorganisation concept, materialising in Christmas presents, thank-you-calls and the like. If there was one difficulty in sight for call centre agents, it was the threat of splitting up the call centre into first- and second-level support. This had (for special reasons) been done in one of the six call centres and might possibly be repeated in the other units in the future.

Working in the Back-office of the Back-office

Things were different in the mass and specialised production teams. Here, the work, that was once performed by a single branch supporter alone had now been split up into numerous functionally differentiated teams. In the specialised production teams, workers performed tasks that required vocational training. The mass production teams dealt with the more routine work for which workers without formal vocational training were employed. Here, work was highly repetitive and there was little chance for further qualification. One head of department remarked: 'Frankly, I would not like to work all day, performing such tasks.'

To those, who had been overburdened with the high demands of being an all-round branch-supporter, the new concept was clearly more suitable. But apart from that, there were a lot of disadvantages for employees. Renewed specialisation was feared as possibly impairing their chances on the bank's internal labour market in the future. Also, for those in the less qualified mass production teams, the chance for slowly learning more complex tasks was no longer present, thus blocking possible mobility into the higher qualified, functionally specialised teams.

Quite importantly, workers had also lost the frequent personal contact with colleagues from branches and the recognition this personal acquaintance afforded them. Of course, they were still in daily contact with employees from the branches, especially if more complex questions had to be sorted out directly. But the number of branches for which they were now responsible had grown to a point where one could no longer build close relationships with branch employees. Close personal contact had been experienced by back-office workers as the basis for fruitful co-operation. As one of the team-leaders described:

> 'Basically, the old concept was not so bad at all. Experience shows that today, branches do miss their personal support, that branch workers ... say: "We don't have anybody personal to contact, who will help us out now?" The Call-Centre is all right, but there are many instances, where one would fare better with direct person-to-person dialogue... But this is not wanted by the bank.'

In the new organisation, service-quality depended on the functioning of complex formalised routines, ranging from apparently simple functions like mail-delivery to the co-operation between call centre and production teams, as small deviations caused great problems. Production team workers were thus forced to stick to the rules rather than to pursue a more flexible co-operation, as was previously the case. This in turn caused frustration with the 'bureaucratic' behaviour of the back-office among the branch staff.

Not surprisingly, there was discontent among employees. Management and team leaders found it difficult to motivate workers for this new kind of work. A team leader in the mass production team recounted workers' reactions in one of the mass production teams:

'For some of my workers it is just a nuisance to go the extra mile. (They just think:) "It's going to be alright." Many things have been sent to the branches anonymously - I had to end this custom - so that nobody would know, just who was responsible for this certain task ... So that nobody could question them in case something was not all right. They hid away instead of taking the bull by the horns.'

I will not elaborate on the particulars of the reorganisation strategy. Suffice to say, that its typical difficulties antagonised many workers in the production teams, who felt that the original state of things had not been bad and who compared their situation to the call agents, who participated in establishing the centre and got to work more closely with the customer.

At this point, one might wonder, just why the bank underwent such a demanding reorganisation process. Enhanced cost-efficiency and service-quality are not sufficient explanations since both were severely compromised due to the shortcomings of the new concept. I argue that the answer must not be sought on the level of work process strategies, but rather at the level of broader organisational strategies.

The Logic Behind the New Organisational Concept

The reorganisation away from an integrative work organisation does not equate with a simple return to Taylorist principles of task fragmentation and a division of decision making and execution. While developments in some work areas, most notably in the mass production teams, are reminiscent of Taylorist rationalisation approaches and while management has clearly strengthened its overall control over the work process, the whole picture is more complex. Rather I would contend that the case study provides evidence of a new approach, which I have tentatively labelled flexible bureaucracy (Dose, 2001). The organisational form is still bureaucracy, but it is a more flexible organisational concept in terms of implementing strategic decisions and answering to customers' demands and wishes. In the flexible bureaucracy, a range of arrangements and concepts are used for shaping different work processes. But notwithstanding all its heterogeneity, there is a unifying principle to the concept. Such organisations bring together formalisation and standardisation (Luhmann, 1964) on the one side and chances for more complex and reflexive decision making on the other. Even more precisely, in a flexible bureaucracy, the latter is supported and enhanced through the former. Reflexive decision making here means to come to decisions, which are conscious of customers' wishes, and companies' interests, and quality and efficiency issues. This is not a trivial task.

While management accepts, that it must give employees some leeway in order to let them come to adequate decisions, it nevertheless tries to structure decision making processes and be it through such simple things as providing employers with some, but not other, information. This ambivalence is characteristic of the flexible bureaucracy.

There are numerous examples of how reflexivity is supported through standardisation and formalisation (Holtgrewe, 2001). The definition of branches as paying customers is an important aspect of the formalisation and standardisation of former service relations. Branches and the back-office were now organised in two completely different divisions and joint regional responsibility for branches and back-offices were done away with. This created new demands for efficiency and quality from the branches. They had paid for it, now they wanted to see something delivered in return. If their expectations were not met, there was no reason, not to escalate dissatisfaction into conflict. One symbol for the new way of dealing with other units within the same company was the creation of a new database, in which complaints were entered with the intention of proving, that most of them were unwarranted. Remarks one project specialist:

> 'This (the complaints-database) will be an instrument, which will put us into a position, to demonstrate to branches, that either their complaint is unjustified, because they are responsible for the problem themselves, or that the delay is not as they claim it is. This will clearly help us.'

This standardisation of services had a productive side. Problems and difficulties could not be covered up, and were regularly articulated. Whereas in the former organisation, everyone depended on the good will of the other side and was thus inclined to overlook delays, small errors, etc. in exchange for that same benevolent negligence, such customer-worker-coalitions were no longer present. Requests were not issued to a specific person, but to the organisation as a whole. Likewise, complaints could not be held confidential by a certain worker or even team. All this engenders new reflexivity about the work process. Workers, down to the last person in the back-office archive, had constantly to ask themselves, what the customers might expect of them, even if this customer was only present in the form of an official complaint.

Also, while the services to be offered were standardised, numerous new possibilities to reflect upon the question, to whom to offer which service for what price opened up. More specifically, back-office and branch units were in a position to discuss service level agreements about how much branches had to pay for better quality support. Basically, this was negotiated in relation to lines of retail customer segmentation. The ironic turn: the branches' demand for better service quality from the back-offices began to lead to a partial return to integrative forms of branch support, at least for the customer segments of small business financial services and private banking for affluent customers, areas where high quality support is regarded as important by the banks' managers.

Furthermore, with the separation of tasks between the call centre and the production teams, chances for the acquisition of new business was enhanced. The call centre and its immediate management was built up as a highly competent and flexible team, whose demonstrated customer orientation was an advertisement for the whole back-office unit and that was able to take on new tasks quickly. For example, the call centre did some outbound work, trying to fix dates with private customers and their advisers in the branches. This was made possible through the centralisation of lines of communication in the front-line call unit. Associated support tasks could be confined to one of the production teams.

Consider also, that standardisation and formalisation of the work process allowed management to implement further organisational and IT-concepts, aimed at providing employees with added information for their decision making. There were projects under way to set up internal accounting systems, to help to determine the price of services offered. Also envisaged were benchmarking systems, whereby the six different back-office units and maybe even the teams would be compared against each other. Such systems could hardly have been implemented in the less centralised, less structured former organisational concept.

In the light of these findings, the move away from the concept of integrative work organisation can be considered anew. While the integrative work organisation had strengths in engendering processes of reflexive decision making, management lost influence over those processes. The old integrative work organisation had left branch supporters and employees in the branches a lot of freedom to develop specific local arrangements. It thus situated reflexive decision making at a local level. At the same time, it reduced management's influence on these processes. The integrative work organisation was fine concerning questions of customer orientation in the setting of long term customer relationships. On the whole however, it no longer fulfilled upper-management's expectations to direct and orient such decision-making processes.

The analysis of the flexible bureaucratic reorganisation of work by no means justifies an optimistic outlook on changes for workers at the back-office units of the bank. Rather, the concept of the flexible bureaucracy points to the contradictory consequences for workers and customers alike. This is so, because the heightened chances for skilled work, the opportunities for more self-reflexive work practices and the skill demands that come with it, are unevenly distributed. In retrospect, the old concept of integrated branch-support seems a surprisingly homogenous approach. Today, we find a marked division between those who profit from the reorganisation (enlarged discretion, more complex and challenging tasks, better opportunities for skill acquisition) and those who don't. This division does not simply parallel hierarchical position. Team leader positions certainly have become more demanding. But so has the work of those branch support workers, who are now employed in the call centre and those who will soon handle the part of the back-office tasks that serve corporate customers in dedicated production teams. Branch supporters, who have been relegated to mass production teams, but also those in the specialised teams, whose responsibility is now limited to just one product group, have certainly lost in terms of being delegated more routine work with fewer chances for learning more skilled work tasks.

Customer-relations and Chances for Resistance in the Flexible Bureaucracy

Drawing a somewhat more detailed picture of the flexible bureaucracy, changes concerning customer-relations and also for chances for resistance seem worth mentioning. The reorganisation described above is not just about customer orientation and improving service quality. Flexibility towards customer demands has been strengthened in some aspects - but weakened in others. Very clearly, it was management's aim to be able to manage (internal) customer-relations more directly. The reorganisation is closely linked with being able to offer different service levels, whether it be the standardised encounter or the more personal support.

If we analyse this in terms of the triangle of customer-worker-management-relations (Frenkel et al., 1999, p. 201), the concept of the flexible bureaucracy points to breaking up a customer-worker-coalitions, that had been part of the concept of integrative work organisation. But there is no other coalition established. Rather management tries to maintain a delicate balance between (internal) customers and workers, keeping control over customer-worker relations. It uses the (internal) customer as a figure of authority (Korczynski et al., 2000), forcing employees to think about consequences of their decisions for concrete customers. But it also defends employees against illegitimate demands or even ill-treatment, which is necessary, since the old regulating mechanism of dual dependency is not functional anymore. The customer is thus made relevant in both aspects: as an abstract group, that is of importance to the company *and* as an individual customer (Korczynski et al., 2000). Pointing to the customer as an abstract group, employees are asked to accept the drawbacks of formalisation and centralisation. Also, they are forced to accept that service in many instances must be limited, including the loss of close personal relations. But then, the new concept demands the execution of each and every task in reference to a concrete customer as well. This is easiest in the call centre, where these individual customers are at least audible to the agents. But it is also demanded in the production teams. Employees everywhere are constantly being reminded, that complaints are only uttered by concrete individuals.

Quite interestingly, the flexible bureaucracy seems to be both less and more vulnerable to various forms of resistance on the part of workers and their representatives. The formalised nature of the work process makes centralised reorganisation approaches easier, side-tracking workers and their representatives. When the works council in one of the regional units refused the implementation of an automatic call distribution (ACD)-telephone system, reverting to its co-determination rights, management was able to establish a first-level call centre within six months at another site with a more co-operative work council (and much higher unemployment rates). The works council at the old location was completely surprised by this move. Such a regional transfer of complete workflows would not have been possible in the old, less structured organisational concept.

Yet in the new complex work processes of the back-office units, all parts need to function according to their specified role. If they do not, shortcomings multiply in a very short time. Also, reflexive decision making cannot simply be secured through pressure and commands, but demands individual motivation and determination on the part of workers. Consequently, forms of individual resistance can become a serious problem for the flexible bureaucracy. This was very evident in the mass production teams. Management had to discover that speed and quality of service depended on the commitment of those employees who had obviously not profited from the new concept. As a result, the work council was able to at least fend off redundancies and secure pay levels and other pay related arrangements for most employees. Also, management has so far shied away from opting out of collective pay bargaining for the banking sector. It would have meant a significant loss of pay and bonuses for workers and would thus be met with fierce opposition by employees. Still, these forms of resistance are quite defensive: employees and works councils and even lower management were not able to influence the basic rationalisation strategy of renewed task fragmentation.

Conclusion

Which is the appropriate unit of analysis for researching the flexible bureaucracy? In the back-office units of this large bank, we find a call centre with highly motivated, entrepreneurially minded staff. For sure, one can observe many of the same strains and drawbacks as in other call centres. But in the eyes of employees, the advantages overweigh the disadvantages. Also we find customers, satisfied with the new services the call centre offers them. But this is not the whole picture. To get at it, other teams in the back-office unit have to be included in the analysis as well. We then find an array of different workplaces, differing in pay levels, skill demands and career opportunities. The common denominator: all these tasks had once belonged to one type of workplace. It is only by taking into perspective the entire back-office organisation, that we can appreciate the advantages and many disadvantages of the new concept: some employees – namely the call agents – have gained, while others have lost through the reorganisation process, and these are just two sides of the same coin.

Looking solely at the call centre, one might have assumed, that there is a continuation of the concept of integrative work organisation (D'Alessio and Oberbeck, 1999). Looking at the whole picture, this assumption cannot be upheld. Instead, we find a new strategy, best conceptualised as a flexible bureaucracy, with both integrative and fragmenting elements. This holistic discussion of reorganisation cases makes the analysis of aims and consequences more complicated. At the level of the work process, it was not clear why the whole effort was undertaken by the bank against tremendous difficulties and resulting in enormous one-time costs. To answer this, it was necessary to reflect upon the organisational logic of the new concept. This then suggests, that social scientific research will only be able to orient actors in the field, if it engages with the organisational strategies pursued, points to its weaknesses, but also acknowledges its strengths and then hints to alternatives. Industrial sociology in Germany has a good track record of considering such organisational logics. The concept of the flexible bureaucracy is intended to strengthen this line of research, particularly in the service sector, where there has been comparatively little research in Germany. The aim of this chapter has been to explain differential outcomes of rationalisation processes and account for important contradictions facing companies and employees. The empirical results are worrying though. It is very disappointing, that this company did not pursue strategies, which would have made better use of their highly qualified and loyal workforce.

References

Baethge, M. and Oberbeck, H. (1986), *Zukunft der Angestellten. Neue Technologien und berufliche Perspektiven in Büro und Verwaltung*, Frankfurt/Main, Campus.

D'Alessio, N. and Oberbeck, H. (1999), '"Call-Center" als organisatorischer Kristallisationspunkt von neuen Arbeitsbeziehungen, Beschäftigungsverhältnissen und einer neuen Dienstleistungskultur', in *Jahrbuch sozialwissenschaftliche Technikberichterstattung 1998/99. Schwerpunkt: Arbeitsmarkt*, Berlin, Sigma, pp. 13-61.

Dose, C. (2001), 'Jenseits der Automatisierung. Ambivalente Nutzungsformen von Informationstechnik im Finanzdienstleistungssektor', in Matuschek, I., Henninger A. and Kleemann F. (eds.), *Neue Medien im Arbeitsalltag*, Opladen, Westdeutscher Verlag, pp. 71-88.

Frenkel, S., Korczynski, M., Shire, K. and Tam, M. (1999), *On the Front Line. Organisation of Work in the Information Economy*, Ithaca, Cornell University Press.

Gutek, Barbara (1995), *The Dynamics of Service*, San Francisco, Jossey-Bass.

Holtgrewe, U. (2001), 'Organisationsdilemmata und Kommunikationsarbeit. Call-Center als informatisierte Grenzstelle', in Matuschek, I., Henninger A. and F. Kleemann (eds.), *Neue Medien im Arbeitsalltag*, Opladen, Westdeutscher Verlag, pp. 55-70.

Horstmann, M. and Oberbeck, H. (1996), 'Finanzdienstleister zwischen Kundenorientierung und traditioneller Rationalisierung', in Braczyk, H.-J., Ganter, H.-D. and Seltz, R. (eds.), *Neue Organisationsformen in Dienstleistung und Verwaltung*, Stuttgart, Kohlhammer, pp. 29-52.

Kadritzke, U. (1982), 'Angestellte als Lohnarbeiter. Kritischer Nachruf auf die deutsche Kragenlinie', in *Materialien zur Industriesoziologie, Sonderheft 24 der Kölner Zeitschrift für Soziologie und Sozialpsychologie*, pp. 219-249.

Korczynski, M., Shire, K., Frenkel, S. and Tam, M. (2000), 'Service Work in Consumer Capitalism: Customers, Control and Contradictions', *Work, Employment & Society*, Vol. 14, pp. 669-687.

Lane, C. (1992), 'Technologischer Wandel und kaufmännische Angestelltenarbeit in Großbritannien. Ein Vergleich mit der deutschen Situation', in Littek, W., Heisig U. and Gondek H.-D. (eds.), *Organisation von Dienstleistungsarbeit: Sozialbeziehungen und Rationalisierung im Angestelltenbereich*, Berlin, Ed. Sigma, pp. 201-217.

Littek, W. and Heisig, U. (1995), 'Taylorism Never Got Hold of Skilled White-Collar Work in Germany', in Littek, W. and Charles, T., *The New Division of Labour. Emerging Forms of Work Organisation in International Perspective*, Berlin, de Gruyter, pp. 373-395.

Littek, W., Heisig, U., Gondek, H.-D. (eds.) (1992), *Organisation von Dienstleistungsarbeit: Sozialbeziehungen und Rationalisierung im Angestelltenbereich*, Berlin, Ed. Sigma, pp. 219-261.

Luhmann, N. (1964), *Funktionen und Folgen formaler Organisationen*, Berlin, Duncker & Humblot.

Muller, M. (1997), 'Stability or Transformation of Employment Relations in German Banking', in Knights D. and Tinker T. (eds.), *Financial Institutions and Social Transformations*, Basingstoke, MacMillan, pp. 135-157.

PART III
CUSTOMER SERVICE WORK AND INTERACTION

Chapter 9

Call Centre Consumption and the Enchanting Myth of Customer Sovereignty[1]

Marek Korczynski

Much of contemporary interactive service work is structured to promote the consumption of the sign value of the enchanting myth of customer sovereignty. After outlining this concept, the chapter examines the key problems that face call centre management in its attempts to ensure that customers are able to consume this sign value. Management seeks to promote this sign-value through its symbolic representation of call centres in its advertising and marketing, through the overall organisation of call centre operations, and through the structuring of individual interactions between customers and call centre workers. The following section argues that despite these attempts, important factors exist which will lead systematically to some customers' enchantment turning to disillusionment. The call centre worker's job then, often, can revolve as much around the management of disillusionment as around the promotion of the enchanting myth of sovereignty.

Contemporary Service Work and the Enchanting Myth of Customer Sovereignty

> 'When workers and customers meet... that relationship adds a new dimension to the pattern of human relations in industry.' (Whyte, 1946, p. 123)

Central to an adequate sociological understanding of service work, and call centre work specifically, is an analysis of the relationship between customers, on the one hand, and the service organisation and its front line workers, on the other. Are there dominant patterns to this relationship that allow us

---

[1] Thanks to insightful comments from Ursula Holtgrewe on an earlier draft, and for Karen Shire's encouragement in pursuing the argument.

insights into the organisation and experience of service work? What kind of sociological actors are customers in interactive service work, and what kind of constraints are they subject to?

A tempting short-cut in answering these elusive but important questions is to turn to existing images of the customer that litter a wide range of literatures from neo-classical economics and marketing to critical cultural studies (see Gabriel and Lang, 1995; Lee, 2000; Rosenthal et al., 2001; Korczynski, 2001b). A reading of these literatures highlights a polarisation around two starkly contrasting images of the customer. On the one hand, there is an image of the customer as the powerless manipulated pawn, controlled effortlessly by massive producing corporations. Galbraith, in part, employs this approach, stressing the ability of advertising and sales tactics to 'compel in the consumer a sense of want' (1979, p. 43). Vance Packard also famously argues in *The Hidden Persuaders* (1957) that consumers tend to be manipulated by techniques of depth psychology and mass advertising. Adorno's (1976) still widely discussed analysis of music consumption and production portrays the music consumer as close to an unthinking automaton moulded by the routinised labour process of Fordism and duped by dressings of pseudo-individualisation in commodified music. George Ritzer's (2000) famous thesis on *The McDonaldisation of Society* also implicitly contains an image of the customer as subject to the control of McDonaldised organisations.

On the other hand, there is an image of the customer as powerful, even sovereign, as leading the way while producing organisations scramble amongst themselves in seeking to cater to the customer's demands. The sovereign rational customer is a central a priori assumption of neo-classical, marginalist economics. The pre-existing status of these wants in this literature implies that the consumer wants are self-generated, that the consumer is self-constituted (Campbell, 1987, p. 40). The consumer is sovereign in that the allocation of resources is directed by consumer preferences. As Frenzen et al. (1994, p. 405) put it, 'in the marginalist world, consumption provides the raison d'être for production'. This image of the customer extends beyond economics. For instance, McGuigan (1998) makes a convincing argument that both Fiske's (1987) concept of consumers forming a 'semiotic democracy' and Hayek's (1944) version of free-market theory share the assumption of the sovereignty of consumers. Similarly, Campbell's (1987) *The Romantic Ethic and the Spirit of Modern Consumerism* emphasises the active, fluid and often unmanageable agency of customers. Campbell argues that consumption is increasingly driven by the 'autonomous' hedonism of consumers, with producing organisations desperately trying to keep up with the latest form of pleasure-seeking sought by consumers.

Parallels to both of these images can be found in contemporary analyses of the rise of the call centre as a key new mode of consumption. On the one hand, there is the depiction of call centres as a soulless outcome of large corporations search for efficiency and control (Ritzer, 2000), while on the other there is a celebration of call centres as a manifestation of the 'customer's victory' (DuPuy, 1999), of call centres as on the cusp of the breakthrough into *The 24 Hour Society* (Kreitzman, 1999), long-desired by consumers. However, there are real problems with these images of consumers more generally, and of the call centre consumer, more specifically. As Middleton (1990, p. 57) asks of Adorno's picture of the manipulated music consumer: 'could listeners be so unfree?', so we may ask of the counter-image of the autonomous, sovereign customer, 'can consumers really be so free?'

I will address these questions at three levels, proceeding from the level of the general nature of consumption, to the level of the consumption within interactive service work, and then in the following section, to the level of the consumption relating to call centres. Both social structure and agency inform behaviour. Customers should be seen as *mutually constituted* by their own agency and by the structures erected by producing organisations. In addition, in examining which of these holds the greater sway, it is necessary to differentiate whether it is the individual or collective aspect of producing organisations and customers that is being considered. This is important because it is easy to draw conclusion of consumer impotence if an individual consumer is contrasted to a group of multi-national corporations, while conclusions of organisational impotence can be drawn from examining the position of a small local firm confronted by a mass of increasingly informed and mobile consumers. At this point the focus is upon the collectivity of consumers and the collectivity of producing organisation. Except in a situation of monopoly, producing organisation cannot be assumed to have unambiguous determinative power over customer behaviour. Rather, the producing organisations are in a position of *competitive appeal and enchantment* regarding customers. This concept allows space for a consideration of the way in which production organisations still seek to structure customers' behaviour, albeit in a context in which they compete with other producing organisations. That firms seek to appeal to, and enchant, customers also suggests customer agency. The view of passivity is taken away, because an appeal or an attempted enchantment is something that calls for action from the customer. Enchantment, moreover, contains the idea that customers are active participants in the creation of meaning. The story-teller can only enchant his/her audience if the audience members invest part of themselves in the experience. The brand or the logo is a clear contemporary manifestation of competitive enchantment by individual producing organisation. Even Klein, a vehement critic of the dynamic of logo-centred capitalism, concedes that consumers play an active role in this process of enchantment (2000, pp. 141, 143, 149).

When moving from a consideration of the customer at the general level to a consideration of the customer within front line service work an important distinction must be made regarding the individual / collective level of analysis. The individual producing organisation becomes the focus, but regarding the customer, both the collective and the individual level must be considered. It is the case that the producing organisation must be configured to deal with customer behaviour at a collective level. The concept of competitive appeal and enchantment holds good here, therefore. What is different for front line work is that the organisation must also deal directly with individual customers. In the situation of an individual customer interacting directly with an individual service organisation the power shifts strongly to the producing organisation.[2] Service organisations are in a strong position to strongly influence customers' behaviour in service interactions. This power, however, is limited by two key factors. One is the dynamic created by the continuing context of competition with other producing organisations. Service organisations can compete with each other on the basis of the degree to which customer behaviour is directly influenced by the organisation. When one service organisations starts attracting customers on the basis that 'customers are our number one priority', that 'here the customer is the king' then other service organisations are also pushed in that direction. As Zeithaml and Bitner (1996, p. 75) note, there has been a 'rapid escalation of customer expectations' within service industries, and these expectations have been fuelled by fierce competition and advertising. Ritzer (1999a, p. 75) similarly notes, 'once one setting has been reenchanted, competitors must follow suit or risk the permanent loss of business'. The second factor is the incongruity that would be experienced by the customer. They would move from being appealed to and enchanted, to suddenly being subject to dictates. Service organisations seek to reconcile this contradiction by subtly attempting to direct customer behaviour while also attempting to ensure that the customer feels that he/she is in charge. As Leidner (1993, p. 139) puts it, when managers try to manipulate customers, they must 'finesse' their actions so that it appears that the customer is still

---

[2] An analogy can be drawn between this shift and the 'fundamental transformation' that Williamson (1985) writes of as occurring when large numbers competition becomes 'bilateral treaty' with the signing of a contract between two parties.

in charge. Within this, the trick for front line workers, then, is to be 'both deferential and authoritative' (Benson, 1986, p. 159), to direct behaviour but to convey the impression that the customer is in charge.

In short, the service organisation attempts to structure the interaction to promote the consumption of *the enchanting myth of customer sovereignty*. To clarify what is meant by this, below, I lay out the meaning of each term in the phrase, working backwards from the end.

Sovereignty. The meaning of sovereignty is much debated. Here I outline the meanings I put on the term and I locate these meanings in the wider debates on the meaning of sovereignty. The concept of sovereignty used here has both pre-modern and modern connotations. In its pre-modern sense, sovereignty as a concept is tied to the absolute power of a supreme ruler, for instance, a king. Concepts of sovereignty are, in an important sense, relational (Hoffman, 1998). It is the relational sense of *supremacy*, of the sovereign above the other, of the king above the ruled, the subject, which is the pre-modern sense of sovereignty that I would like to retain within the concept of the enchanting myth of customer sovereignty. This sense of sovereignty, while present in contemporary service work, operates *at a secondary level*. The *dominant sense of sovereignty* that operates is a modern one. The classical liberal writers, Hobbes, Locke and Rousseau, heralded modernity with their concept of individuals as the starting point of social theory - individuals were autonomous, private owners, of themselves and their property. While these theorists wrote about the necessity of sovereign state arising to oversee these atomistic individuals as they come into collision, it is the sense of *individual autonomy* that I allude to within the concept of the enchanting myth of sovereignty. This sense is also present in some neo-classical economic writing – for instance, when Thompson (1977, pp. 90-1) writes that 'the consumer is, above all, independent... ultimately, all power is held to lie with the consumer – that is what is meant by consumer sovereignty'. Typically, individual autonomy is played out, and recognised through, the process of self-directed decision-making in a situation where the individual is faced with a *choice* between alternatives. Individual autonomy, played out through self-directed choice, is the dominant sense of sovereignty, then, with relational supremacy constituting the secondary sense of sovereignty.

Customer. A customer is an *individual* who has bought, or is buying, a good or service from a service organisation. The word 'individual' is italicised to emphasise that the enchanting myth does not pertain to the neo-classical economics concept of the sovereignty of consumers as a whole. The economists' concept of resources being distributed according to the overall preferences of consumers cannot be taken to suggest that the individual consumer is sovereign. Indeed, it can be the case that a consumer with idiosyncratic wants will find that producers do not produce for his/her wants because there is not sufficient demand. Customer, then, is deliberately used in a singular sense, alluding to the specific problem that arises when an individual customer interacts with employees of an individual service organisation. The term 'customer' is used rather than 'consumer' for similar reasons. 'Consumer' relates to general consumption, whereas the term 'customer' brings to mind direct interaction with service employees. Further, the term customer reminds us that a customer may only have sovereignty to the extent that he/she has money to buy goods or services. It is not a myth of sovereignty relating to inherited position at birth or to citizenship. These points of first principle will be seen to have great significance in the later discussion of how sovereignty is promoted, and, systematically, can turn to disillusionment.

Myth. A myth is taken to relate to a widely held notion. Further, the meaning ascribed to myth here leans on Levi-Strauss's thesis that 'the purpose of myth is to provide a... *model capable of overcoming a contradiction*' (1963, p. 229). The specific contradictory position in this myth is the customer beguiled with messages of appeal and enchantment by the service organisation suddenly confronted with a situation in which he/she is subject to the influence, policies and procedures, of the service organisation. Barthes argues that myths, through their mode of naturalisation, tend to hide their ideological basis, i.e. the fact that they systematically uphold certain interests. In this case, the myth supports the interests of service organisations. It acts as a lubricant to encourage continued purchasing decisions by customers in a potentially troublesome social situation. Finally, a myth should not only be believed but should also be *believable*. In Bauman's (1988; 1992) terms, the new freedom of consumer choice is both imagined and real. As Barthes (1972) argues, the power of a myth is that it appears natural, it involves a superficially obvious narrative. In this case, it alludes to the superficially obvious narrative of customer sovereignty that is taught in classrooms all over the world in introductory economics courses, and that is reinforced in advertising messages that colonise more and more of the spaces within people's daily lives (Klein, 2000).[3] As Edwards (2000) and McDonald and Sirianni (1996) note, the norm of 'the customer as king' is a widespread one in many capitalist economies. This myth is also believable because it potentially gives a customer greater power in his/her nego-

---

[3] Miller (1995) argues that although there remains a 'wide discrepancy between economic theory and the world', marginalist economics has increasingly colonised aspects of economy and society as an ideology, informing people's perceptions and images of the world.

tiations with a service organisation. If a customer feels poorly treated by a service organisation he/she can allude to the myth, either in terms of the general norm of customer sovereignty, or in terms of the specific advertising messages put out by the firm. It makes the complaining customer a figure who has legitimacy. This specific myth is also believable because it is seductive and ...

Enchanting. A myth of one's own sovereignty, i.e. individual autonomy expressed through choice, with perhaps intimations of supremacy, is a myth that beguiles and enchants. As Lynch dryly notes, 'any action which increases the self-esteem of the customer will raise the level of satisfaction' (1992, p. 128). It also draws the customer into a fantasy world in which he/she has a role in meaning-making. As Campbell (1987) has brilliantly argued in *The Romantic Ethic and the Spirit of Modern Capitalism*, Weber's vision of a rational capitalism systematically stripping the world of its fantastical, magical, or enchanting qualities was wrong. A central part of consumption within capitalism involves the evocation of enchantment: the music bought that evokes a first kiss; a comfortable chair bought to lounge and day-dream in. Even the mundane can involve a level of enchantment. Consider, for instance, Wolf's (1999, p. 70) description of a customer's experience in a superstore: 'the lights, the music, the furniture, the cast of clerks create a feeling not unlike a play in which you, the shopper, are given a leading role'. This in turn echoes Williams (1982) analysis of the first French department stores as arenas of enchantment and seduction where customers were invited to live out fantasies. In these 'palaces' of consumption the customer, addressed as 'Sir' or 'Madam', becomes, mythically, the sovereign. The process of enchantment suspends disbelief - a process that a number of writers see as central to customer behaviour. Although individual customers, at some level, may know that notions of their sovereignty are mythical the fact they may still go along with this myth reflects the 'distinctively modern faculty, the ability to create a illusion which is known to be false but felt to be true' (Campbell, 1987, p. 78). The process, then, is another of the important structured forms of social denial that have been shown to pervade everyday existence (Cohen, 2001). Consumers know that they are sovereign and, at the same time, know that they are not. If Campbell's arguments forces us to look for the dreams and fantasies of consumption, then, in the specific arena of consumption within service interactions, that search leads us to the enchanting myth of customer sovereignty.

Indeed, the enchanting myth of customer sovereignty can be seen as the *key meta-level sign value of contemporary interactive service work*. The term 'sign value' relates to Baudrillard's distinction between the 'use value' and 'sign value' of a good or service. The use value of a good relates to its utility, its functionality. The sign value of a good relates to what it signifies, to what meanings are attached to it. So, for instance, if I buy a car, its primary use-value will be its utility in transporting me from A to B. A car may have many sign-values – advertisers, for instance, may try to attach a sign-value that the driver is a reckless, freedom-loving figure, or that the driver is a careful, considerate, family-centred figure, while drivers themselves may create other, quite distinct, sign-values (de Certeau, 1984). In service work, the use-value of a service interaction may be one's hair cut in a certain style, it may be a transfer of money between different bank accounts, it may be the efficient serving of a pleasant meal. While, there can be a range of sign-values specific to types of service interactions, I am arguing that there is a broad tendency for the enchanting myth of customer sovereignty to exist as a sign-value that is promoted across all service interactions that involve workers below the professional or knowledge worker level.[4] Whether in hospital or in hospitality, whether in a bank or in a supermarket, the customer increasingly finds himself/herself in a situation structured to encourage not only efficient service but also the consumption of the enchanting myth of customer sovereignty (Korczynski, 2001b, ch. 5).[5] This is not to say that customers are assumed to simply go along with this process of enchantment, but rather that this is the sign-value that is systematically promoted by management in a range of service settings. The following section turns to examine the main ways in which call centre management attempt to promote the consumption of this meta-level sign-value.

Call Centre Management and the Promotion of the Enchanting Myth

The call centre is a mode of service delivery typically set up in an organisation following a form of business process re-engineering (Hammer and Champy, 1995). A central driving factor in the creation of call centres is the cost savings that can be made, when compared to traditional face-to-face service delivery modes. But the organisation of call centre work is not solely driven by the aim of cost savings through rationalisation. Call centres, like other forms of service work, are also structured to promote the

---

[4] Even in service interactions involving professionals, there is a tendency for management to seek to promote the enchanting myth of customer sovereignty. For instance, see Cohen et al. (2001).

[5] Also see Korczynski (2001b) for a discussion of how widespread 'tools' that management use to structure and measure service quality in effect promote the enchanting myth of customer sovereignty.

enchanting myth of customer sovereignty. This section examines three main ways in which this occurs: through the symbolic representation of the call centre in advertising and marketing, through the overall operation of the call centre, and through the organisation of the service interaction between front line worker and customer. Greater emphasis is placed on the last way because this has more direct implications for understanding the social relations of call centre work.

Symbolic Representation

In the longer term, with the operation of a degree of competition, customers are likely to benefit, through lower prices, from cost savings that arise from the establishment of call centres (Miller, 1995). However, in the shorter term, when price reductions are unlikely to immediately accrue, management is left facing an important problem: it must maintain the enchanting myth of customer sovereignty but the organisation has just established call centres without customers actively petitioning for this change in service delivery. Even if call centres are established after focus group research with customers it is the case that the vast majority of customers will not have been consulted about such a change. The problem, then, for management is to somehow reconcile this with the customer sensing that she or he is in charge. Here the symbolic representation of the establishment of the call centre plays an important role. Within marketing and advertising the establishment of a call centre can be described in terms that help promote the enchanting myth of sovereignty. So, for instance, in advertisements I have received from service organisations setting up call centres, I have been advised, variously, that 'this new service has been set up for you', 'we're waiting for your call', 'anytime you want, just pick up the phone', 'we're driven by you', 'another service improvement at the company where the customer is number one'. These advertisements serve to reassure the individual customer that although he or she has not directly asked, for instance, for a call centre to be set up and a local bank branch closed down, he or she is still sovereign.

Overall Organisation of Call Centre Operations

The enchanting myth of customer sovereignty is also promoted by the overall organisation of call centre operations. It is easier for a sense of sovereignty to be conveyed in call centres because of the spatial and temporal implications of the organisation of call centres. Spatially, a customer is no longer compelled to travel to the physical location of a service organisation in order to conduct business. Organisations setting up call centres often use them to extend the hours in which they are open for business with customers. As Kreitzman (1999, p. 107) notes, now 'one in five banks is open 24 hours 365 days a year'. This means that, temporally, the customer faces fewer constraints in contacting the organisation at times specified by the organisation. DuPuy's (1999, p. 56) description of the traditional spatial and temporal constraints on the customer ties these constraints to the dominance of the producing bureaucracy over the customer: 'the customer who has to give in to the producer is also the one who has to... run to the local retailer not when there is a pressing need, but when the store is open. This is the customer who has to follow a complex process of rules and procedures, running from one place to the next, all because the system was not designed for the customer's convenience but for the bureaucrats who have certain tasks to do'. The relaxation of the spatial and temporal constraints that arise from the establishment of call centres promotes the enchanting myth of sovereignty because the customer, increasingly, can become the autonomous arbiter of where and when to do business.

The overall organisation of call centre operations can promote the enchanting myth of customer sovereignty in another sense. In very many call centres a key management aim is for customers to have a short wait in the telephone queue before they are dealt with by a customer service representative (Cleveland and Mayben, 1997; Durr, 1996). Linking information technology to the telephone system allows for queuing time to be measured, and for operations to be structured to meet short waiting time targets. In traditional, face-to-face service delivery considerably less systematic information is available on queue-waiting times and so operations are less likely to be structured with queue waiting time targets in mind. In call centres, management use software programmes to build up predicted patterns of customer behaviour and arrange staffing to meet these predicted patterns. If this works the enchanting myth of customer sovereignty is further promoted because the organisation's advertising message of 'we're waiting for your call' is matched by the customer's experience.

Structuring the Moment of Myth

Carlzon (1985) has described the encounter between the front line worker and the customer as the '*moment of truth*' for the service organisation, the decisive moment that shapes whether the customer will begin or continue to do business with the organisation. The analysis so far, however, suggest that this encounter is not so much about truth as about myth. The service encounter, then, is more appropriately thought of as the *'moment of myth'*, the key moment at which the enchanting myth of sovereignty must be further promoted; it is also the moment at which the consumption of this myth is at its most fragile. Research into call centre work indicates a number of ways in which management structure this service encounter to be the 'moment of myth', when the enchanting myth of sovereignty is consumed.

First, the customer service representative (CSR), the call centre worker, is trained to take charge of calls with customers to ensure that customers are dealt with speedily and efficiently. But taking charge on its own is not enough, the CSR must structure the interaction such that *it appears to the customer that he or she is in charge of the call*. In this, the CSR is aided by the relaxation of spatial constraints on the customer. No longer is the customer obliged to follow a spatial 'assembly-line' through a service organisation, such as in a traditional bank branch where a customer might be sent from one specialist window to another and to another, queuing in each. The business process re-engineering underpinning the establishment call centres often aims to create call centres as 'one-stop shops' in which an individual CSR can deal with a range of customer issues. Although the customer is not obliged to spatially follow signs, the CSR seeks to ensure that the customer follows the subtle verbal signals put forward by the CSR. Typically, the CSR will begin with an open-ended question which allows the customer to set the agenda, 'how may I help you?'. From the customer's answer, the CSR then will follow a procedure to solve the problem or conduct the business, all the while allowing the impression that the customer is in charge, and the course taken has been autonomously chosen by the customer. The CSR will attempt to finish the call within the prescribed target time, perhaps three or four minutes, without giving the impression to the customer that he or she is being rushed. The ability of a CSR to structure an encounter with a customer while giving the impression to the customer that it is he or she who is in charge is one of the key skills of call centre work. As Holtgrewe (2001, p. 45) has argued, women are more frequently socialised into roles with similar demands, and this helps to explain why call centre work is predominantly undertaken by women.

In call centre work, as in many other types of service work, the enchanting myth of customer sovereignty is also promoted in service encounters through the promotion of empathy for customers among CSRs, and through the terms of address used in the interaction. While deference is the adjunct of pre-modern sovereignty, empathy is the adjunct of the modern mythically sovereign consumer. CSRs tend to be hired on the basis of their empathy, and identification with customers, and are encouraged by management to feel and exhibit such empathy during service interactions

(Korczynski et al. 2000). Empathy shown towards customers promotes the enchanting myth of sovereignty because it positions the customer's viewpoint as dominant in one sense but not necessarily dominant in another. The customer is portrayed as important because it is the CSR who should see through the customer's eyes, and think about themselves 'in the customer's shoes' not the other way around. But unlike deference which implies that action should be directed by the sovereign, empathy does not necessarily mean that action will be determined by the mythically sovereign customer, just that the customer's importance has been acknowledged, and his or her viewpoint would have directed action had this been possible. The terms of address used by the CSR and the customer respectively in service interaction in call centres also promote the enchanting myth of sovereignty. The CSR typically addresses the customer in formal terms, using Mr., and Ms., Sir and Madam, while management ensure that the customer is invited to address the CSR in informal, first-name terms. Here the secondary relational sense of sovereignty is evoked.

The Systematic Cracks of Disillusionment

So far the discussion has shown how call centre management seeks to promote the enchanting myth of sovereignty and it has emphasised the factors that support this process. Consumption, however, is a fragile process (Edwards, 2000). Systematically, the contradiction upon which the myth stands and which it serves to obscure will show through. In these moments the customer's enchantment can turn to disillusionment. This section examines the main ways in these *systematic cracks of disillusionment* are likely to be manifest within call centres: the customer in poverty with no phone; the intrusion of the rationalising logic within the service encounter; the experience of waiting in the phone queue, and the challenge to customer autonomy that occurs in sales work and particularly in outbound calls. Each in its own way appears mundane, but can be interpreted on a more abstract level as manifesting a more fundamental element in the fragility of consumption within the contemporary service society.

Take the case of the customers who do not own a phone, for instance. It is not hard to foresee the disillusionment of these customers when confronted with the closure of a local bank branch or shop and, to add insult to injury, the announcement that the service organisation is restructuring for their benefit. Disillusionment here cuts right to the heart of one of the key contradictions of the myth of customer sovereignty: the term customer implies that the sovereignty is conditional upon the individual having money which allows he or she to buy goods and services. The quid pro quo is that if an individual does not have the money to have a phone, or be a customer, there is no enchanting myth of sovereignty to be consumed. This can also be interpreted in terms of Bauman's (1988; 1992) analysis of contemporary consumer choice. Bauman articulates how freedom in late modernity has come to revolve more and more around the concept of consumer choice. He argues that as this freedom has increased for many, for those denied this freedom this lack of choice becomes ever more keenly felt. As Bauman puts it, choice liberates some but exacerbates the oppression of others. So the growth of call centres liberates many from temporal and spatial constraints, while at the same time denying access to consumption for members of a new underclass.

Another important way in which disillusionment may become manifest in call centre consumption is through the intrusion of the rationalising logic within the service encounter. As I have argued elsewhere (Korczynski, 2001a; 2001b), the organisation of much of contemporary service work can be usefully analysed in terms of a *customer-oriented bureaucracy*, in which there are dual logics of rationalisation and customer-orientation at play. Within the customer-oriented bureaucracy, workers are expected to display not just emotional labour, but *rationalised emotional labour*; they are often expected to form a *pseudo-relationship* (Gutek, 1995) with customers, and have to work to *quantitative as well as qualitative goals* within the labour process. For instance, a McDonald's trainer told Leidner (1993, p. 217), the firm's goals for customer service were that 'we want to treat each customer as an individual in sixty seconds or less'. Efficiency and rationalisation are prioritised in the emphasis on service within sixty seconds or less, but customer-orientation is also prioritised with the emphasis on treating the customer as an individual. The enchanting myth of sovereignty may be consumed to the extent that the consumer can feel like he or she is being treated like an individual without consciousness of being pushed through the service encounter in sixty seconds or less. Cracks of disillusionment occur when the consumer becomes conscious of the latter rationalising logic at play.

Disillusionment will be prompted, for instance, when the rationalised element of emotional labour displayed by the front line worker becomes evident, and when the pseudo part of the pseudo-relationship comes to the surface. In call centre service interactions, these could occur, for instance, when a customer recounts a problem with a product or service and the CSR empathises with the problem in a way that the customer perceives as inauthentic. It would not be surprising if expressions of emotion over the phone from a person never to be met would be frequently perceived as inauthentic. In call centres, pseudo-relationships are underpinned by the CSR's ability to use information technology to call up a wide range of information on the customer (Frenkel et al., 1999). An important part of this information are the 'notes', written up by CSRs on a customer's on-screen file, which summarise noteworthy or idiosyncratic elements of a previous service encounter. For instance, such notes might summarise the reasons given by the customer for a request of an extension of a due-date of payment of a bill. The 'pseudo' element of the CSR-customer relationship may become manifest in call centre service interactions if these notes are incomplete - which will systematically occur if a CSR's quantitative goals prevent him or her from typing comprehensive notes on a customer - or if the notes written in by one CSR cannot be unambiguously interpreted by another CSR who reads them when dealing with the customer on a subsequent occasion. In these cases a customer finds him or herself having to repeat or explain his/her story again, becoming conscious in the process that he/she is not so much a sovereign individual in a relationship in a moment of truth, but more a processed case in a pseudo-relationship in a moment of myth.

The disillusionment that can come from waiting in a call centre phone queue in part also relates to the intrusion of the rationalising logic - the customer, while waiting, may become increasingly conscious that he or she is just another call to be processed. Further, the customer will systematically face the necessity of waiting in the phone queue precisely because of the presence of the rationalising logic. In searching for heightened efficiency and cost savings, call centre management seek to minimise the amount of time that CSRs sit around waiting for customers to call - in rationalised, managerial, terms this is 'unproductive' time. Call centre management are seduced with promises of the power of software programmes to rationally predict the number of phone calls at any period of the day in any part of the year, and management tailors the number of CSRs taking calls to match these predictions. However, call centres are forms of 'boundary-spanning' organisations (Kerst and Holtgrewe 2001) and so are subject to unpredictable shocks stemming either internally within the organisation, or externally from customers. Because of this, there will, systematically, be occasions in which rational predictions prove to be incorrect, and lengthy queues will arise.

There are also other aspects to the disillusionment that comes from holding on to that phone and waiting. Waiting in the phone queue represents the reappearance of temporal constraints that the symbolic representation and overall operation of call centres promised to abolish. In addition, waiting in a phone queue is subtly but importantly different from waiting in a queue behind embodied people. In the embodied queue, the individual customer becomes necessarily aware of other customers. Potentially these other customers come to be seen as other sovereign individuals who have demands which compete with the individual's own interests. Here, the service organisation and its staff become the necessary Hobbesian sovereign figure which arbitrates between these demands, by forming a legitimately ordered queue. In the embodied queue, then, there is potential for the enchanting myth of sovereignty to become recomposed in terms of the necessity for a figure at a higher level of sovereignty. In large part, this recomposition may be prompted by the physical proximity of other customers in the queue. Such physical proximity is lacking in the call centre phone queue. Therefore, the potential for the enchanting myth of sovereignty to become recomposed is diminished, and the possibility of enchantment turning to disillusionment is increased.

Customer enchantment may also turn to disillusionment in call centre interactions when the CSR is charged with making sales, particularly when this is done in the context of outbound calls, i.e. when the CSR, rather than the customer, initiates the phone call. Sales work involves the front line workers actively stimulating demand, encouraging customers to purchase a good or service. At its most extreme form, sales work tends to prioritise the role of the firm, and its front line sales workers, in constituting the 'real' interests of the customer, and to marginalise the role of the customer in this process. For instance, this is captured clearly in the widespread belief among insurance managers and sales workers that 'life assurance is never bought, it is always sold' (Clarke, 2000; Morgan and Knights, 1990). This process is likely to come into conflict with the aim of maintaining the enchanting myth of customer sovereignty, particularly the idea of sovereignty as involving autonomous choice. Already as a person answers his or her phone at home and finds a call centre worker trying to sell something the illusion of autonomous choice is thrown into question. The most fundamental choice of whether to place oneself as a potential customer is potentially taken away by the CSR's phone call. The temporal and spatial reordering that call centres entail, on the one hand free many consumers from constraints, but on the other hand allow and promote the invasion of an individual's space away from the process of new consumption. In Bauman's terms, such are the ambiguities of the freedom of consumer choice. If the phone call progresses, the CSR's job is to persuade the customer to buy a good or service while giving the appearance that all the key decisions made arise autonomously from the customer. When a customer raises an 'objection', for instance that he or she does not actually need the product being pushed, the CSR is trained to redefine this as an 'opportunity' to further persuade the customer of the benefits of the good or service (Korczynski et al., 2000). In this process, the myth of customer sovereignty is likely to be put under heavier and heavier strain, and enchantment will turn to disillusionment if not all the time, then certainly frequently and systematically.

If in some important senses call centres are well-suited to promote the enchanting myth of customer sovereignty, in a number of other important senses, they are also well-suited to create systematic and frequent cracks of disillusionment among customers. Crucially, the nature of call centres will also affect how this disillusionment becomes translated into customer behaviour. As Bauman (1989) and Millgram (1974) have shown the greater the technological and social distance between two people the greater the potential for one party to act in a dehumanised way to another. Call centres create a greater distance between parties by turning a face-to-face interaction into an interaction mediated by telephone technology, and thus increase the likelihood for disrespectful and dehumanised behaviour. Qualitative research into the nature of call centre work often throws up the importance of abusive and irate customers for how CSRs experience their work (Frenkel et al., 1999). One call centre consultant notes that, 'we are not dealing with face-to-face transactions. People feel free to rant and rage at a disembodied voice' (quoted in *The Guardian*, 2nd June, 1998). The issue is far from a trivial one. Another report notes (*The Guardian*, 14th June, 1999):

> 'According to research by the Industrial Society, more phone calls, fewer staff and higher expectations are just some of the growing trends contributing to the dramatic increase of "phone rage". "It's obvious that the problem is widespread", says... a training consultant for the society... Phone rage can be very costly in terms of lost customers, stressed out employees and low morale.'

It appears that call centre customers, piqued and pained as enchantment turns to disillusion in call centre interactions, vent the contradictions of their social situation through anger directed at the CSR, immediately available, but also distant. Further, this anger and abuse that comes out of enchantment turning into disillusionment also represents one last attempt to reclaim vestiges of sovereignty, in this case the secondary, pre-modern, sense of sovereignty as supremacy. Just as the supreme subjects knows that his or her subjects must put up with whatever he or she says, so the customer knows that the CSR's job is to put up with virtually whatever is said at them, and in so doing reclaims a feeling of powerfulness. All this suggests that a central priority of the CSR's jobs lies not only in the promotion of the enchantment of customer sovereignty but also in the *management of disillusionment*.[6]

Conclusion

Consumption via call centres can be called on by a range of theorists of consumption as lending evidence to their positions. The theorists that portray the consumer as emblem of freedom and choice (see Gabriel and Lang, 1995) can point to the greater freedom afforded to customers by call centres. At the same time, critical theorists, such as Lasch (1980), who emphasise the dangerous hedonistic, aggressive and amoral nature of modern consumption, can point to the anger of the disembedded call centre customer directed at CSR's in support of their arguments. But the analysis presented in this chapter suggests that call centre interactions, as with other modes of service delivery, are imbued with the fragility of contemporary consumption. Just as shopping in a mall can be experienced as delightful or painful, and sometimes both at the same time (Edwards, 2000), so too can consuming via a call centre. Arguably, in fact, call centres *heighten* the sense of both the enchanting myth of sovereignty and the corresponding disillusionment. Call centres free consumers from temporal and spatial constraints, and allow management to impose more systematic practices among staff that can promote the enchanting myth of sovereignty. At the same time, by the nature of their social organisation, call centres create the conditions both for systematic cracks of disillusionment, and for this disillusionment to become manifest in anger and abuse.

The chapter's analysis has not only been necessary in its own right, because the process of consumption via call centres is an important social phenomenon, but also because it has clear implications for the experience of call centre work. I have argued elsewhere (Korczynski, 2001b) that with service work becoming increasingly structured in terms of a customer-oriented bureaucracy the experience of service work can be usefully analysed in terms of the *tensions*, *spaces* and *fine lines* of this work. The dual logics of customer-orientation and rationalisation mean that front line workers are frequently placed in a tension-ridden social situation. However, at the same time these dual logics open out the possibility of spaces for front line workers to find meaning and pleasure, perhaps by carving out spaces that are comfortable to them by playing one logic off against another. This analysis of call centre consumption suggests that the fine lines that CSRs have to tread along should be seen as finer than in most other

---

[6] Thanks to Colin Hales for this term.

modes of service delivery. The heightened fragility of call centre consumption means both that CSRs' ability to balance on their journey is severely constrained, and that the consequences of their stepping off this line are more likely to be painful.

Finally, a caveat. The analysis here has, in a sense, gone along with the logic of call centre management. It has focused upon how *management* promotes the enchanting myth of customer sovereignty, and has followed the disillusionment that flows from this - which itself assumes that the customer has gone along with the process set in place by management. While this process is likely to be an important one it is nevertheless the case that individual customers can and do resist the type of social interactions promoted by management. The ways in which customers may subvert the promotion of the enchanting myth of sovereignty, and potentially manage their own disillusionment, clearly requires further analysis. Perhaps a customer, through dry ironic relaying of phrases, may seek to show that he or she is conscious of and resistant to the promotion of enchantment. Perhaps, a customer will seek to break through the structures guiding the economic interaction with a CSR and attempt to create a meaningful, socially embedded, exchange. Even in call centres, CSRs recount stories of the 'regulars' (Frenkel et al., 1999) – the customers who phone individual CSRs and have an ongoing series of conversations with them. These are all important social processes within call centre consumption and Sturdy (2001) is clearly right to suggest that customer resistance to enchantment is an important subject for further research. Indeed, potentially, customer experience, as well as worker experience, can be usefully conceptualised in terms of the tensions, spaces and fine lines thrown up by the customer-oriented bureaucratic structures of contemporary call centres.

References

Adorno, T. (1976), *Introduction to the Sociology of Music*, New York.
Barthes, R. (1972), *Mythologies*, London, Jonathan Cape.
Bauman, Z. (1988), *Freedom*, Milton Keynes, Open University Press.
Bauman, Z. (1989), *Modernity and the Holocaust*, London, Polity Press.
Bauman, Z. (1992), *Intimations of Postmodernity*, London, Routledge.
Benson, S. (1986), *Counter Cultures*, Chicago, University of Illinois Press.
Campbell, C. (1987), *The Romantic Ethic and the Spirit of Modern Consumerism*, Oxford, Blackwell.
Carlzon, J. (1987), *The Moment of Truth*, Cambridge, Ballinger.
Clarke, M. (2000), *Citizens' Financial Futures*, Aldershot, Ashgate.
Cleveland, B. and Mayben, J. (1997), *Call Center Management on Fast Forward*, Annapolis, Maryland, Call Center Press.
Cohen, S. (2001), *States of Denial*, Cambridge, Polity.

Cohen, L., Musson, G. and Duberley, J. (2001), *Flexible experts: Doctors, scientists and customers*, paper delivered at Work, Employment and Society conference, University of Nottingham, September 2001.
de Certeau, M. (1984), *The Practice of Everyday Life*, Berkeley, University of California Press.
DuPuy, F. (1999), *The Customer's Victory*, Basingstoke, MacMillan.
Durr, W. (1996), *A World-Class Inbound Call Center*, Teleprofessional.
Edwards, T. (2000), *Contradictions of Consumption*, Milton Keynes, Open University Press.
Fiske, J. (1987), *Television Culture*, London, Methuen.
Frenkel, S., Korczynski, M., Shire, K. and Tam, M. (1999), *On the Front Line: Organisation of Work in the Information Economy*, Ithaca, ILR/Cornell University Press.
Frenzen, J., Hirsch, P. and Zerillo, P. (1994), 'Consumption, preferences, and changing lifestyles', in Smelser, N. and Swedberg, R. (eds.), *The Handbook of Economic Sociology*, Princeton, Princeton University Press, pp. 403-425.
Gabriel, Y. and Lang, T. (1995), *The Unmanageable Consumer: Contemporary Consumption and its Fragmentations*, London, Sage.
Galbraith, K. (1979), *The Affluent Society*, Harmondsworth, Penguin.
Gutek, B. (1995) *The Dynamics of Service*, San Francisco, Jossey-Bass.
Hammer, M. and Champy, J. (1995), *Reengineering the Corporation: A Manifesto for Business Revolution*, London, Nicholas Brealey Publishing.
Hayek, F. (1944), *The Road to Serfdom*, Chicago, University of Chicago Press.
Hoffman, J. (1998), *Sovereignty*, Milton Keynes, Open University Press.
Holtgrewe, U. (2001), 'Recognition, intersubjectivity and service work: Labour conflicts in call centres', *Industrielle Beziehungen, The German Journal of Industrial Relations*, Vol. 8(1), pp. 37-54.
Kerst, C. and Holtgrewe, U. (2001), *Flexibility and customer orientation: Where does the slack come from?*, paper presented at the Work, Employment and Society conference at the University of Nottingham, September.
Klein, N. (2000), *No Logo*, London, Flamingo.
Knights, D. and Morgan, G. (1990), 'Management control in sales forces', *Work, Employment and Society*, Vol. 4(3), pp. 369-89.
Korczynski, M. (2001a), 'The contradictions of service work: The call centre as customer-oriented bureaucracy', in Sturdy A., Grugulis I. and Willmott H. (eds.), *Customer Service*, Basingstoke, MacMillan and Palgrave.
Korczynski, M. (2001b), *Human Resource Management in Service Work*, Basingstoke, MacMillan and Palgrave.
Korczynski, M., Shire, K., Frenkel, S. and Tam, M. (2000), 'Service work in consumer capitalism: Customers, control and contradictions', *Work, Employment and Society*, Vol. 14(4), pp. 669-687.
Kreitzman, L. (1999), *The 24 Hour Society*, London, Profile Books.
Lasch, C. (1980), *The Culture of Narcissism*, London, Abacus.
Lee, M. (2000), *The Consumer Society Reader*, Oxford, Blackwell.
Leidner, R. (1993), *Fast Food, Fast Talk*, Berkeley, University of California Press.
Levi-Strauss, C. (1963), *Structural Anthropology*, New York, Basic Books
Lynch, J. (1992), *The Psychology of Customer Care*, Basingstoke, MacMillan.
Middleton, R. (1990), *Studying Popular Music*, New York, Norton.
Millgram, S. (1974), *Obedience to Authority*, London, Tavistock.
Miller, D. (1995), 'Consumption as the vanguard of history', in Miller, D. (ed.), *Acknowledging Consumption*, London, Routledge, pp. 1-57.
Packard, V. (1957), *The Hidden Persuaders*, Harmondsworth, Penguin.
Ritzer, G. (1999), *Enchanting a Disenchanted World*, California, Pine Forge Press.

Ritzer, G. (2000), *The McDonaldization of Society: An Investigation into the Changing Character of Contemporary Life*, Newbury Park, CA., Pine Forge Press.

Rosenthal, P, Peccie, R. and Hill, S. (2001), 'Academic discourses of the customer', in Sturdy, A., Grugulis, I. and Willmott, H. (eds.), *Customer Service*, Basingstoke, MacMillan, pp. 18-37.

Sturdy, A. (2001), 'Servicing societies?', in Sturdy, A., Grugulis, I., and Willmott, H. (eds.), *Customer Service*, Basingstoke, MacMillan, pp. 1-17.

Thompson, A. (1977), *Economics of the Firm*, Englewood Cliffs, N.J., Prentice Hall.

Whyte, W.F. (1946), 'When workers and customers meet', in Whyte W.F. (ed.), *Industry and Society*, New York, McGraw-Hill, pp. 123-147.

Williams, R. (1982), *Dream Worlds: Mass Consumption in Late Nineteenth-Century France*, Berkeley, University of California Press.

Williamson, O.E. (1985), *The Economic Institutions of Capitalism*, New York, The Free Press.

Wolf, M. (1999), *The Entertainment Economy*, New York, Times Books.

Zeithaml, V. and Bitner, M. (1996), *Services Marketing*, New York, McGraw-Hill.

Chapter 10

Quality Time and the 'Beautiful Call'[1]

Catrina Alferoff and David Knights

Introduction

The transfer of customer service work to dedicated call centres is now routine practice for many service and (albeit fewer) manufacturing sector organisations. The redistribution of customer service activities from local retail outlets or branches to large telecomputing centres has followed an earlier concentration of back office processing work within financial services and this has spread widely across all sectors of the economy. In the UK alone, the call centre industry now employs more people than the coal, steel and automotive sectors combined. Between 1997 and 2002 Datamonitor predicted a growth of approximately 120,000 agent positions in the UK call centre market, extending from around one per cent to around two and a half per cent of total employment in five years (1998).[2] Call centres employ large numbers of staff arranged in serried ranks and glued to their headphones in personal tele-computing workstations. Early commentators on this radical change in the workplace have centred attention on the heavy discipline and surveillance facilitated by the power of the technology to monitor and drive staff to ever increasing levels of production in these modern sweatshops (Fernie and Metcalf, 1997). More recently, the crude character of these attempts to liken call centres to 19th century sweatshops or satanic mills have been challenged (Taylor and Bain, 1999).

There is no question that work for many call centre employees is highly standardised and routinised because of tight job designs and technological

---

[1] We acknowledge funding from the ESRC Grant Number R022250186. We thank participants of the conference which preceded this volume (see introduction) for their constructive criticisms.
[2] Estimates of the growth of call centres and other statistics on call centre work are notoriously unreliable and expensive to obtain. This is because until the government employment statistics are adjusted to meet the change in categorisation expected to be late in 2001, private surveys produced largely for commercial purposes are the only source.

surveillance (Frenkel et al., 1998; Hutchinson et al., 2000).[3] It is also often emotionally exhausting as a result of, amongst other things, a quotidian round of time-measured calls and performance pressures (Deery, Iverson and Walsh, 2001). Call centre managers in certain organisations are clearly prepared to deploy the new technology coercively to intensify work (Fernie and Metcalf, 1997) regardless of the quality outcomes. But faced with increased competition, poor performance, high labour turnover and low morale, some call centres have been forced to re-evaluate their operations, to promote conditions that are more conducive to advancing quality customer service. They have recognised the tension between quantity and quality and the danger of undermining customer service by concentrating exclusively on output performance. It would be to oversimplify the argument to assert that this represents a break with strict systems of control and surveillance, since the call centres may attempt to monitor quality customer responses as rigidly as it had previously monitored call-handling times (Alferoff and Knights, 2001). Tape recording the service encounter facilitates such close monitoring, for, as with Bentham's panopticon (Foucault, 1979), the sheer awareness of the recording and that it may be examined in detail by management is sufficient to ensure considerable self-discipline. However, on the downside for management, it is a low-trust strategy that can reinforce the very work-to-rule behaviour that customer service needs to eradicate.

What we find is that certain organisations vacillate between the extremes of coercive control through strict time-discipline and its relaxation in the pursuit of a 'better' service (Knights and Odih, 2000). In the process, they create a level of indeterminacy and ambiguity (May 1999) around the quality discourse that opens up a field of possibilities for resistance. In this chapter, we seek to argue that, within certain well-defined limits, staff may resist management controls partly by transforming their work into a more aesthetic, pleasurable and creative experience. Staff in our case study research at Commsco CSC (a pseudonym) had developed a discourse that envisaged achieving 'quality-time' in what they perceived as an almost perfect telephone encounter with the customer. These might be seen as 'joyful discoveries' (De Certeau, 1988, p. xix) whereby the 'weak' can begin to win tactical victories over the 'strong' (ibid.). On the other hand, for the call centre manager, aesthetic achievements were not so much about the use of informal skills that staff had gained over time; rather the manager was more concerned with correct performance of the expected call structure

---

[3] Staff may also experience undue pressures as both a condition and consequence of attempting 'to find and suggest ways of improving service levels and organisational effectiveness' (Hutchinson et al., 2000, p. 71).

that involved four stages – scripted openings, specified content, recap and closure. It seems that management was so single-mindedly focused on control that it was incapable of seeing how the aesthetic resistance of staff offered a solution to its problem that was almost perfect in its capacity to economise on power. For it traded on the desire of staff to perform to the best of their abilities, a performance that management control was likely to disrupt. However, managers find it almost impossible not to intervene in an attempt to standardise and manage knowledge and routinise organisational practice. They do so in ways that deny the significance of staff wisdom, gained through experience, in this case through interactions with customers, and this may well encounter ambivalence, or even resistance from employees who take pride in their work as an aesthetic project. Resistance is then much more likely to take a disruptive character.

The potential for what one of the managers termed the 'beautiful call' rests to a very large extent on the particular focus and conception of time. A preoccupation with chronological time fails to take account of the diversity of temporal repertoires organisations accumulate over their histories (Whipp, 1994). Bureaucratic and standardised systems of monitoring, surveillance and control that lead to work intensification (Sewell and Wilkinson, 1992) depend on a linear sequencing of time that is frequently disrupted by the demands of call centre work. Consequently managing a call centre as if it were a linear process is likely to result in some difficulties.

The chapter is organised as follows: We begin by providing a brief introduction to the case study company and the methods deployed in the research. The chapter then focuses on the introduction of a quality customer response initiative that followed from consultation with call centre staff after a day of industrial action. What is addressed here is the tension that derives from the twin concerns of management to measure performance and maintain or improve service quality. This is manifested in an almost permanent oscillation between excessive management controls through targets and time measured performance and their relaxation as the organisation shifts from output to service quality crises and back again. In discussing this tension between task-driven output performance and process-centred service quality, we occasionally complement the data from this case study by drawing on material from other research in which we have been involved. This section is succeeded by an analysis of the limited assertions of identity on the part of staff who resist the time constraints and pressures that management seeks to impose on the service or sales encounter. Drawing on the discourse of quality and aspirations for 'the beautiful call', this resistance is difficult for management to counter. Finally, in a discussion and conclusion, the issue of emotional labour is examined critically before we conclude that call centre staff, in our case study, are not merely passive victims of management preoccupations with controlling them. Rather they engage in a variant of what de Certeau (1988, p. 25) describes as 'la peruque' – where a worker

> 'takes pleasure in finding a way to create gratuitous products whose sole purpose is to signify his (sic) own capabilities through his *work* and to confirm his solidarity with his fellow workers or his family by *spending* his time in this way.' (ibid. orig. emphasis)

'La Peruque' is not dissimilar from what Gouldner (1951) described as the 'indulgency pattern' where management turned a blind eye to workers using limited amounts of company time and materials for personal and private purposes. By contrast, while pleasurable and inspiring, the aesthetic work of our call centre staff was extremely beneficial for the company in terms of producing high quality service.

The Case Study: Context and Methods

Commsco is a national telecommunications organisation operating across a variety of fields both nationally and internationally. Commsco call centre operations encompass both in-bound customer services and outbound telemarketing. Commsco CSC deals with inbound service, sales and billing enquiries, mainly to residential customers. Two hundred advisors are employed at the Commsco Customer Service Call Centre where the research took place. Staff are divided into 3 streams as follows:

- dual-skilled sales and services helpdesk staff, employed on full-time or part-time company contracts
- single-skilled agency staff who deal with billing traffic and a small group of calls
- access employees who deal with other service providers that lease telephony products, or services from Commsco.

Of the approximately 200 advisors in all at this call centre, 120 have company contracts of some sort. The remaining 80 are contracted through employment agencies. Some helpdesk staff with extra training spend up to 80 per cent of their time processing letters and other documents for their team, but all advisors spend some time online.

The case study took place over four months from late spring to early autumn 2000, with frequent visits sometimes for a few hours, or full days. In-depth, unstructured interviews were audio-taped with 30 customer service advisors. In most cases these were one-to-one, but these interviews also included two group discussions comprising one group of three: One coach and two CSAs and another group of five CSAs. The call centre manager was interviewed twice, once at an early stage in the quality pilot and a second time at its conclusion. Three team managers and a further three coaches and the resources manager participated in the research. In order to gain insight into the underlying industrial relations background, the on-site union convenor was also interviewed. Since the organisation provided unmonitored, open access, the researcher was also able to spend time observing the conduct of activities and chatting to individuals in the restaurant and smoking room. Documents on the new roles and responsibilities of coaches and team managers were made available as were the instruments used in remote and internal monitoring and weekly performance statistics. A request for documents on induction and quality training was refused. Prior to the research, a strike had taken place and the union convenor provided extensive documentation on its development, its resolution and outcomes. Triangulation (Denzin, 1978) of documentary materials, analysis of transcriptions and field notes provided the rich data on which this chapter draws.

The Quality Centre Pilot

A few months before this research, Commsco customer services advisors had taken industrial action over a number of issues including recruitment, employee development and the intensification of work that they were presently experiencing. This, they claimed, worked against their ability to deliver a quality service to customers. In this chapter we focus on only the issue of work intensification. At the time of the one-day strike, CSAs had complained about the rigid and stressful call-handling time. This is a typical remark on the pressure experienced by staff at the time:

> 'I was under a great lot of pressure because calls were continually coming in. Continuous! And no sooner had you put your finger on there, you see there? There was another call coming in. There was no breaks. Sometimes – you can do that for a couple of hours, you know, mornings or afternoons, but other types of calls were dropping out – you know? You do have a little break 30 seconds, or 15 seconds between each call, but you, literally, soon as you finished a call there was another call coming in.' (Male CSA)

In response to worker dissatisfaction on the pressure of call-handling times, Commsco commenced a series of consultative sessions with customer service advisors at sites in various parts of the country while negotiations continued on the other issues. The 'Quality Centre' pilot at Commsco CSC was the outcome of the consultative process. Shortly before this research, therefore, a shift in orientation from a 'task' oriented approach to productivity towards a 'process' concern with the quality of the service encounter had occurred. This is part of what was described earlier as an oscillation between 'tough' management controls and their relaxation that we discovered in other cases studies, and especially at Brand Name Financial Services (Knights, Calvey and Odih, 1999). Here is an excerpt revealing the shift in the direction of relaxation from one of our respondents in that study.

> 'The attitudes towards that [i.e. pressure] from management is a lot better than it used to be. To be very honest you were always taught to be aware of the wallboards, "watch the walls" "X number of calls are queuing". At one point supervisors used to walk round which was very annoying. You'd be taking calls and they would be walking round to check that every detail was correct. I mean if somebody was in call work for a couple of minutes bit too long, they'd say have you got a problem... There was a lot of pressure then, always being told how many calls how long they've been waiting... Now it is more relaxed. The wallboards are strategically placed so that you can see them wherever you are. But you don't watch them constantly; well I don't because you also got it on the console. As long as you're aware, to now and again check your console if you are perhaps finishing something off or you have gone unavailable into call work, just keep an eye in there... But there is not the pressure there that there used to be. They have relaxed a lot more and I think the staff are grateful for that. Because we can only take one call at a time[Senior Customer Adviser].' (ibid., p. 7)

The process approach reflects a concern with the social context in which measurement takes place and seeks to complement quantitative calculations of performance with qualitative support of staff to improve customer service. It contrasts with the earlier approach to the service encounter where a much 'harder' preoccupation with results and performance output was maintained (ibid., p. 13). For the duration of the Quality Centre trial, the volume of calls taken by the call centre became less of an issue as calls were only taken from one regional database in order to facilitate the evaluation process. Call-handling times were extended from the pre-existing 300 seconds to 360, but 'wrap times'[4] remained at 75 seconds as the stated aim of the programme was to reduce repeat calls by giving CSAs more time to deal with customer requirements within the call, rather than at its conclusion. Along with this relaxation of call-handling times, new participative structures had been instituted – weekly coach-led 'huddles', monthly team meetings, a staff-led 'Care Forum' and occasional team social events. To counteract employee complaints about the previous bullying style of management, a more rounded approach to performance appraisal had been introduced covering both personal elements of self-management and customer effectiveness and business elements of revenue-generation.

Restructuring the workforce provided the context for introducing an extra layer of employee support in the form of coaches drawn from the ranks of the more experienced customer service advisors and some de-intensification of work. It also involved team-based performance measurement and a new integrative style of management. It is clear that the quality initiative met some of the most pressing employee demands that had emerged during the industrial action, but ironically, this was at the cost of increased surveillance and monitoring. Whereas staff had been accustomed to managers listening-in to their calls for two hours per month, the success of the quality initiative was evaluated by statistics gathered internally by managers and coaches and externally by the 'quality customer response' team. Added to these measures, data from telephone surveys of customer complaints were also presented on a weekly basis. Even though, the actual time that these groups listened-in to any one CSA's calls may not have varied, the very fact that this could happen at whim proved unsettling, especially given the competitive conditions between teams that had been fostered by management:

> 'I think the issue is with the quality centre initiative, it's got erh, we get a quality call review score and the guys from () and the girls down there, they listen to the calls and then they score it and then we get a team score and it's like anything, if we get a team score and we want to be competitive we want to have the best team score that we possibly can. And, we get lots of information back from them and then we talk about that information all the time. So, that may create the impression that they're listening more than they are. But, actually, they're not listening as much as our people think that they are.' (Team Manager)

---

[4] Wrap time refers to the amount of time allowed to complete any administration before moving to the next customer call in the queue.

Here is an example of panopticon-like discipline where management are happy to let staff think that surveillance is greater than is actually the case. In the belief that management are listening-in, staff are self-disciplined in their performance. The team managers are just preoccupied with having 'the best team score that we possibly can' but in the absence of knowledge to the contrary, staff cannot but think that surveillance is continuous. Quality can be constructed as a method of organising or an end product and the tensions between these two constructions are reflected in the organisation's attempt to produce effects on both fronts. Management may have to cede control over some elements of 'linear-time' output performance whilst retaining bureaucratic measures over what has been variously described as 'interaction-time' (Lewis & Weigart, 1990), or the 'process-time' (Davies, 1994) involved in delivering the desired 'quality customer response'. Management strategy, however, does not evolve in a continuous and progressive manner for the pattern of development is most commonly iterative and uncertain (Whipp, 1994, p. 107). The consequences of this stop and start process of change are often highly precarious as decisions are deeply influenced by the social and political texture of the organisation. The change in focus from a regime that prioritised quantity over quality was not without tension, as is demonstrated in the debate amongst team managers and the coaching manager during the managers' forum.

At the start of the forum, the centre manager announces that this is:

'Part of the sector rollout to refocus coaching back on customer satisfaction, because we are all a little bit nervous about what is happening to customer satisfaction results. And I think we've seen more pain here particularly on our complaints management.'

The aim then was to develop sharing between managers and coaches and to work on:

'What we are actually doing on our calls and then how we move on and coach on what things we are looking for in that beautiful call that delivers customer satisfaction.' (Centre Manager)

The whole group then listens to two staged calls and the discussion commences with the ways in which a feedback session might go with an advisor in order to bring about desired behaviours. The quality control officer starts the discussion, '*it should be positive*', the centre manager responds by emphasising conformance to the internal pro-forma used by coaches post the listening-in sessions: '*the first thing in coaching sessions with tracker notes*[5] *is to paint a picture, ask the advisor what they want to work on'*. Model one[6] team manager poses a general question on *'if you would go in negative?'* To this the coaching manager responds: *'I'm not going to clutch at straws to give positive feedback'*. The centre manager notices this, *'we have an issue with not giving positive feedback, we need a standard approach – how far to go putting positive feedback in'*. The model one team manager (who adopts a somewhat hands-off style of management, possibly because his team includes a high proportion of experienced CSAs dealing with off-line processing, complaints and access for other service providers) takes issue with the coaching manager on this negative approach to giving feedback, saying that he, *'thinks his way will lead to the advisor showing disinterest to coaching'*. The coaching manager defends his position, *'if the advisor respects you, he will take it'*. The model one manager finishes this antagonistic conversation by saying; *'you never get respect if you go in negative'*.

As the workshop progressed this lack of unity on performance and its necessary elements continued with the coaching manager emphasising the significance of hard statistics derived from customer surveys carried out nationally, and the model one team manager arguing for the softer elements of customer care.

> 'You can get statistics to do anything you want. What does performance mean to the CSA? Customer service is a perception, I think the whole lot of it is thrown in, but it doesn't go very well together because, on the one hand you've got the customer you want to go away happy, and a group of people you want to go away happy (CSAs), but on the other side you've got all the business needs – you know? What you've got to understand is that the two don't go very well together.' (Team Manager)

As we have intimated, the national process of involving CSAs in the design stage of the quality customer service initiative created expectations that it would deliver a level of quality-time to their interactions with customers. On the other hand, for the centre manager conducting this forum, the 'beautiful call', was a matter of changing recalcitrant behaviours on the part of CSAs to ensure that they conform to structured and measurable instruments and, in particular, the four-part customer interaction script. Monitoring correct performance involved both internal and external groups 'listening-in' to service encounters and compiling statistics that were then

---

[5] A standardised format used by coaches and managers when giving feedback after a session of 'listening-in' to calls.
[6] For the duration of the trial four experimental team models were in operation with different combinations of mixed or single-skilled teams.

used as the basis for the quality trial. The need for further training to change recalcitrant behaviours was one objective of the coaching but there was little opportunity for staff to engage in the formulation of the problem since management insisted that the four-part (i.e. scripted openings, content, recap, and closure) call structure be rigidly adhered to. Eventually constructive resistance on the part of staff to the four-part structure had some effect (see below p. 194).

The title of this chapter 'Quality Time and the Beautiful Call' is, to say the least, highly ambiguous. It reflects the ways in which the discourse of time-measurement and its relationship to customer care and its inherent quality controls became a site of struggle in Commsco CSC. We wish to underline the contested nature of the discourse of time and its usage in the social relations involved in the delivery of customer services by the different groups. It could have been either quality-time and the beautiful call, or quality, time and the beautiful call, both at different stages in the call centre's recent history and for different groups within the organisation.

The existing management strategy that prioritised call volume and time scarcity proved to be self-defeating for this organisation. A report by Reed (2000) has argued that '(o)ver emphasising "hard" measures of performance is still standard in the telephony industry, (e)specially statistics generated by the ACD on call volumes, agent activity and centre productivity'.[7] The Reed report acknowledges that, 'companies that aim to evolve from a cost base towards a customer focus will find the use of such measures both insufficient and tend to disguise many underlying problems' (ibid., p. 4). In our case study, this was reflected in the persistence of a low-trust management style as demonstrated in the extreme dependence on monitoring and surveillance. The on-site union convenor describes the ways in which time-based performance was used competitively by Commsco Customer Service Centres managers nationally.

> 'We had a different manager you see. Different managers have different approaches. But generally, across the country, the resource-based climate encourage managers to actually, they were given statistics and performance and, therefore it drives managers to get as much performance and in a sense there's a deep tradition to get better results. So, by competing – so one centre will do the best in this and another centre will do the best on that. So managers, obviously, if they can get the best results for their centre, presumably they get some sort of reward or bonus.' (Commsco CSC Union Convener)

Alongside the management forum, a series of site briefings also tackled the problem of meeting company objectives by delivering the structured call

---

[7] By kind permission of Financial Times Retail and Consumer and the author.

correctly. Although purporting to be participative, they were essentially instructional and as such were not entirely successful. Moderate further improvement was made, but the programme did not reach the targets expected. The weekly statistics gathered by the remote site demonstrated that CSAs were not delivering the structured call in desired format. A coach conducting a 'crèche' for non-conforming CSAs attributed this to:

> 'They don't like it to be scripted- it's more like, "you're asking us to more or less use a script..." The problem with it, well, I've heard people comment that they think it is too much pressure and if they don't do it, it won't be brought in.' (Coach)

Identity and Resistance

Prescriptive, managerialist texts on quality promote the benefits of agile, anti-bureaucratic organisations by recommending a series of performance control and human resource management measures to achieve these aims. These generally include some elements of devolved autonomy accompanied by the institution of quality controls (Crosby, 1979), or Peters and Waterman's loose-tight properties (1974). These are intended to minimise defects by means of statistical monitoring, flattened hierarchies, teamworking, entrepreneurship, culture management and a customer satisfaction orientation; directed both internally and externally to the organisation (see Peters and Waterman, 1974). The questionable assumption underlying such programmes is that culture can be readily manipulated.[8] There is a naive belief that members of the organisation will thereby begin to derive their sense of meaning and understanding solely from the new cultural discourse without reference to history or processes of social interaction. Despite extreme claims to the contrary (Hammer and Champy, 1990), the past cannot simply be removed or eradicated (Grint and Case, 2000); more accurately, the past and present serve to reconstitute one another and remnants of old struggles will be recovered or reconstructed in present contests and conflicts (McCabe, 1996). Seduced by guru panaceas, management often fail to recognise this. Quality programmes are seen as a novel means of control through culture management, by way of the construction of an 'ideal', self-managed worker, sensitive to the dictates of the market (Tuckman, 1994). There is little challenge to the view that cultural

---

[8] This assumption has been severely challenged by Smircich (1983) when she argues that culture is something that an organisation *is* not that it *has*. Therefore culture cannot be fine-tuned like an engine in a racing car.

transformations can erode individual autonomy and reconstruct worker initiative in a manner that (again) allows management to determine outcomes (ibid.).

In the initial stages of this innovative programme of change, employees welcomed what they initially perceived to be its beneficial elements especially as this had not been a unidirectional top-down imposition of change by management. Early enthusiasm, however, began to fade as the pressure of increased monitoring and standardisation of the call structure reduced the personal element of their interactions with customers:

> 'I've always felt for me to, like, or for people to be different. Because they are and that's the way it is, so I don't know if I like the idea of it all being scripted. Like, if I ring a company myself and go through customer services, sometimes I don't like hearing them say the same thing, you know, when they say, "thanks for calling British Gas". I don't want to sound like a robot, that's all it is. I don't want customers to tell that I'm saying what I've been told to say. As long as it comes naturally it's not so much of a problem, but...' (CSA)

Staff complaints about the 'robotisation' of the service encounter eventually forced management albeit reluctantly to make some concessions on the structure of the call. Basically staff were given much more autonomy in the second content part of the four-part structure as long as they complied with the other three: scripted openings, recap, and closure. Partly this was because the coaching manager realised the old adage that while you take a horse to water you can't make it drink. As he put it:

> 'It's very much down to, you can only coach someone so much, you know, and then it's down to whether somebody wants to be coached, whether somebody wants to try harder, or are they just happy with the performance they are just doing.' (Coaching Manager)

Yet as the following team manager indicates, the company deplores the efforts of CSAs to exercise their local knowledge of the customer base in making decisions on the products they will promote:

> 'Actually, they'll promote budget accounts because it's free and easy the customer to pay. I think if we look at the National results – every time we produce a league table of national results for budget accounts, you'd find () at the top. It's this perception, rented products, they think it's good to rent round here, so every time we have competitions to drive rentals up we do really well, but when we switch round to selling phones, we'll sell hundreds at £22.99, £25.99, £29.99, which is good, but we don't sell so many in the 70, 80, 90, £100 bracket...'

Management were unhappy about staff using their knowledge of customers in the local market to pre-judge what they could afford. While probably correct in their assessments of customers, this resistance to the company drive for increased profits was unacceptable to management.

As Strati (1999) argues, the organisation that we know has an ephemeral quality that we can only see in action, in the skills and know-how of its members. By drawing on the skills they derive in their interactions with customers, individual CSAs work on the knowledge they gain and develop a body of knowledge. This is a complex combination of tacit and explicit skills and of formal materials and informal experiences. Despite the current faith in knowledge management,[9] it is difficult for organisations to formalise and thereby transfer this knowledge from one party to another. But this does not stop staff from using this experience and knowledge to resist management control. The quality programme provided them with ammunition to legitimise their resistance. For they could turn the discourse of quality back on management, arguing that the imposition of rigid frameworks on the customer response was not only experienced as de-humanising for themselves but also for the customer. Managers could then be criticised for a failure to deliver on their promises of quality. CSAs contrasted the formal and bureaucratic preoccupation with meeting targets and other measures with what they (and in principle the quality programme) considered more important – giving good customer service:

> 'And what you've got to really consider is what is better – to hit all these statistics so the company looks good on paper, or to have the company having a good reputation by word of mouth, by reputation, because the advisors are prepared to take the time and not just rush them off, which I think a lot of people have generally found with customer service centres generally. People generally know that they work with call handling time, more well informed people certainly do, and know if you're trying to rush them off, get rid of them, and it's so important not to do that, of course.' (CSA)

> 'I feel that the personality has been taken away from the job. I've been in Commsco quite a while and I was in helpdesk when it was just sales and that was predominantly taking sales just in the local area, so you're getting local experience and you dealt with local engineers. Obviously, the technology was a little bit slower in them days. But you were doing areas with people that you knew or could build up a relationship.' (CSA)

---

[9] Knowledge management is the latest of a long line of innovations promoted by gurus and consultants and largely concerns the formalisation of culturally embedded, tacit and localised knowledge through such information technology devices as the intranet or chat-rooms.

Those commentators (e.g. Taylor and Bain, 1999; Bain and Taylor, 2000) who perceive subjects as ineluctably harnessed to the discipline of goal-oriented, 'linear time' mechanisms are inclined to view resistance in one or other of two contrasting ways. Either it is collectively organised through a union or it is an individualistic form of opting-out. However, labour can deploy more creative strategies in order to escape the time constraints, discipline and surveillance of call centre regimes, including either de-territorialising the workspace, or subverting the work process (Knights and McCabe, 1998). When the focus is predominantly about protecting one, or a series of identities as a way of appearing competent, resistance often takes the form not of an escape from, so much as an escape into work (Sturdy, 1999). Indeed, such constructive forms of resistance can occur at all levels of the organisation and may frequently involve the criticism of management by employees and other managers for their failure to comply with the internal norms and goals of the organisation. (Knights and Odih, 2000, p. 10-11). This form of resistance often encapsulates a projection on to significant others (especially managers) of a failure to behave competently, or deliver what has been promised. As such, it is relatively risk-free since it is resistance that can claim its legitimacy from the organisation and its proclaimed objectives (ibid.). The resistance of CSAs was then primarily targeted at managements' preoccupation with retaining a rigid control over staff and the service encounter. However, the majority of staff linked the pleasure they gained in their work to the more processual elements of the interaction with the customer and viewed this conflictual period in the organisation's history as a time when:

> 'You're meeting the company needs, but it's not to say that you're actually meeting the customer's needs. In addition, you're just giving yourself that much more pressure, really. Umm, because you know yourself you're not giving the customer the service they would like, or that you would like to give them. At the same time, you are trying to meet the company's targets. Bit like a pig in the middle.' (Female CSA)

Discussion and Conclusion

Service personnel are situated at the point where the organisation and customer meet; whether in a face-to-face encounter, or in the ether of the inbound telephone call, they represent the organisation to the customer. The encounter, therefore, contains an element of uncertainty since how the customer participates in the encounter can never be entirely predicted. This gives the encounter a dynamic and emergent quality and the way it is managed is crucial as it can affect the customer's perception of the product or service (Ashforth and Humphrey, 1993). Self-management in the customer-focused service sector is argued by some, therefore, as including an element of dramaturgy that is exploitative in its impact on the individual's emotional states and well-being. It involves the employee in inducing, or suppressing, feelings in order to sustain an interaction in the encounter. This can be at a cost of estranging the worker 'from an aspect of self - either the body or the margins of the soul - that is *used* to do the work' (Hochschild, 1983, p 7). Such literature tends to be critical of the damage or cost to the subject of this exploitation of emotional labour. This commercialisation of emotional labour involves the purchase, or transfer of an experience in which the quality of the social interaction is vital - whether or not it is formally part of the exchange (Filby, 1992). But the range of acceptability in certain service roles enables agents to embrace the role and to project at least some of an 'authentic self' into it and thereby, emotional labour may facilitate self-expression (Ashforth and Humphrey, 1993, p. 94-95). For this reason, employees may be perfectly willing to draw on their emotional labour as well as their technical skills in service encounters. But any task that involves a social communication is difficult to conduct independently of some emotional energy, so staff hardly have a choice. In some senses, we would argue, the emotional labour literature is misplaced for at least three reasons. First, employees would be more unreal or 'alienated' if they were to try and communicate independently of their emotions. Second, in certain contexts and for some purposes, staff are able to express themselves and a sense of their work as an aesthetic experience, partly at least through emotional labour. And third, their emotional commitment to the activity can serve as a source of resistance to management's attempts to routinise the work and thereby render it more tedious.

Emotional labour arguments tend to be essentialist with regard to the 'natural' expression of human emotion that is violated by its exploitation by employers for instrumental purposes. If the humanistic ideology that reflects and reproduces these essentialist views of human nature is rejected, the emotional labour thesis is seen as little more than romantic idealism. As we have suggested, service staff may find their work relationships with customers quite satisfying as long as they are not constrained or condemned to behave in a scripted way where their emotional labour is readily exposed as dissembled or false. Indeed, far from wishing to resist deploying their emotions, the staff in our case study sought only to resist any controls that would constrain or prevent them from developing their relationships with customers as an emotional and aesthetic experience.

This raises two further issues, firstly, emotional labour arguments are unable to tell us how knowledge discourses come to be changed and modified over time, since their preoccupation is on preserving privacy around the emotions. 'All in all, a private emotional system has been subordinated to commercial logic' (Hochschild, 1983, p. 186). What seems to be ignored or overlooked here is that power can only be exercised over 'free' subjects that are faced with a field of possibilities (Foucault, 1986, p. 221). That being so, it cannot be assumed from some idealistic position concerning the privacy of human emotions that workers are violated by emotional labour. Secondly, emotional labour arguments tend to suggest that individuals have the choice of 'smiling and not meaning it', or 'smiling and sometimes meaning it'; that is, behavioural compliance or ambivalence (Sturdy, 1998, p. 36). Where we know that employees are behaving as they do out of simple compliance to the normative controls of employers, we may suggest an element of cynicism. But this would be a projection based on a distinction between a supposed 'real' self as opposed to a 'false' or enacted self that if it ever could, can no longer, be sustained. As Sturdy (1998, p. 46) asks rhetorically, 'to what extent does this inform a receptivity or relativism towards normative controls?' If, as has been argued, cultural norms of politeness and gender roles (Sturdy, 1998) or discourses on the sovereignty of the customer (du Gay, 1996) act as pre-suppositions of identity formation in the customer service organisation, is there any space for resistance?

Throughout this chapter we have been suggesting that staff have been highly resistant to the rigid scripting and control of their service encounter work but this resistance has not so much challenged as endorsed the norms of the quality programme regarding service quality. In short, they have embraced the identity of serving the customer not just as a compliant response to management demands but as part of an aesthetic project for the self. Following Foucault (1988, p. 18):

> 'technologies of the self' ... 'permit individuals to effect by their own means or with the help of others a certain number of operations on their own bodies and souls, thoughts, conduct and way of being, so as to transform themselves in order to attain a certain state of happiness, purity, wisdom, perfection, or immortality.'

Indeed they have resisted management demands when they have been perceived to disrupt these technologies of the self and their identification with the customer.

On this topic of role embracement and identification, Knights and Morgan (1993) observe that the corollary of the construction of service recipients as customers is the construction of self-disciplining employees devoted to delivering customer services, acting in accord with their company's strategic aims and objectives. Exemplifying this, a couple of the more experienced CSAs interviewed in this case study chronicled their experiences when, in the capacity of customer, they have made calls to utilities in order to compare the presentation to the service with that they themselves delivered at work. In this sense the CSAs are treating their work as an aesthetic performance – or skillful knowing (Polanyi, 1962) that has to be continually practiced and improved even by learning off the job, as it were.

Skillful knowing arises from the use of maxims, or subsidiaries developed by mastery, internalising of moral values, or apprenticeship. As in the use of a hammer, or in learning to ride a bicycle, we would find it difficult to explain the process. So with the tools essential for service work, it is only when we understand the framework that we can put the knowledge into action as this quote from a customer service advisor suggests:

> 'I mean when I first came to (Commsco CSC), it was a job and it was no more than that – umm it paid my wages and that was it. And then I wanted to go a bit further, I was thinking "well I'm earning so much that I want to earn more", instead of just being a job I started then to make a bit more of an effort to understand things and, obviously, when you been here a while you pick up a lot of things. Sometimes you'll explain things and you'll go on and on a bit, you'll hear somebody else explain it and you'll think "yes, that's good, I'll use that in the future". I think a lot of that goes on and if you take things in you can use them.'

By using the terminology of 'the beautiful call that delivers customer satisfaction', at both management fora and site briefings the centre manager created a linguistic artifact that appealed (Gagliardi, 1990) to individuals engaged in the process of transforming their work into an aesthetic experience. As we have shown, there was a considerable discrepancy in the usage of the term, since beauty for staff was associated with freedom and self-expression whereas for management it was compliance with the regulations they believed were the route to perfect customer relations. Despite this, these could be seen as merely different means to the same end as staff were clearly as concerned as management with having good relations with the customer.

Now it is one thing to describe this concern to make of work an aesthetic experience or the telephone call a beautiful event but how do we account for this theoretically? Foucault (1985; 1986) was largely concerned to trace back these technologies of the self to a time in ancient Greece and Rome when 'taking care of oneself' was just as important as 'knowing oneself'. The precedence of the latter in post-existentialist modern western cultures has driven subjects to pursue projects that derive their meaning from securing social confirmation from significant others. Combined with the 'success ethic' and competitive pressures of capitalist relations, this has encouraged if not enforced a preoccupation with an egocentric, narcissistic self. Where this project fails or when its pursuit generates more anxiety than it solves, post-Freudian psychotherapy or other alternative means of 'knowing the self' are on hand that usually have the effect of re-normalising the self and ensuring subjective self-discipline in the pursuit of projects. Yet, what if this account, as Foucault (1988) intimates, is one-sided and that individuals have always sought to make of their work an aesthetic experience that is more responsible to the self and others[10] than to success in the pursuit of competitive material and symbolic status? In negotiating a position outside humanistic or narcissistic explanations of the self we might then want to argue that employees are ordinarily positive and productive in their work. Negative or disruptive behaviour is largely restricted to the way that work is socially organised around hierarchical controls. When such controls interfere with their work as an aesthetic project where they draw past experience into present activity, employees are prepared to exploit the quality discourse to demonstrate the inconsistencies of certain management demands (e.g. scripting, strict time measurements) to the realisation of customer service.

In this chapter, we have indicated how management strategy occurs in a specific environment with its own history (Whipp, 1994). Encroachment into spheres of employee autonomy or discretion, is likely to be met with resistance, although this may not merely take the form of opting out (Bogard, 1996; Bain and Taylor, 1996; Taylor and Bain, 2000). Drawing on the work of Hochschild (1983), some theorists believe there will be resistance to the artificial world in which self is made to perform to order (see Fineman, 1993; Gabriel et al., 2000). But we have found resistance taking the form of staff embracing, or escaping into, their work (Sturdy, 1992; 1996; 1998). This is a comparatively risk free strategy where staff can use aesthetic knowledge (Polanyi, 1962; Strati, 1999) to evaluate and resist the prevailing knowledge regime (Foucault, 1982). They can do this by engaging in a morally righteous critique of the managers who were seen to fail to live up to their responsibilities for service quality (Knights, 2000).

---

[10] In a challenge to the primacy of ontology, Levinas (1986; 1998) argues that moral consciousness in our face to face relation with the other is the condition of consciousness per se and hence of all language and knowledge. They should not, however, be seen as 'subordinate to the *consciousness* we have of the presence of the other, or of his (sic) proximity, or of our community with him, but as a condition of that conscious realisation (Levinas, 1998, p. 6).

References

Alferoff, C. and Knights D. (2001), *Violence at work: The uneasy process of re (form)ing the people-by numbers approach. Captivating hearts, minds and bodies?*, A Paper Presented at the Standing Conference on Organisational Symbolism SCOS XIX 'Organisations, Institutions and Violence', Trinity College, The University of Dublin, 30th June – 4th July.

Ashforth, B.E. and Humphrey, R.H. (1993), 'Emotional Labor in Service Roles', *The Academy of Management Review*, Vol. 18(1), pp. 88-115.

Bain, P. and Taylor, P. (2000), 'Entrapped by the electronic panopticon? Worker resistance in the call centre', *New Technology, Work and Employment*, Vol. 15(1), pp. 1-8.

Bogard, W. (1996), *The Simulation of Surveillance: Hypercontrol in Telematic Societies*, Cambridge, Cambridge University Press.

Crosby, P.B. (1979), *Quality is Free*, New York, McGraw Hill.

Datamonitor (1998), *Call Centre Markets in the UK up to 2003*, London, Datamonitor.

Davies, K. (1994), 'The Tensions Between Process Time and Clock Time in Care Work: The example of day nurseries', *Time and Society*, Vol. 3(3), pp. 277-303.

De Certeau, M. (1988), *The Practice of Everyday Life*, University of California Press.

Deery, S., Iverson, R. and Walsh, J. (2001), *Work Relationships in Telephone Call Centres: Understanding Emotional Exhaustion and Employee Withdrawal*, unpublished paper, The Management Centre, University of London.

Delbridge, R., Turnbull, P. and Wilkinson, B. (1992), 'Pushing Back the Frontiers: management control and work intensification under JIT/TQM factory regimes', *New Technology, Work and Employment*, Vol. 7(2), p. 97-106.

Denzin, N.K. (1978), *The research act: A theoretical introduction to sociological methods* (2nd edition), New York, McGraw-Hill.

Du Gay, P. (1996), *Consumption and Identity at Work*, London, Sage.

Filby, M.P. (1992), 'The Figures, The Personality and The Bums: Service Work and Sexuality', *Work, Employment and Society*, Vol. 6(1), pp. 23-42.

Fineman, S. (1993), *Emotion in Organisations*, London, Sage.

Foucault, M. (1979), *Discipline and Punish*, Harmondsworth, Penguin.

Foucault, M. (1979a), *The History of Sexuality Vol. 1*, Harmondsworth, Penguin.

Foucault, M. (1980), 'Two Lectures', in Gordon, C. (ed.), *Michel Foucault, Power Knowledge: Selected Interviews and Other Writings 1972-1977*, Harlow, Harvester Press, pp. 48-108.

Foucault, M. (1985), *The Use of Pleasure*, New York, Pantheon.

Foucault, M. (1986), *The Care of the Self*, New York, Pantheon.

Foucault, M. (1986), 'The Subject and Power', in Dreyfus, H. and Rabinow, P. (eds.), *Michel Foucault: Beyond Structure and Hermeneutics*, Brighton, Harvester Press, pp. 208-226.

Foucault, M. (1988), 'Technologies of the Self', in Martin, L.H., Gutman, H. and Hutton, P.H. (eds.), *Technologies of the Self: A Seminar with Michel Foucault*, Amherst, The University of Massachusetts Press, pp. 16-49.

Frenkel, S., Tam, M., Korczynski, M., and Shire, K. (1998), 'Beyond bureaucracy? Work Organisation in call centres', *The International Journal of Human Resource Management*, Vol. 9(6), pp. 957-979.

Gabriel, Y., Fineman, S. and Sims, D. (2000), *Organising and Organisations*, (2nd Ed.), London, Sage.

Gagliardi, P. (1990), 'Artifacts as Pathways and Remains of Organisational Life', in Gagliardi, P. (ed.), *Symbols and Artifacts: Views of the Corporate Landscape*, Berlin, Walter de Gruyter, pp. 3-38.
Gouldner, A.W. (1951), *Patterns of Industrial Bureaucracy*, London, Routledge & Kegan Paul.
Grint, K. and Case, P. (2000), 'Now Where Were We? BPR Lotus-Eaters and Corporate Amnesia', in Knights, D. and Willmott, H. (eds.), *The Re-engineering Revolution?*, Critical Studies of Corporate Change, London, Sage, pp. 26-49.
Hochschild, A. (1983), *The Managed Heart: Commercialisation of Human Feeling*, Los Angeles, University of California Press.
Hutchinson, S., Purcell, J. and Kinnie, N. (2000), 'Evolving high commitment management and the experience of the RAC call centre', *Human Resource Management Journal*, Vol. 10(1), pp. 63-78.
Jaques, E. (1982), *The Form of Time*, London, Heinamann.
Knights, D. (2000), 'Writing Organisational Analysis into Foucault', forthcoming in Linstead, S. (ed.), *Postmodern Organisations*, London, Sage.
Knights, D. and McCabe, D. (1998), 'What Happens When the Phone Goes Wild? Staff, Stress and Spaces for Escape in a BPR Telephone Banking Regime', *Journal of Management Studies*, Vol. 35(2), pp. 163-194.
Knights, D. and Morgan, G. (1993), 'Organisation theory and Consumption in the Post-Modern Era', *Organisation Studies*, Vol. 14(2), pp. 211-234.
Knights D., Calvey D. and Odih, P. (1999), *Social Managerialism and the Time Disciplined Subject: Quality – Quantity Conflicts in a Call Centre*, 17th Annual International Labour Process Conference, School of Management, University of London, Royal Holloway, 29th – 31st March 1999.
Knights D. and Odih, P. (2000), '"Big Brother is watching you!": Call centre surveillance and the time disciplined subject', presented at the Annual British Sociological Association Conference, Making Time/Marking Time, York University, 17th – 19th April, to be published in Crow, G. and Heath, S. (eds.), *Times in the Making: The Political Economy of Time Change*, Palgrave, forthcoming.
Levinas, E. (1986), *Face to Face with Levinas*, edited by Cohen, R.A., State University of New York Press.
Levinas, E. (1998), *entre nous: Thinking-of-the-Other*, Trans. by Smith, M.B. and Harshaw, B., London, The Athlone Press.
Lewis, J.D. and Weigart, A.J. (1990), 'The Structures and Meanings of Social Time', in Hassard, J. (ed.), *The Sociology of Time*, Basingstoke, MacMillan, pp. 77-101.
McCabe, D. (1996), 'The Best Laid Schemes of 'O': TQM, Strategy, Politics and Power', *New Technology, Work and Employment*, Vol. 11(1), pp. 28-38.
May, T. (1999), 'From Banana Time to Just in Time: Power and Resistance at Work', *Sociology*, Vol. 33(4), pp. 767-783.
Peters, T. and Waterman, R. (1974), *In Search of Excellence*, New York, Harper Row.
Polanyi, M. (1962), *Personal Knowledge: Towards a post-critical philosophy*, London, Routledge & Kegan Paul.
Reed, D. (2000), *Call Centres – The Next Generation: Strategies for evolving from cost base to customer focus*, London, Financial Times, Retail and Consumer.
Rose, N. (1989), *Governing the Soul*, London, Routledge.
Sewell, G. and Wilkinson, B. (1992), 'Empowerment or Emasculation? Shopfloor Surveillance in a Total Quality Organisation', in Blyton, P. and Turnbull, P. (eds.), *Reassessing Human Resource Management*, London, Sage, pp. 97-115.
Smircich, L. (1983), 'Concepts of culture and organisational analysis', *Administrative Science Quarterly*, Vol. 28, pp. 339-359.

Strati, A. (1999), *Organisation and Aesthetics*, London, Sage.
Sturdy, A.(1992), 'Clerical Consent, "Shifting Work" in the Insurance Office', in Sturdy, A., Knights, D. and Willmott, H. (eds.), *Skill and Consent*, London, Routledge, pp.115-148.
Sturdy, A, (1998), 'Customer Care in a Consumer Society: Smiling and Sometimes Meaning It?', *Organisation,* Vol.5(1), pp.27-53.
Taylor, P. and Bain, P. (1999), 'An assembly line in the head: work and employee relations in the call centre', *Industrial Relations Journal*, Vol. 30(2), pp. 111-117.
Tuckman A. (1994), 'The Yellow Brick Road: Total Quality Management and the Restructuring of Organisational Culture', *Organisation Studies*, Vol. 15(5), pp. 727-751.
Whipp, R. (1994), 'A Time to be Concerned: A Position Paper on Time Management', *Time and Society*, Vol. 3(1), pp. 99-115.

Chapter 11

Co-Production in Call Centres: The Workers' and Customers' Contribution

Kerstin Rieder, Ingo Matuschek and Philip Anderson[1]

Call centre work is a form of service employment which is characterised to a considerable extent by interaction between service provider and service recipient. A co-production between both actors is required in order to enable the service to be put into effect. The growing number of studies in the field of service work in the last few years have given rise to an increasing focus on the customer. Among other things it is the part the customer plays in the process of service delivery which is of interest. This goes beyond the limits of the concept of customer orientation. The customer is no longer seen as a passive recipient but as being actively involved. This broadening of perspective requires consideration of preconditions for meaningful co-operation between service provider and customer and of the problems which can arise in service interactions.

The following article attempts an analysis of the process of co-production in call centre work. The point of departure is a case study of call centre agent and customer interactions in the financial services sector. Competence and motivation on the part of the agents and customers involved are highlighted as important preconditions for successful co-production of service work. Further, both actors have to be able to make a correspondence between the content of their interaction and the procedures and rules set by the service organisation. Nonetheless we argue that call centre agents and customers also develop independent personal styles, which can not be completely steered and canalised by the organisation. Our case study illustrates how management attempts to regulate the employee side of service provision (through such instruments as personnel selection and development). Appropriate selection and training of customers on the other hand is not generally an option for companies. How can the preconditions for customers' co-operation in performing service be influenced? The results of

---

[1] For constructive criticism and stimulating discussion we thank Karen Shire, Wolfgang Dunkel, Michael Heinlein, Frank Kleemann, Christoph Klotter, Gertraude Krell, Angela Lutz and G. Günter Voß.

our study indicate that this type of influence is also common, but it happens in an indirect manner, for instance through structuring the conversations of call centre agents with customers. Management justifies its attempts to structure service interactions on the basis of principles like 'customer orientation' and 'efficiency'. We question the extent to which these principles create a basis for an active contribution on the part of the customer in service provision. We suggest an alternative to managerial attempts to shape interactions in the extension of principles of humanised work organisation onto the 'work' of the customer.

In this essay we first briefly discuss the co-production of service interactions in the context of previous research about service interactions and the role of the customer. We then present evidence from a case study of a call centre in the financial services sector. The empirical analysis of transcribed service interactions is the basis for a conceptualisation of four types of service interactions. In the conclusion we discuss the preconditions for co-production of service work and options available to influence service interactions on the part of the organisation.

Service Work and the Role of the Service Recipient

Leidner (1993) critiques research in the field of service work for being too strongly based on concepts of industrial work. The characteristics of service work, however, have not yet been covered sufficiently. For analyses of service work it is important to bear in mind that it often implies the active involvement of the service recipient (Gartner and Riessman, 1978; Gross and Badura, 1977; Gross, 1983). Service work can be described as a co-production of employee and customer (for consideration of co-production in public health see Badura, 2001). While the active role of the service recipient has often been mentioned, there has been little research concerning the question of how co-production is achieved and what both of the actors contribute to it. In the following we want to describe briefly several lines of research on the role of the service recipient in service work in general and especially in call centres.

In managerial publications on service work the customer is an important issue. However such publications have concentrated on the question of how service work can become more customer orientated (starting with the bestseller by Peters and Waterman, 1982, in Germany cf. Bruhn, 1999; Reinecke, Sipötz and Wiemann, 1998). It is only in recent years that some publications on the customers' active role in service work have appeared. The customers' activity is described as a potential resource for enterprises (Meyer, Blümelhuber and Pfeiffer, 2000; Schmid and Gouthier, 1999). This is seen as a means of raising the efficiency of a service organisation. Customers for instance may be used to check the performance of service workers (for a critical view of this see Fuller and Smith, 1991).

Discourses and measures taken to develop customer orientation have led researchers in the field of sociology to the thesis that the customer has gained greater power in service work (Frenkel, Korczynski, Shire and Tam, 1999). These considerations refer to more general assumptions about power relations in service work: with the customer being involved in the process of service work the 'two-way struggle between management and labour' is replaced by a 'triangular pattern of shifting allegiances and interests among workers, managers, and customers' (Leidner, 1993, p. 41). Conflicts of interest may occur not only between workers and management. Customers too may have notions differing from those of the management and / or the workers.

The relationship between employee and management is nonetheless special in as much as the employee is integrated into the hierarchy of the organisation (Krell, 2001). Employees can not decide the goals followed in service interactions on their own. They may have greater or lesser room for shaping these goals and their attainment. But employees remain part of an organisational hierarchy, which typically can sanction departure from its regulations.

The organisation's regulations relate to the service recipients in so far as they avail themselves of its services. This involvement of the service recipient becomes particularly apparent in so-called total institutions (Goffman, 1973), e.g. old people's homes. In institutions of this type the organisation determines many aspects of conduct of life of the service recipient.

As a rule however service recipients are not bound to the organisation by a hierarchical relationship. Service recipients can turn to organisations with their own personal aspirations. They may then conclude that these can be attained more or less effectively. The relative 'freedom' of customers to follow their own personal goals is one possible source of problems in the process of co-producing service interactions.

The different perspectives and interests of management, employees and service recipients provide the basis for several possible alliances. What kinds of alliances are typical for which kinds of work? Gutek (1995) shows the relevance of the type of interaction (encounter or relationship) for the development of ties among the three parties involved in service work. Encounters for instance increase the employees' dependence on the organisation and weaken the employees' ties to customers. Relationships however provide a better background for strong ties between customer and service provider.

Frenkel, Korczynski, Shire and Tam (1999) elaborate on these considerations. They distinguish between three types of workflows in front line work: service, sales and knowledge work. They show that relations between management, employees and customers are influenced by the type of workflow. Alliances between management and employees are most likely in service workflows which are shaped to a greater extent by bureaucratic structures. However, in practice only one such case was found and this gave evidence of more empathy towards customers than was expected. In sales workflows a more entrepreneurial approach was encountered and alliances between management and customers predominated. Knowledge work workflows showed several variations of alliances.

Reflections and empirical research on the customers' role in service work can also be found in the field of standardised service work (Gundtoft and Holtgrewe, 2000; Leidner, 1993; 1996; Voswinkel, 2000). In her study of *McDonalds* and the *Combined Insurance Company* Leidner (1993; 1996) for instance shows that the standardisation of work in the service sector – in contrast to that in the industrial sector – conforms to rules of its own. In the field of service work not only the employees' activity has to be standardised, but also that of the customer. The customer in that kind of service process has to assume his or her role in a quite narrowly defined 'script' which the organisation writes (see also Frenkel, Korczynski, Shire and Tam, 1999). This can give rise to problems: at McDonalds for instance customers are expected to give their order quite quickly. If they can't decide which meal they prefer, staff may become impatient and push them to hurry up.

Rationalisation also plays a central part in call centre work. The establishment of call centres is bound up with the hope of connecting rationalisation, standardisation and customer orientation (Gundtoft and Holtgrewe, 2000). From a managerial point of view the relationship between enterprises and customers is increasingly becoming an important element in the strategy to secure or expand market share (Heskett, Jones, Loveman, Sasser and Schlesinger, 1994). Within this perspective call centres seem to be one of the most effective ways to tie customers to the enterprise. In the last decade the number of call centres has increased – but it is still exceeded in Germany by the number of manuals on how to organise them (Bittner, Schietinger, Schroth and Weinkopf, in this volume). The focus of these manuals lies on the (technical) management of call centre work (Böse and Flieger, 1999; Briese-Neumann, 1996, Menzler-Trott, 1999). Issues are for instance the technical preconditions involved in setting up call centres, the organisation of shift plans or the selection and training of the employees. If the issue of interaction between agent and customer is addressed, this is usually done in the form of guidelines for the structuring of the conversation by the agent. 'Efficient customer dialogue' (Menzler-Trott, 1999) is a major guideline on this.

In contrast to the flood of publications from the practice side, academic studies on call centre work have only begun to be conducted in Germany in recent years (Bittner, Schietinger, Schroth and Weinkopf, in this volume). Call centres are discussed as a new form of organisation of work that creates a specific relationship with the customer and changes the conditions of employment (D'Alessio and Oberbeck, in this volume; Gundtoft and Holtgrewe, 2000; Dose, in this volume). Alongside organisational problems the analysis of work in the call centre tends to concentrate on workplace evaluations (e.g. Isic, Dormann, Zapf, 1999; Metz, Rothe and Degener, 2001; Richter and Schulze, 2001). Job-control and stress factors at the workplace are main aspects of such evaluations.

One important characteristic of call centre work is the central role of technology. The *workplace studies* approach has shown the relevance of communication in employment areas that are to a great extent characterised by the use of information and communication technology (Knoblauch, 1996). Work in call centres entails a special combination of communication and technology. Thus the interaction between employee and customer is conveyed through technology, usually by telephone (Höflich, 1996). Communication by e-mail is viewed as becoming an important extension in the future. Moreover, the use of computers is quite common. The technical nature of call centre work gives rise to the question of the extent to which the technology is appropriate to the requirements of the interaction (Maaß, Theißing and Zallmann, 2001). Moreover, the central importance of technology has specific consequences as regards the customer's contribution to making service possible. This issue has already been handled in ethnographic studies on the micro-logic of telephone interactions (e.g. Zimmerman, 1992). Gundtoft and Holtgrewe (2000, pp. 194-195) draw attention to the fact that call centre work makes specific demands on the customer: in a sense he or she is unwittingly involved in the processing of information to deal with his or her case.

Service Interactions in the Media-Based Financial Services – A Case Study of a German Call Centre

In Germany, representative studies on call centres are only recently available. A number of reports have been published by commercial research institutes or consultancies. The most comprehensive overview of the situation is provided in a literature survey by Bittner, Schietinger, Schroth and Weinkopf (in this volume).

In this chapter we analyse a call centre in the financial services sector. Approximately 40 per cent of all call centres in Germany are located in banking and insurance. All major banks and insurance companies offer telephone-based customer services. In contrast to call centres that concentrate on simple tasks like taking orders or checking addresses, the media-based financial services cover a broad spectrum of activities of varying complexity. Thus dealing with bank account transfers by phone is part of the routine job, whereas giving advice can be counted among the more demanding tasks. For employees in this field, vocational skills provided by vocational training in banking is favoured by banks, but not essential for recruitment to call centres. Communication skills however, have become crucial: for example being able to speak standard German, being capable of emotional labour and having the ability to show empathy with the customer's concerns.

The Call Centre at X-Bank[2]

The X-Bank call centre is an independent subsidiary of its parent company, a German bank. The call centre was initially founded in the nineties as an entirely independent Telebank servicing a middle to upper-middle class clientele. It was then acquired by the present parent bank, but continues to operate relatively autonomously, servicing a clientele similar to its original one.

Work at the X-Bank call centre entails relatively complex financial services for retail customers. The call centre is focussed on two major types of service: complex investment banking and loans where only vocationally-trained bank clerks are employed and general banking services, operated both by vocationally-trained employees and agents without a banking background.

A total of 160 employees, including team managers, work in the call centre. Working hours vary and many different shift models are in place. More than half of the workers are full-time personnel, roughly 30 per cent are students who work the legal limit of a 19-hour-per-week schedule for students. The other 20 per cent of the staff have individual arrangements ranging between 20 to 32 hours a week.

The general banking services section of the call centre formed the focus of our study of service interactions. General banking services were divided

---

[2] To preserve the anonymity of the bank studied, the name has been changed.

into four departments, within which several teams of 7 to 13 agents comprised the basic work unit. In the inbound service department, five teams were devoted to answering inbound-service inquiries from potential new customers. In this department the calls were mostly dealt with in short interactions involving simple requests for information. A second financial transactions department was comprised of 11 teams, which were also inbound-operators. In this department, only one senior agent in each team had the right to place outbound calls to customers. A third outbound department with three teams of call centre agents was devoted to sales and marketing activities, directed through the use of the bank's gathering of financial information on its customers. Some calls in this department lasted up to one hour. The fourth department, complaints management, consisted of three teams involved in both in- and outbound call centre service for handling customers' complaints or correcting bank mistakes. The agents in this department all had special competence in handling complaints outside the routine procedures of the bank and in so doing, their calls could last more than half an hour.

The financial transactions department, because of its size (11 teams) was lead by two managers. The other three departments were headed by a single manager. Each team was supervised by a team-leader. The entire call centre was managed by a general manager.

Human Resource Management at the call centre of the X-Bank focused mainly on recruitment and training activities. Faced with a high rate of turnover, the permanent telephone application hotline was evidence of the strong emphasis put on recruitment. From the point of view of the management the key criteria for the job were the personality and the personal motivation of the applicants, their social and communicative skills and their team-working ability. Previous knowledge of banking was not necessary in general call centre services, but welcome. Employee assessments were also conducted regularly. As is common in most German call centres, wages were below the level of the standard wage for bank clerks.[3] Wages were individually negotiated between management and the agents and were split into basic pay and a contingent performance component which comprised nearly 10 per cent of the total wage. Each new recruit was normally assigned to inbound-services. To join outbound-services agents usually had to demonstrate or acquire experience and have completed vocational training in banking. Complaints-counsellors had all worked in one of the other

---

[3] As discussed by Arzbächer, Holtgrewe and Kerst in this volume, many call centres in Germany have been established as independent subsidiaries of their parent banks in order to evade inclusion in collectively bargained wage rates for the financial services industry.

departments for at least two years. Because of the low number of managerial positions, there was little chance of promotion for the call centre's employees. Many team leaders and managers were recruited from among the centre's staff or had been in their position since the call centre was established.

Once recruited, employees underwent an intensive six-week training. They received information on general banking matters, the department's specific products and the handling of the information management system. Training conveyed the company regulations regarding length and range of conversations. These regulations varied by department and were checked regularly for enforcement. The average number of conversations during a shift extended from about a dozen in the outbound section to around 80 calls in the inbound areas. Role-plays of customer-interactions were used to train general communication skills and sales techniques. All employees – those engaged in inbound transaction services as well as those devoted to outbound marketing and sales – were expected to engage in sales.

Most important for our analysis of the co-production of service work by call centre agents and customers was the attempt at X-Bank to structure service interactions through the development of a loose interaction sequence. This sequence received a name – *Effect* – marking it as an official procedure for the call centre agents. Managers viewed *Effect* as a strategy for combining customer-orientation with an efficient method of controlling customer interactions. Employees were instructed to use this framework to structure all sorts of conversations with the customers.

Effect prescribed employee-customer interactions according to the following sequence: Contact – Analysis – Offer – Transaction/Sale. In the first step of the interaction, *contact*, the customer is identified by his or her personal code number in a Computer-Telephony-Integration-System with interactive voice recognition. The customer is asked for his or her code number by the system and when the agent takes over the call the relevant data about the customer comes up on the computer screen.[4] The agent then says the standard greeting used by the bank. The contact phase may also include strategies to 'warm up' with the customer, e.g. engaging in small-talk or making a joke. In the second step, the *analysis*, the agent tries to determine the customer's needs. This implies, for instance, questions about the (financial) situation and the intentions and preferences of the customer. The *offer* is the third step of the interaction. With it the agent tries to find a solution for the problem or need the customer has articulated in the course of the conversation. This solution might be a new product or just a piece of

---

[4] For outbound calls agents give a password to identify themselves as an employee of the X-Bank and then ask for the personal code number of the customer.

information the customer required. With the *transaction* the agent brings the interaction to an end. He or she summarises the result of the conversation. If it is about a *sale,* the employee will try to reach a binding agreement with the customer. The X-Bank encourages its employees to combine these general elements of the interactions with a personal 'authentic' speaking style. The aim is to make the conversation appear to be a 'natural' one, despite the prescribed structure.

In the company's training program coaching-sessions are employed with senior agents who explain technical matters or conversational behaviour aspects of call centre work. On the job every agent is coached several times by team-leaders or senior agents. This forms part of the continual training and is obligatory for half an hour per week. Usually on the basis of a monitored call with a customer, conversational behaviour is focussed on in the coaching-sessions. In addition some 'sensitivity training' is employed in order to convey to the agents the meaning of good service. Training in sales is also offered. All qualifications attained at the company and through on-the-job training are validated with certificates issued by the bank. Training and coaching sessions provided by the X-Bank have a reputation of high quality throughout the whole branch. With such certificates in hand agents have a good chance of promotion when leaving for other call centres, where former X-Bank-agents are welcomed with open arms.

The turnover rate at the X-Bank call centre is as high as is customary in call centres in Germany. In spite of the good work atmosphere referred to by both call centre agents and managerial staff in interviews, there are, apart from the minimal chances of promotion, two main reasons for leaving the X-Bank. Distinct symptoms of burnout (this applies especially to workers in the inbound area), for most workers becoming apparent after three years at the latest, is one source of turnover. Second, agents find that working at the call centre becomes boring in the long run.

Research Strategy and Methodology

In this article we present the first analysis of an empirical study of work at the X-Bank call centre. The research was conducted at the Chemnitz University of Technology, Germany, by members of two projects funded by the DFG.[5] The data from the call centre study includes:

---

[5] The first project is concerned with 'New practices of work in the context of daily life in media-related autonomous forms of work' (supervision: G.Günter Voß).
The second research project, 'Service Work as Interaction' is concerned with the development of a theoretical concept of interaction in service work (supervision: G. Günter Voß and Wolfgang Dunkel).

- 89 recordings of customer interaction sequences
- 22 semi-structured interviews with call centre agents
- 10 semi-structured interviews with members of the management, team-leaders and the chairperson of the works council at the X-Bank
- 13 semi-structured interviews with customers
- 12 non-participant observation sequences at the workplace and
- 1 participant observation block from an in-house training course.

In this analysis we focus on transcripts of recordings of interaction sequences. The transcripts were recorded and used by the bank itself as part of its training program. Using linguistic (e.g. Gumperz, 1982; 1992) and ethno-methodological conversational analysis techniques (e.g. Garfinkel, 1967; Garfinkel and Sacks, 1970; Sacks, 1992), we analyse critical situations arising in the course of the interaction sequences. We also take into account assumptions derived from previous research in another field of interactive service work (Rieder, 1999).

Examples of Service Interactions at the X-Bank

The service interactions at the X-Bank reflect in part the instructions which the bank gives for interactions. We can find the four steps of the *Effect* sequence in most of the calls recorded. At the same time however, *Effect* is conditioned by the respective personal speaking style of the agents, a fact that the agents themselves were keen to emphasise in the interviews. This combination of instructions and personal style turned out to be a good basis for understanding quite a range of calls and our first example is representative of the typical interaction at the X-Bank call centre.

Some interactions however, showed critical situations where the Effect sequence broke down or turned out not to be helpful. With the notion of *critical situations* we refer to problems arising in the course of the interaction which endanger performance of the service and/or potentially detract from the quality of the service. Following the presentation of one uncritical and several critical situations, we conceptualise preconditions of co-production in service interactions on the part of the actors.

Empirical Case 1: Immediate Agreement

The following transcript is of a complete telephone service interaction (KB203). The occasion for the customer to call was the wish to revoke a direct deduction order (in the transcripts C stands for customer and E for employee).

E: A very good morning, customer services here. I am (agent's name).[6]
C: (customer's name) want to get something of mine back.
E: Get something back. A direct deduction I hope?
C: Yes.
E: So when did this happen Mr. (customer's name)?
C: Third of July.
E: Could you tell me the client as well?
C: (client's name).
E: One thousand two hundred and seventy-seven Marks and thirty-seven Pfennigs?
C: Exactly.
E: And you'd like to revoke this and have it put back?
C: That's right.
E: OK, just a moment. So, I'll repeat that again. I shall get the direct deduction from the third of July to (client's name) returned, for one thousand two hundred and seventy-seven Marks and thirty-seven Pfennigs.
C: Exactly, it's not justified.
E: OK I've done that Mr. (customer's name).
C: I'm very grateful to you.
E: Thank you. Goodbye.
C: Bye.
E: Bye, have a good day.

In this case reaching agreement did not prove problematic. The customer knew that it was possible to cancel commissions which have already been transferred to another account. The call centre agent, too, quickly grasped the issue despite the shorthand expression of the customer's wish. After a short query, ('A direct deduction I hope') the agent carried out the necessary procedure in a professional manner. The customer followed the process and gave further proof of his competence in telebanking.

The customer introduced his aim as the singular point and kept this up until the end of the conversation. The call centre agent realised this and confined himself to carrying out the transaction without trying to interest the customer in another product; he even dispensed with the otherwise customary standard expression 'Can I do anything else for you?', after having completed the transaction. The customer who was annoyed at the unjustified transfer is probably not a fitting interlocutor for a sales talk. To try it anyway would have been to put the bank in a bad light. This way the call centre agent spared himself what would presumably have been a fruitless endeavour. In view of the targets set by the organisation for successful

---

[6] Here the agent says his name. Names were removed to preserve the anonymity of the persons involved.

product promotion it was more astute for the agent to wait for a more communicative customer.

A range of calls at the X-Bank proceeded in such an unproblematic fashion. These were more or less the routine interactions, like transfers or requests for statements of account. The aims pursued by the actors complemented one another and often both parties had a lot of practice in the procedures. Requests for advice provided further examples of conversations without problems. Inasmuch as the customer needed to be advised, the interactions fit in well with the call centre agents' 'advisory task'. In the interviews we carried out with the employees it was apparent that the conversations in which the agents were able to provide the customers with thorough information and advice were the ones they perceived as being particularly satisfying (see also Frenkel, Korczynski, Shire and Tam, 1999). In conversations such as these they experienced their own professionalism and strengthened their identity as 'customer advisers'. The interests of employees and customers complemented one another well at this point. These were the calls which gave rise to alliances against the management, such as when questions like rational structuring or length of conversations were raised. Connections can be made here to a study on struggles for recognition in call centre work (Holtgrewe, 2001). This shows that the criteria of quality of work can be employed strategically by the workforce in the fight for recognition of their performance.

The rest of our examples focus on problematic cases. As representative cases of particular interaction problems, we use these cases to develop an analysis of types of interactions based on the competence of the agents and customers and the convergence of goals of these actors.

Empirical Case 2: What is the Question?

The following is an excerpt of a transcribed conversation between an employee of the inbound area of the X-Bank and a customer (KB108). The excerpt is taken from the middle part of the interaction, where the problem in this conversation became most obvious. The aim of the customer was to get a statement of his account through the internet. He phones the bank because he does not understand the presentation on the computer.

> C: And where do I get, like, why is there written balance? Shouldn't it be in credit or is that just what it's called?
> E: Do you mean the statement page?
> C: Yes.
> E: You have two windows, one page above and one below, above are the two accounts, so one is the joint account, the other shows the individual ac-

count and if you click on each you'll get the current balance in the lower window.
C: Yes, where do I have to click? Like, right in the middle?
E: Yes, click just right in the middle of the account in the upper frame.
C: Nothing's happening.
E: And then you see the interest giro account below with the state of the account for sure, don't you?
C: Yes, but there it says balance 4,130. That's in credit isn't it?
E: That is both accounts added together.

From this short extract from the conversation it is evident that the service employee and the customer did not understand one other. The customer misunderstood the meaning of 'balance'. This probably goes back to the fact that the German word for balance, *Saldo*, is phonetically similar to that for debit (in German: *Soll*). The customer mixed up the terms. He feared his account could be in debt. The employee, however, believed that the customer had problems using the internet platform of the bank (this may also be the case).

The problem in this interaction sequence can be viewed as one of a lack of behavioural conformity on the part of the customer with the expectations, which the service provider (and possibly the bank *in toto*) had of him. The customer was not familiar with bank vocabulary. His competence in the field of banking was far below that assumed by the call centre agent. The employee obviously expected a customer who had basic bank knowledge and just needed the usual support for internet banking. This discrepancy between the employee's expectations of the customer's competence and the latter's actual skills made the conversation difficult. The customer was not typical for this bank regarding his level of competence, a fact which helps explain the misunderstanding.

For the management, customer competence was not such an important problem. The communication technique *Effect* aimed at dealing efficiently with the broad spectrum of wishes and preferences of the customers. But it did not take into account the level of customer competence. For instance it did not go so far as to provide those customers who did not know the range of products the bank had on offer with the appropriate information. Instead the agents concentrated on getting information on customers needs. In the course of investment consulting for example, agents asked if a customer would prefer a high risk or a safe strategy. If a customer was unfamiliar with investment consulting *per se* however, he or she may not have been able to answer such questions adequately.

Empirical Case 3: A Small Compensation

The following excerpt (CuCa1) is an example of an interaction where the customer's goals differ from those of the call centre agent. The customer argued that he was confronted with financial loss in his bonds portfolio because an employee of the X-Bank gave him the wrong advice. He draws attention to the bank's liability and this is confirmed by the call centre agent. However, the employee makes clear that the question of whether his colleague in fact gave false advice will have to be checked and clarified. He promises to take care of the matter. In the following sequence the customer expresses his idea of how the situation might be sorted out.

C: Perhaps, I mean this is, er, just an idea. You give a little present (laughing), perhaps a bigger one, for instance a Nokia.
E: Yes (laughter).
C: Like if I recommend customers. Right? Of course I can only recommend the bank if everything is all right in the future. Right?
E: Good.
C: That's obvious. Well that direction because,
E: (Inaudible) yes?
C: would just, er, er, because that'd be a good thing.
E: Yes indeed.
C: It's up to you. Right? (agent's name) get on with it so I can forget about it. Yes (agent's name)?
E: Ahh, naturally. Ah, I shall sort the matter out to your satisfaction first.
C: Yes (agent's name).
E: I'll talk to our bonds specialist.
C: Mmm.
E: Erm, I think it'll take up to the end of the week to sort the whole thing out, then I'd phone you again at the end of the week.
C: Yes this is er,
E: Yes, and then we can think up something nice.
C: yes, yes.
E: Something to make you happy, a little something.

The customer wants compensation for a mistake which in his view the bank has made, as well as thanks for his support of the bank. He connects this compensation with current advertising gifts common in the branch and which the bank has on offer: a well-known brand of mobile phone would cause his anger to evaporate into thin air and he would even be willing to become a promoter of the bank. However, the employee hints that the customer will at best be able to reckon with some small compensation: 'a little something'.

The conversation is an example of a situation in which the service provider and the customer pursue *divergent goals*. They have differing notions of the service to be provided (i.e. of how the customer's complaint should be dealt with). Nonetheless the service provider suggested there will be clarification at some later point in time. It remains a moot point as to whether this will satisfy the customer.

In contrast to the first example of a critical interaction, both actors revealed a high degree of competence. The customer was for instance well informed on the options available from the bank for compensation and material reward, if recommending the bank to other people. He employed this knowledge in the course of the call in a strategic fashion. An example of the high social skills of the actors was the fact that both parties managed to stay calm over the course of the conversation and not to lose face. Moreover the service provider did not allow the customer's demands to harry him into acting too quickly. Thus the actors were able to keep the conversation in objective terms despite their divergent intentions. The interaction did not develop, as in other similar cases in our sample, into an emotionally-laden exchange or escalate into a quarrel.

Critical Aspects of Interaction in the Call Centre: Competence and Motivation

The critical situations described above have to be set within the framework of the procedures and rules that the service organisation provides for service interactions. These instructions guide service providers' actions. At the same time these instructions make up the framework for customers' behaviour. Thus the expectations which face a customer in the course of a service interaction are determined to a large extent by the work organisation and technical provisos of management.

As has been illustrated with the examples presented above, competence and motivation are also important on the part of the customer or client (see also Rieder 1999). Thus the service recipient has to show the competence which the service organisation expects him or her to contribute to the service. A discrepancy between the skills expected and those at hand is a main source of critical situations in service interactions. Moreover, problems in service interaction can be traced back to the fact that service provider and recipient do not develop a shared aim of how the service is to be performed. Companies will therefore have an interest in as *few discrepancies* as possible occurring between the customary procedures and the actions of the customer. Organisations can approach this from two sides: they can try to adapt company procedures as far as possible to the customers (this path is generally discussed under the term customer orientation) or they can try to control the customer's behaviour. As a rule both strategies will play their part in enterprises and be interconnected.

In influencing the customers, however, the companies do as a rule have to adopt different methods from those used to influence their staff. While personnel selection and development are designed to ensure the staff work as smoothly as possible, many enterprises will not be able to afford to choose their customers. It is uncommon to provide skills or motivational training for customers.

But it is possible to discern a *hidden* or *ad hoc* form of influence on the skills and motivation of the service recipient via the instructions and the structuring of customer calls. Thus numerous strategies employed by the call centre agents in the course of a conversation are intended to achieve a compatibility of the customer's aims with those of the organisation. One such strategy is the systematic consideration of the service recipient's feelings. Thus a personal remark or little joke at the beginning of a call is supposed to put the customer in a positive mood and help to create a personalised atmosphere. In addition the customers come to know the expectations the employees have of them in the course of an interaction through their conversational style. Customers are for instance expected to have their secret number ready at the beginning of the call. If it is an advisory interaction about a bank product the questions put by the employees show that the bank expects them to give some thought to their preferences. In addition to telephone interactions, information about bank services is provided to customers through advertising, word of mouth and the bank's own presentation on the internet. In contrast to its employees, the bank does not have the option of systematically training its customers.

The amount of effort that the organisation must put in, in order to get customers' behaviour to conform to company procedures depends partly on the kind of service that is provided by an organisation. Leidner (1993) for instance shows that at McDonalds the customers' wishes usually fit in well with those of the employees and the organisation. The insurance concern *Combined*, on the other hand, employs a wide range of techniques to manipulate potential customers, thus getting them into line with the organisation's goals. It is the employees' task to create this harmony or at least to get near to doing so. They do this by falling back on their experience in dealing with non-conforming customers. Employees keep interactions going by improvising on the basis of feelings and in this way permanently varying the course of the conversation as envisaged by the company. In this sense, the active role of the worker's subjectivity, what in Germany is called 'subjectivising working behaviour' (Böhle, 1994; 1998) is a prerequisite for an advisory interaction, which can scarcely be planned and therefore constitutes a minefield of potentially critical situations. The objective instructions of the organisation which have been moulded into a code of conduct are, so to speak, transformed and adapted through step-by-step procedures to suit the specific interaction. Moreover, additional rules may be developed by the actors during the process of communication (e.g. joking is allowed during conversations) – this is one aspect of co-production.

It is in relation to co-production that employees initiate and permanently develop 'personal working styles', which in their complexity can only be steered and canalised to a limited extent by company procedures and rules (cf. the problem mentioned above of varying alliances between employees, customers and management). Personal working styles do not conform exclusively to company instructions; they adapt themselves continuously to the conditions of daily work. Alongside the undoubtedly important framework provided by work organisation, the sensory perceptions of employees, their biographical experiences as well as their social contexts all play a substantial part in the ongoing process of developing a personal style (Matuschek, Kleemann and Voß, 2002; Kleemann and Matuschek, 2001).

Potential Scenarios for Interaction Processes in Call Centre Work

The two critical situations presented above demonstrate the relevance of two factors in the successful co-production of service interactions: the competence of the actors (especially customers) and the convergence of the goals of the actors. Taking these categories together we can describe four potential scenarios for service interactions.

Table 11.1 Four-Cell Scheme to Depict Potential Constellations of Service Interactions in Call Centre Work

Competence of the actors	Correspondence of goals of the actors	
	Convergent	Divergent
High	Co-operative interaction (empirical case 1)	Potentially conflictual interaction (empirical case 3)
Low	Potentially error-prone interaction (empirical case 2)	Potentially out-of-control interaction (empirical case 4, see below)

The four-cell scheme in Table 11.1 shows these constellations. The section on the top left of the table indicates interactions where *goals* are *convergent* and *competence* of the actors is *high*. Typically those interactions can be referred to as co-operative interactions. Empirical case 1 provided an example of such successful co-production.

The sector on the right at the top in Table 11.1 indicates critical situations in which call centre agent and customer act *competently* but follow *divergent goals*. Interactions in this sector can be referred to as potentially conflictual. The actors will try to attain their respective goals. Open conflicts can develop or manipulative tactics may be employed. The third empirical case is an example of goal divergence among competent actors, where the customer tries to manipulate the agent to compensate a mistake with a gift, while the agent stalls the decision in order to check the accuracy of the complaint. From interviews and observations we know that there are also other typical interaction scenarios where goals are divergent, but this divergence fails to become evident to one or the other actor in the course of the conversation. Thus employees act in part in accordance with the customer's demands, without explicitly showing their goal divergence during the conversation – this is an aspect of the imperative of customer orientation. The divergence of goals in such cases however, is sometimes the subject of discussions about an interaction with a third person. Where divergence is present, a conflictual interaction can result, resulting in either the withdrawal or dominance of one actor. In empirical case 3 however, there is a hint of a compromise which will presumably fall some way short of the customer's expectations.

In interactions where goals of the actors are divergent various *alliances* might occur. In empirical case 3 we can assume that the employee acts in accordance with management when he sets limits on the customer's expectations as regards compensation. There are other cases where the employee tends to show solidarity with the customer, yet has to keep to the rules established by management. Examples of such interactions can be found when customers request a loan but do not meet the conditions. Interactions with so-called VIP customers provide examples of alliances between management and customers. Employees are instructed to be particularly co-operative with these customers. They are obliged to meet the special wishes of customers in this category, but sometimes compensate for this by making jokes with their colleagues about the airs and graces of this particular clientele.

The cell at the bottom left of Table 11.1 depicts a scenario in which the *goals* of the actors are *convergent* but *competence* of one of the actors (or both) is *low*. Our example above of the customer who mixed the meaning of the German banking terms for balance and debit is a case in point. 'Low competence" here means that the competence does not match the expectations of the service organisation. Such expectations may be explicit (e.g. expectations of agents expressed in job advertisement) or implicit (e.g. expectations of customers set by forms of work organisation – such as dealing with a voice recognition system in the call centre). Problems concerning competence may relate more to the instrumental or the social aspect of behaviour (for this distinction see Nerdinger, 1994). Low competence may lead to errors and misunderstanding in the course of the interaction. In empirical case 2 for instance the customer is lacking in the basic knowledge of the interpretation of an account statement, a competence that can normally be assumed of banking customers. Moreover the actors do not succeed in finding a common language to deal with this problem. It can be assumed here that they also lack the social competence necessary to resolve the situation. The employee is not able to understand the customer's question about the meaning of 'balance'. The customer however does not pose his question clearly.

The most critical situations in service interactions however, occur when both kinds of problems analysed in this contribution occur together – lack of competence and divergence of goals. Interactions of this type are indicated in the cell at the bottom right of Table 11.1. The following transcript gives an example of this kind of interaction.

Empirical Case 4: Please Not Now

Empirical case 4 is an example of an outbound call (KB210). The employee wants the customer to get her overdrawn account back into balance. The transcript in this case extracts the beginning of the conversation.

E: (customers' name) I am with the *X-Bank* (agent's name). Your password is (password).
C: Yes, that's right, yes.
E: OK. I've got an important piece of information for you, if you have your six figure secret number at hand, then we can talk about the matter.
C: Oh, please not now. My husband has died.
E: Oh, your husband has died. When can we reach you again then?
C: Oh, next week.
E: Yes. What does that mean, next week, when actually, so we can make an appointment, 'cos this is a really important thing. Or you phone back when you're feeling better.
C: Ah, god, if it's so important, then I'll have to look for the number.
E: Yes, it is important. It's about your money.
C: Yes.

The transcript only gives a small part of the whole conversation which lasts about 20 minutes. During the course of the interaction many banking subjects were discussed, for instance how to get the husband's death certificate to the central office of the bank. At the end the customer lost control of herself and started crying.

The conversation posed a real emotional challenge for both parties. The customer tried to keep control of her feelings in a situation where she had just experienced a great loss. The worker who was prepared for an exchange about bank business stumbled into a completely different situation that would even be difficult to cope with in the context of a more personal relationship. The agent obviously lacked the social competence necessary to respond to the customer's emotions. Following the usual rules of courtesy the most sensible course of action might have been to end the conversation as soon as politely possible with an expression of sympathy and the agreement that the customer calls back when she feels able to do so. However, the agent limited the conversation to the business nexus and tried to solve the problem that was the reason for his call: the agent's main, possibly his sole, goal was to get the account back into balance. The goals of his co-actor in the given situation, however, did not include doing business with the bank. But she seemed not to have the knowledge or the strength necessary to put an end to the conversation. A situation resulted in which she allowed the employee to determine her conduct.

The lack of emotional empathy with the customer's situation on the part of the agent may have helped him to attain the bank's immediate goal of getting the account out of the red. But in the long run it may equally have negative consequences for the X-Bank. For instance the customer could decide to leave the bank because of the lack of sensitivity evident in the agent's behaviour in this sequence.

Conclusion

Recent research in the field of service work has thematised the central importance of the customer's behaviour. Studies of interactive service work require consideration not only of the service provider's contribution but also that of the customer. Our article has analysed critical situations in service interactions with reference to the behaviour of employee and customer. Moreover relationships between the behaviour of both of the actors and the framework of service interactions set by the organisation have been taken into account.

The analysis of critical situations based on 89 service interactions shows the relevance of two factors for the successful co-production of service interactions – competence and goals of the actors. Should for example skills be expected from the customer (explicitly or implicitly) in the course of the service interaction which the latter does not possess, then the completion of the service is endangered.

The inclusion of the behaviour of the customer in analysis of service work entails consideration of a whole series of questions which have as yet scarcely been touched upon by academic research. Examination of the customer's co-operation also gives rise to the question of his or her 'working conditions'.[7] To what extent can concepts of the humanisation of work be applied to customer activity (Theißing, 2001)? What room for manoeuvre is accorded to customers (Rieder, 1999)? Which stress factors do customers face? To what extent do customers meet the qualification requirements which are assumed to 'do the job' of a customer? Engaging these questions could contribute to a better understanding of co-production in service work. In so doing, it would be particularly important to bear in mind the specific role of the service recipient. Customers are not integrated into the hierarchical structure of the organisation, in contrast to employees.

Reflections along these lines are not only of academic interest. For the practice side too, reflections on the organisation of service interactions could be made use of which transcend the limited concept of customer orientation. Thoughts on how to organise customer co-operation could for instance be of interest to consumer protection groups. These are primarily concerned with questions relating to the quality of products. Research on customers' 'working conditions' could provide inspiration for further areas of activity for consumer groups (as well as for other groups representing the interests of customers, clients or patients). Concepts of humanised work might focus on different topics than those bound up with customer orientation concepts. It is quite possible for customer orientation to go hand-in-hand with telling the customer what to do. An example of this is the X-Bank's structuring of conversations with the medium of *Effect*. This conversational structure is supposed to put customer orientation into practice in that in the course of giving advice the customer is asked about his or her needs, and this information then provides the basis for the subsequent offer. But within this structure the customer does not have the chance to first find out about the range of products actually available. Selection of the 'appropriate' offer is instead made by the agent on the basis of the information obtained. In this sense the conversational structure does entail telling the

---

[7] It may be doubted whether there is any sense in denoting the customer's contribution to service performance as 'work'. Reference to criteria for procedures analysing work in the home might help clarify this issue (Resch 1999).

customer what to do. If a customer just wants to get information for the moment, then *Effect* does not meet this need.

For the health care sector there is already a discussion about how to organise the context for patients' co-operation in service provision (cf. von Reibnitz, Schnabel and Hurrelmann, 2001). There is a need to review whether approaches of this type might be developed for call centres as well.

References

Badura, B. (2001), 'Thesen zur Bürgerorientierung im Gesundheitswesen', in von Reibnitz, C., Schnabel, P.E. and Hurrelmann, K. (eds.), *Der mündige Patient. Konzepte zur Patientenberatung und Konsumentensouveränität im Gesundheitswesen*, Weinheim, Juventa, pp. 61-69.
Böhle, F. (1994), 'Negation und Nutzung subjektivierenden Arbeitshandelns bei neuen Formen qualifizierter Produktionsarbeit', in Beckenbach, N. and van Treeck, W. (eds.), *Umbrüche gesellschaftlicher Arbeit, Soziale Welt, Sonderband 9*, Göttingen, Schwartz, pp. 183-206.
Böhle, F. (1998), 'Technik und Arbeit. Neue Antworten auf "alte" Fragen?', *Soziale Welt* Vol. 49(3), pp. 233-252.
Böse, B. and Flieger, E. (1999), *Call Center – Mittelpunkt der Kundenkommunikation. Planungsschritte und Entscheidungshilfen für das erfolgreiche Zusammenwirken von Mensch, Organisation und Technik*, Braunschweig and Wiesbaden, Vieweg.
Briese-Neumann, G. (1996), *Professionell telefonieren. Kompetenz, Kundenorientierung und Corporate Identity am Telefon*, Wiesbaden, Gabler.
Bruhn, M. (1999), *Kundenorientierung: Bausteine eines exzellenten Unternehmens*, München, Beck.
D'Alessio, N. and Oberbeck, H. (1999), '"Call-Center" als organisatorischer Kristallisationspunkt von neuen Arbeitsbeziehungen, Beschäftigungsverhältnissen und einer neuen Dienstleistungskultur', in IAB, ISF, INIFES, IfS and SOFI (eds.), *Jahrbuch Sozialwissenschaftliche Technikberichterstattung*, Berlin, Edition sigma, pp. 157-180.
Frenkel, S., Korczynski, M., Shire, K. A. and Tam, M. (1999), *On the front line. Organisation of work in the information economy*, Cornell University Press, New York.
Fuller, L. and Smith, V. (1991), 'Consumers Reports: Management by Customers in a changing Economy'. *Work, Employment and Society*, Vol. 5, pp. 1-16.
Garfinkel, H. (1967), *Studies in Ethnomethodology*, Prentice Hall, Englewood Cliffs (NJ).
Garfinkel, H. and Sacks, H. (1970), 'On Formal Structures of Practical Action', in McKinney, J.C. and Tiryakian, A. (eds.), *Theoretical Sociology*, New York, Appleton-Century-Crofts, pp. 337-366.
Gartner, A. and Riessman, F. (1978), *Der aktive Konsument in der Dienstleistungsgesellschaft. Zur politischen Ökonomie des tertiären Sektors*, Frankfurt a.M., Suhrkamp.
Goffman, E. (1973), *Asyle. Über die soziale Situation psychiatrischer Patienten und anderer Insassen*, Frankfurt a.M., Suhrkamp.
Gross, P. (1983), *Die Verheißungen der Dienstleistungsgesellschaft*, Opladen, Westdeutscher Verlag.
Gross, P. and Badura, B. (1977), 'Sozialpolitik und soziale Dienste: Entwurf einer Theorie personenbezogener Dienstleistungen', in v. Ferber, C. and Kaufmann, F.-X. (eds.), *Soziologie und Sozialpolitik (Sonderheft 19 der Kölner Zeitschrift für Soziologie und Sozialpsychologie)*, Opladen, pp. 361-385.

Gundtoft, L. and Holtgrewe, U. (2000), 'Call-center – Rationalisierung im Dilemma', in Brose, H.G., (ed.), *Die Reorganisation der Arbeitsgesellschaft*, Frankfurt a.M. and New York, Campus, pp. 173-203.

Gumperz, J.J. (1982), *Discourse Strategies.* Cambridge, Cambridge University Press.

Gumperz, J.J. (1992), 'Contextualisation Revisited', in Auer, P. and Di Luzio, A. (eds.), *The Contextualisation of Language*, Amsterdam and Philadelphia, Benajmins, pp. 39-53.

Gutek, B.A. (1995), *The Dynamics of Service. Reflections on the Changing Nature of Customer / Provider Interactions*, San Francisco, Jossey-Bass.

Heskett, J., Jones, T., Loveman G., Sasser E. and Schlesinger, L. (1994), 'Dienstleister müssen die ganze Gewinn-Kette nutzen', *Harvard Business Manager*, Vol. 4, pp. 50-61.

Höflich, J.R. (1996), *Technisch vermittelte interpersonale Kommunikation. Grundlagen, organisatorische Medienverwendung, Konstitution 'elektronischer Gemeinschaften'*, Opladen, Westdeutscher Verlag.

Holtgrewe, U. (2001), 'Recognition, Intersubjectivity and Service Work: Labour Conflicts in Call Centres', *Industrielle Beziehungen*, Vol. 8, pp. 37-54.

Isic, A., Dormann, C. and Zapf, D. (1999), 'Belastungen und Ressourcen an Call-Center-Arbeitsplätzen', *Zeitschrift für Arbeitswissenschaften*, Vol 3, pp. 202-208.

Kleemann, F. and Matuschek, I. (2001), 'Zur Erfassung subjektiver Leistungen in informatisierter Arbeit', in Matuschek, I., Henninger, A. and Kleemann, F. (eds.), *Neue Medien im Arbeitsalltag. Empirische Befunde – Gestaltungskonzepte – Theoretische Perspektiven*, Wiesbaden, Westdeutscher Verlag, pp. 257-279.

Knoblauch, H. (1996), 'Arbeit als Interaktion. Informationsgesellschaft, Postfordismus und Kommunikationsarbeit', *Soziale Welt*, Vol. 47(3), pp. 344-362.

Krell, G. (2001), 'Zur Analyse und Bewertung von Dienstleistungsarbeit. Ein Diskussionsbeitrag', *Industrielle Beziehungen*, Vol. 8(1), pp. 9-36.

Leidner, R. (1993), *Fast Food, Fast Talk: Service Work and the Routinisation of Everyday Life.* Berkeley, University of California Press.

Leidner, R. (1996), 'Rethinking Questions of Control – Lessons from McDonalds', in Macdonald, C.L. and Sirianni, C. (eds.), *Working in the Service Society*, Philadelphia, Temple University Press, pp. 29-49.

Maaß, S., Theißing, F. and Zallmann, M. (2001), 'Computereinsatz und Arbeitsgestaltung in Call Centern', in Oberquelle, H., Oppermann, R. and Kremse, J. (eds.), *Mensch und Computer 2001*, Stuttgart, Teubner, pp. 61-69.

Matuschek, I., Kleemann, F. and Voß, G.G. (2002), 'Personaler Arbeitsstil – ein Konzept zur Untersuchung "subjektivierter" Arbeit', forthcoming in Moldaschl, M. and Voß, G.G. (eds.), *Subjektivierung von Arbeit*, München and Mering, Hampp.

Menzler-Trott E. (ed.) (1999), *Call Center Management. Ein Leitfaden für Unternehmen zum effizienten Kundendialog*, München, C.H. Beck.

Metz, A.M., Rothe, H.-J. and Degener, M. (2001), 'Belastungsprofile von Beschäftigten in Call Centers'. *Zeitschrift Arbeits- und Organisationspsychologie*, Vol. 3, pp. 124-135.

Meyer, A., Blümelhuber, C. and Pfeiffer, M. (2000), 'Der Kunde als Co-Produzent und Co-Designer – oder: die Bedeutung der Kundenintegration für die Qualitätspolitik von Dienstleistungsanbietern', in Bruhn, M. and Strauss, B. (eds.), *Dienstleistungsqualität. Konzepte – Methoden – Erfahrungen*, Wiesbaden, Gabler, pp. 50-70.

Nerdinger, F.W. (1994), *Zur Psychologie der Dienstleistung: Theoretische und empirische Studien zu einem wirtschaftspsychologischen Forschungsgebiet*, Stuttgart, Schaeffer-Poeschel.

Peters, T. and Waterman, R.H. (1990), *Auf der Suche nach Spitzenleistungen. Was man von den bestgeführten US-Unternehmen lernen kann*, München, mvg-Verlag.

Reibnitz, C. von, Schnabel, P.E. and Hurrelmann, K. (2001) (eds.), *Der mündige Patient*, Weinheim, Juventa.

Reinecke, S., Sipötz, E. and Wiemann, E.M. (1998) (eds.), *Total Customer Care: Kundenorientierung auf dem Prüfstand*, St. Gallen, Thexis / Ueberreuter.

Resch, M.G. (1999), *Arbeitsanalyse im Haushalt. Erhebung und Bewertung von Tätigkeiten außerhalb der Erwerbsarbeit mit dem AVAH-Verfahren*, Zürich, Vdf.

Richter, P. and Schulze, F. (2001), 'Arbeitsorganisation als Möglichkeit der Beanspruchungsoptimierung an Call Center-Arbeitsplätzen', in Matuschek, I., Henninger, A. and Kleemann, F. (eds.), *Neue Medien im Arbeitsalltag. Empirische Befunde – Gestaltungskonzepte – Theoretische Perspektiven*, Wiesbaden, Westdeutscher Verlag, pp. 131-146.

Rieder, K. (1999), *Zwischen Lohnarbeit und Liebesdienst. Belastungen in der Krankenpflege*, Weinheim, Juventa.

Schmid, S. and Gouthier, M.H.J. (1999), 'Dienstleistungskunden – Ressourcen im Sinne des resource-based-view des Strategischen Managements?', *Diskussionsbeiträge der Wirtschaftswissenschaftlichen Fakultät Ingolstadt*, Vol. 131, Ingolstadt, Katholische Universität Eichstätt.

Sacks, H. (1992), *Lectures on conversation*, Oxford, Blackwell.

Theißing, F. (2001), *Probleme softwareunterstützter Dienstleistungsinteraktionen – das Beispiel Call-Center*, paper presented at the 2. Tagung der Fachgruppe Arbeits- und Organisationspsychologie at the Friedrich-Alexander-Universität Erlangen-Nürnberg (19. 9. 2001).

Voswinkel, S. (2000), 'Das mcdonaldistische Produktionsmodell – Schnittstellenmanagement interaktiver Dienstleistungsarbeit', in Minssen, H. (ed.), *Begrenzte Entgrenzungen. Wandlungen von Organisation und Arbeit*, Berlin, edition sigma, pp. 177-201.

Zimmerman, D.H. (1992), 'The interactional organisation of calls for emergency assistance', in Drew, P. and Heritage, J. (eds.), *Talk at Work. Interaction in institutional settings*, Cambridge, Cambridge University Press, pp. 418-469.

Index

abuse 178
aesthetic work 184, 186, 198-200
age 69
ambiguity 6, 10, 179, 184-185, 188, 192
authenticity 212-213

back office 149-151
boundary-spanning 24, 176
burnout 54-55
business process reengineering 170

call length 93, 109
career 120
centralisation 150
coaching 33-34, 74, 115, 189-192, 212
collective bargaining 26, 29, 51-57, 59, 91, 93, 97
complaints 115, 155, 217-218
computer-controlled work 92
consumption 164-166, 179-180
control 94, 109
co-production 204-212
critical situations 223-225
customer competence 216-225
customer focus 133
customer sovereignty 167, 175
customer-oriented bureaucracy 106, 175
customer relations 157
customers 10-11, 87-88, 105-106, 120, 163-168, 204-224

deference 173-174
de-regulation 9, 19-40
deskilling 118
disciplinary procedures 57
disillusionment 174-175

efficiency 175
emotional labour 11, 95, 105, 115-118, 124, 197-198, 222
empathy 113, 173-174
employers' associations 49-50, 59
employment data 20, 42, 45, 65-66, 68-69, 91, 99, 128
employment perspectives 99
employment relations 5-9, 42-60
Employment Relations Act 52-53

enchantment 169
enthusiasm 110
ergonomics 8, 77-78
external call centre 90-91

financial services 4-5, 26-27, 44-45, 52-53, 66, 108-121, 149-157, 209-212
flexible bureaucracy 154-159
flexibility 2, 8, 19-40, 71
formalisation 154-156

gender 7, 68, 111-112, 123-142, 173
gender inequality 124
globalisation 9, 46

heterogeneity 3, 5, 43, 66
hierarchy 206
history 3-5, 19-20, 44
human resource management 210
humour 110

information and communication technology 3, 87, 125, 128, 184
industrial action 56, 187
industrial relations 8, 25-30, 43-60
influence 219
innovation 22
institutions 19-40
integration of services 42, 149-150
intensification 48-49
interaction 173, 197, 204-225
internal call centre 90-92
internal labour market 152
internet 42

labour contract, types of 94
labour market 37
labour relations 90-92
language 20, 46
leadership 135

mail order 66, 128
managerial discourse 193
media attention 35, 40, 126
modernisation 39-40
monitoring 56, 93-94, 115
motivation 218-220

myth 168, 172-173

National Vocational Qualifications 119
neo-institutionalism 21-25
Netherlands 43-60
non-union states 48

organisational fields 23-25
organisational strategy 154
outsourcing 5, 8, 23-24, 29, 45-46, 53-54, 129

part-time work 90-92
performance measures 6, 30, 55, 78-79
professionalism 215
pseudo-relationship 175
public support policies 47, 98

qualification 69-70
quality 11-12, 33-34, 39, 100, 113, 155, 183-200

rapport 113, 115
rationalisation 1, 88-89, 146-148, 175, 207
recognition 11, 140, 142
recruitment 7, 31-32, 109-111, 132, 152, 210
reflexivity 155
regions 20-21, 34, 47-48, 67-68
remuneration 71-72, 97-98, 108, 141, 210
re-regulation 9, 19-40
resilience 138
resistance 1, 80, 125, 158, 185, 196, 200
routinisation 58, 126, 136-140, 183, 194

sales 177
sectoral developments 44-46
segmentation 40
service encounter 206-207
service relationship 89, 206-207
service sector 123, 147-148
service work 105-107, 205-207
sign value 163, 169-170
similarities 58
skilful knowing 199
skill formation 105-121
skill requirements 106, 114, 118-121
social skills 7, 33-34, 95, 96, 107, 109-110, 118-121, 124, 127, 132-142
space 172, 177

standardisation 2, 4, 78, 87-89, 93, 154-156, 185, 191, 194, 207
strain 94-95
strategic action 21-22
stress 8, 48-49, 54, 71, 79, 208
students 7, 32, 37, 70
subjectivity 219
surveillance 8, 79, 115, 184, 190-196

target setting 55, 56
target time 173, 185, 188
Taylorism 10, 79, 86, 93, 127, 147-148, 154
teamworking 79-80, 133-136, 189
technical skills 109-110, 134
telecommunications 4, 6, 27, 51-52, 186
time 172, 176-177, 190
time-discipline 184
training 8-9, 35, 70, 72-76, 95-97, 112-113, 211
turnover 25, 32, 55, 70, 118, 212

uncertainty 190
union representation 5, 9, 25-30, 37, 50, 59
union strategies 27, 60-61
USA 43-60

virtual call centre 82
vocational training 96, 119

work cultures 139
work organisation 76-82, 150-153, 156, 207
working conditions 90-92
working styles 220
working time 7, 30, 56-57, 68-70, 90-92, 108
workplace studies 208
works councils 26-30, 158

For Product Safety Concerns and Information please contact our EU representative GPSR@taylorandfrancis.com
Taylor & Francis Verlag GmbH, Kaufingerstraße 24, 80331 München, Germany

www.ingramcontent.com/pod-product-compliance
Lightning Source LLC
Chambersburg PA
CBHW071829300426
44116CB00009B/1489